IMAGES
of America

MYRTLE POINT AND VICINITY 1893–1950

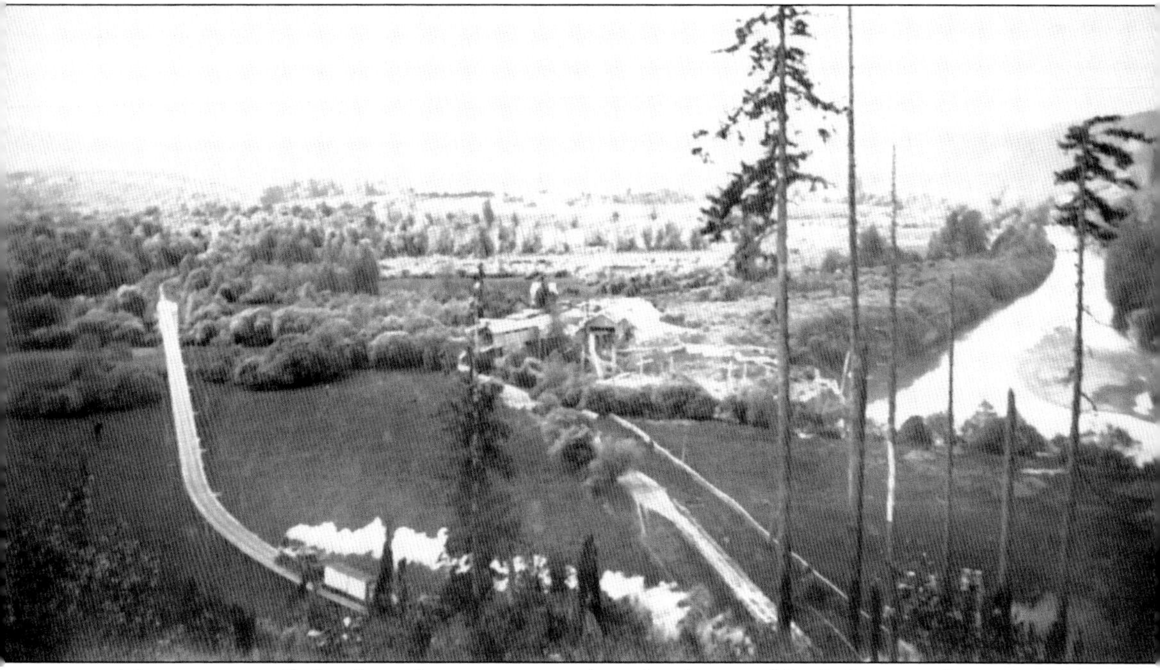

A locomotive pulls freight and passengers south to the depot in Myrtle Point in the early 1900s. West of the elevated tracks are a road and a wooden fence. A covered bridge crosses the North Fork of the Coquille River near the Rackleff Mill. This area was known as "the Forks." West of the mill is the South Fork of the Coquille River. (*Myrtle Point Herald.*)

On the Cover: Paul Davis (right), Gary Davis (center), and their sister Dian Davis (left) showed Guernseys at the Coos County Fair. In 1948, Paul won fourth place with a yearling he took to the state fair in Salem. The Davis farm was located at the west end of the Gravelford Bridge, seen in the background to the right in this 1950 image. The adult leader of the Gravelford 4-H Club, which had its own one-room clubhouse near Cooper Bridge, was Orvus Miller. (Coos Historical and Maritime Museum 177 995-1.9021.1.)

IMAGES
of America

Myrtle Point and Vicinity 1893–1950

Chuck King, Linda Kirk, Carolyn Prola,
and Mary Ellen Robertson

ARCADIA
PUBLISHING

ISBN 978-1-4671-3098-1

Published by Arcadia Publishing
Charleston, South Carolina

Printed in the United States of America

Library of Congress Control Number: 2013941929

For all general information, please contact Arcadia Publishing:
Telephone 843-853-2070
Fax 843-853-0044
E-mail sales@arcadiapublishing.com
For customer service and orders:
Toll-Free 1-888-313-2665

Visit us on the Internet at www.arcadiapublishing.com

Contents

ACKNOWLEDGMENTS

Viewing old photographs collected by our families, friends, and neighbors was a joy and a privilege as we four authors gathered the images for this book. Picture us sitting at a kitchen table with a cardboard box of family photographs in the middle. One by one, photographs are held up, and one by one, stories are told.

When we ran low on boxes of family pictures, we browsed the photograph collections of museums in southwestern Oregon, each museum offering treasures. We talked to as many people as we could, asking questions about the images we had gathered.

In our search, we were guided by our interest in genealogy. Always, we looked for names to match the faces in the photographs. Knowing we would make mistakes, we exerted our very best effort to accurately record names and dates. We tried to learn the stories behind the images. Why had the picture been taken? What happened next, after the camera was put away? We focused on finding photographs that showed how ordinary people lived in times past. This collection of images of the Myrtle Point area from about 1893 to 1950 is the result of our search.

This book is sponsored by the Coquille Valley Genealogy Club. We gratefully express our appreciation to the club's members for their enthusiastic assistance and unflagging support as we worked on this project.

At every turn, we relied on authors who came before us. To them, whose books we studied again and again, we extend our deepest gratitude. We also thank our acquisitions editor at Arcadia, Jared Nelson, whose steady guidance made this book possible, and we thank our families, who helped us more than they can know.

To every person who contributed photographs we pledged our best efforts to tell the story of our community with open hearts and with all the wisdom we could muster. We can never fully express our thanks to the individuals and groups who preserved old photographs and who shared them with us.

Key to Photograph Credit Abbreviations

AD: Alice DeSoto
AR: Allen Reed
AS: Al Stibitz
BA: Barbara Anderson
BB: Beverly Borzone
BM: Bill Mast
BMM: Betty M. McRoberts
BW: Bruce Whitaker
CB: Connie Barnard
CCFM: Coos County Fair Museum
CCFN: Catching Creek Friendly Neighbors
CCS: Cecilia Caughell Schultz
CHMM: Coos Historical and Maritime Museum
CK: Chuck King
CL: Clell Laird
CP: Carolyn Prola
CVM: Coquille Valley Museum
DCM: Douglas County Museum
DH: Dale Hoffman
DK: Dave Kirk
DL: David Laird
DPL: Dora Public Library
EHK: Evelyn Hall Krantz
FS: Florence Schmidt
GO: Glen Olson
HL: Howard Leatherman
HR: Harold Robison
KLD: Kay L. Davis
JLP: Julie Lancaster Puett
JM: Joanne Mulkey
KD: Kim Daniels
KH: Ken Haughton
KL: Kathy Larsen
LK: Linda Kirk
LW: Lin Wilson
MB: Miriam Brown
MC: Mel Craven
MER: Mary Ellen Robertson
MJC: Mapril J. Combs
MPH: *Myrtle Point Herald*
MTBM: Miriam Train Brown Mast
MW: Madonna Wilson
PD: Paul Davis
RB: Richard Bushnell
RG: Robyn Greenlund
SD: Sam Dement
SJ: Sharon Jarman
WL: Wanda Labart
WS: Winnie Sjogren

INTRODUCTION

Three questions guided the search for photographs and facts that would shed light on the history of Myrtle Point and the land that surrounds it. The year 1893 was chosen as the beginning date of the investigation because the train and the telephone—two pivotal developments that signaled the beginning of an era—both arrived that year. As we dug into the past, we focused on our first question: What was it like to live here in 1893?

This inquiry into the past closes with 1950 because it seemed to be the end of an era. World War II was over. Passenger trains no longer stopped in Myrtle Point. Loggers and farmers were mechanizing to meet the demand for lumber and milk. In thinking about the end of an era, we formed a second question: What was it like to live here in 1950?

As we considered images and information about the years from 1893 to 1950, a third question developed: How did life here change during that period? We looked for pictures that showed changes in the way people carried on their routine activities—washing clothes, milking cows, making hay, felling trees, transporting logs, and traveling to the Coos County Fair. This book is the result of our search for answers to those three questions—a collection of images that lets us guess at what it was like to live here between 1893 and 1950, and how that life changed.

To supplement the photographs, we looked at the written record for answers. We found two early descriptions of Myrtle Point that hinted at what life was like in 1893. In 1900, seven years after our target date, Malinda Catherine Baldwin wrote, "Myrtle Point is quite a nice little town of about 500, situated on the bank of the Coquille River which has been widening and deepening until from this point it commences to carry the commerce of the country." A newspaper article from two years later describes the town's attractions and resources in detail:

> Myrtle Point has two hotels, two saloons, five churches, (Presbyterian, Methodist, Dunkards, Christian and Methodist South), six general merchandise stores, three livery stables, three blacksmith shops, one harness shop, two hardware stores, two racket [variety] stores, two drugstores, two cigar stores, one jeweler, one dentist, three doctors, three attorneys, one newspaper, one feed store, two millinery stores, one house furnishing store, one furniture factory, two furniture stores, two bakeries, one restaurant, one barber shop, one shoemaker, one bank, one butcher shop, one opera-house, no photograph gallery, no water works, no sawmill, one billiard hall, express office, telephone exchange, besides various secret society lodges, public school, etc.

To answer our second question and learn about what life was like in 1950, we turned to a brochure prepared by the Myrtle Point Chamber of Commerce three years later, in 1953. The brochure describes a small, vibrant town that serves a wider community of farmers and loggers:

> *Population of Myrtle Point—2,250.
> *Located on Highway 42—60 miles west of Roseburg from Highway 99; 9 miles east of Coquille (county seat), where Highway 42 connects with Highway 101; 27 miles east of Bandon; and 27 miles southeast of Coos Bay.
> *Myrtle Point has a Chamber of Commerce; the oldest Grange in Coos County; Rotary; Lions; Business & Professional Women; and Junior Women clubs. Masonic and Odd Fellows lodges own their own property and buildings.
> *Myrtle Point has the largest bank deposits per capita of any town in the county. Security Bank is housed in a modern concrete building.
> *In the Mast Hospital, Myrtle Point has one of the most up-to-date and modern hospitals in Southern Oregon.
> *Myrtle Point has a modern theater in which all the latest movies are shown—The Hiland.

*Dairying is the main agricultural enterprise.
*Myrtle Point has, in the Superior Cheese Co., the second largest [*sic*] cheese manufacturing plant in the state—taking care of the production of 6,410 cows.
*Myrtle Point is surrounded by several thriving communities, including Arago, six miles to the northwest where a new modern cheese factory handles the production of the major portion of the dairy cattle of that section, connected with Myrtle Point by macadam road and a new $125,000 bridge across the Coquille River.
*Myrtle Point is the center of the livestock industry of the county, with most of the grazing lands which support around 7,000 head of beef cattle and 24,000 sheep.
*Logging is the leading industry in Myrtle Point.
*Industrial operations such as sawmills, veneer and other subsidiaries of the lumber industry; trucking, etc., constitute a large portion of the industrial activity of the Myrtle Point area.
*Myrtle Point is in the center of the only section in the world, outside of the Holy Land, that grows the famous myrtle trees.
*The myrtlewood novelty industry flourishes in Coos County, these novelties being sold widely here and exported as well.
*Port Orford white cedar furnishes most of the wood for the manufacture of arrow shafts in the United States.
*G. R. Kirk & Co., dealers in huckleberry brush greens, fern, cedar boughs, and Christmas cedar, pays out to local residents annually more than $64,000.
*Myrtle Point is the home of the Coos County Fair, an annual show that is one of the finest county fairs in the state—held just prior to the State Fair.
*Myrtle Point's climate will compare with the most ideal in the nation, being even and mild; the rainfall is fairly heavy; the summers are clear and cool; the winters warm and rainy; the mean annual temperature being approximately 55 degrees with only 17 degrees separating the mean maximum and the mean minimum.

Our first two questions had been partially answered, but the third question remained. How had life changed between 1893 and 1950? We returned to the written record, looking for clues.

Transportation changed. In the early days, river travel took precedence along with horses pulling wagons and carriages. Then, in 1893, the first locomotive from Marshfield pulled into the Myrtle Point depot. Soon after, automobiles offered an alternative to riverboats and horses. Slowly, roads improved. Verne Lundy remembered road conditions in 1910: "The streets were rocked as they didn't have crushed gravel; even then they often got pretty muddy. When traveling to town by horse the only place to trot was on the bridges—the rest of the road was too muddy." By 1950, the riverboats had vanished. The only passengers and cargo on boats were fishermen and whatever they caught that day; the trains transported nothing but logs, all roads were graveled (if not paved), and cars and trucks had displaced horses and hacks.

Communication changed. First came the telegraph. In 1889, the Myrtle Point City Council approved a contribution of $50 toward the completion of the telegraph line from Coquille. Then, in 1893, the telephone line between Myrtle Point and Coquille was completed. By 1950, telephones were everywhere, and telegraphs were a thing of the past.

Energy sources changed. In the early era, woodstoves heated homes, and wood ranges cooked food. Wood-fired boilers powered steam donkeys in logging operations, threshing, and pile driving, and coal oil burned in streetlights in Myrtle Point. Then, in 1901, electric wires were strung from Johnson's Mill to Myrtle Point. Areas outside Myrtle Point waited many years, however, for electrification. Dale Hoffman remembered electricity coming to his house near Powers Junction on Christmas Eve 1940. By 1950, even the remote areas surrounding Myrtle Point were electrified.

Health concerns changed. Outbreaks of smallpox, diphtheria, typhoid, scarlet fever, and Spanish flu prompted the city council to approve quarantines, close schools, and forbid public gatherings several times between 1898 and 1919. In 1892, the city council approved the hiring of guards to protect the town "in view of the epidemic of small-pox being at Coquille City." As an additional precaution that year, the council decided "to provide a suitable location for a pest house, to procure suitable nurses, and regulate the traffic and travel to and through the town." Nine years later, the city paid $40 for the use of the Buckmaster house as a pesthouse. A smallpox patient was moved there, and a nurse was hired. In later years, these diseases were tamed.

Even a cemetery changed. In 1891, the council voted to end burials in the cemetery located near today's high school. In 1896, the council approved paying $6 each to move 114 bodies to a cemetery on the hill above town.

Animal control changed. In the 1890s, when every family in Myrtle Point seemed to have a barn, city council dealt with roaming hogs and cows. In 1893, the council ruled that "no persons shall be allowed to have more than two cows running at large at one time." By 1950, having even one cow on the loose in town was frowned upon.

Cattle prices changed. On June 15, 1916, several loads of prime grain-fed beef steers sold for $9.85 each, while good fat dairy steers went for $8 to $8.50. By 1953, beef steers and heifers brought an average of $170.

Jobs and salaries changed. Smith-Powers Logging Company listed its daily and monthly wage rates in the Myrtle Point newspaper:

> "Commencing May 10, 1917 the following scale of wages will be in effect:
>
> Hooktenders: $5.25
> Head Rigging Men: $3.50
> Choker Men: $3.25
> Snipers: $3.25
> Chasers: $3.25
> Whistle Boys: $2.50
> Head Loaders: $3.50
> Second Loaders: $3.25
> Donkey Engineers: $3.50
> Loading Engineers: $3.25
> Filer: $3.50
> Wood Scaler: $3.50
> Wind Fall Buckers: $3.00
> Pump Men: $3.00
> Pile Driver Engineers: $3.50
> Donkey Firemen: $3.00
> Wood Bucks: $2.75
> Railroad Construction Labor: $2.75
> Pile Driver Foreman: $4.25
> Pile Driver men: $3.00 to $3.25
> Cooks: $75 to $90
> Cook's helpers: $40 to $45
> Chore men: $45
>
> In addition to the above, the regular bonus will be paid. We will not raise the price of board in the camps. We will continue to sell all commissary supplies as low as possible."

In the years that followed, advances in mechanization made some of these jobs obsolete. Improvements in roads made it possible for workers to live at home, so logging camps began to close.

Through photographs shared with us, we have been privileged to catch glimpses of the period between 1893 and 1950. In searching for answers about those earlier times, we developed the deepest respect for the people who preceded us—those men and women who built lives in this corner of Oregon where the four forks of the Coquille River spill down the hills and flow through fertile farmland; where myrtle, maples, fir, and cedar grow on the hillsides; where the winter rains bring floods, and in the summer, cattle graze the bottomland. Received from those pioneers are enduring human values passed down to us: work hard, have fun, share with others, stay humble, enjoy nature's abundant beauty, and, especially in the winter, keep your feet dry.

One

Town Life
From Livery Stable to Butcher Shop

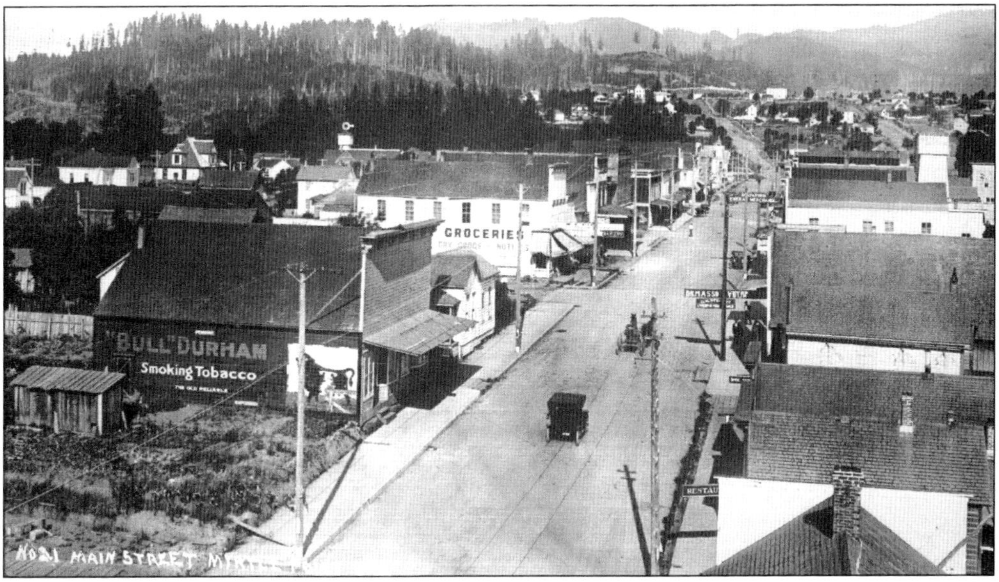

A car and a horse-drawn carriage travel east on Spruce Street in 1910. On the far right is the water tower for the Guerin Hotel, built in 1897 with George H. Guerin as proprietor. A tall house with dormers is visible on the left, built by Nicholas G.W. Perkins in 1903. Perkins opened Perkins' Drug Store in 1888. Telephone service came in 1893, and electric lights were available by 1911. (RG.)

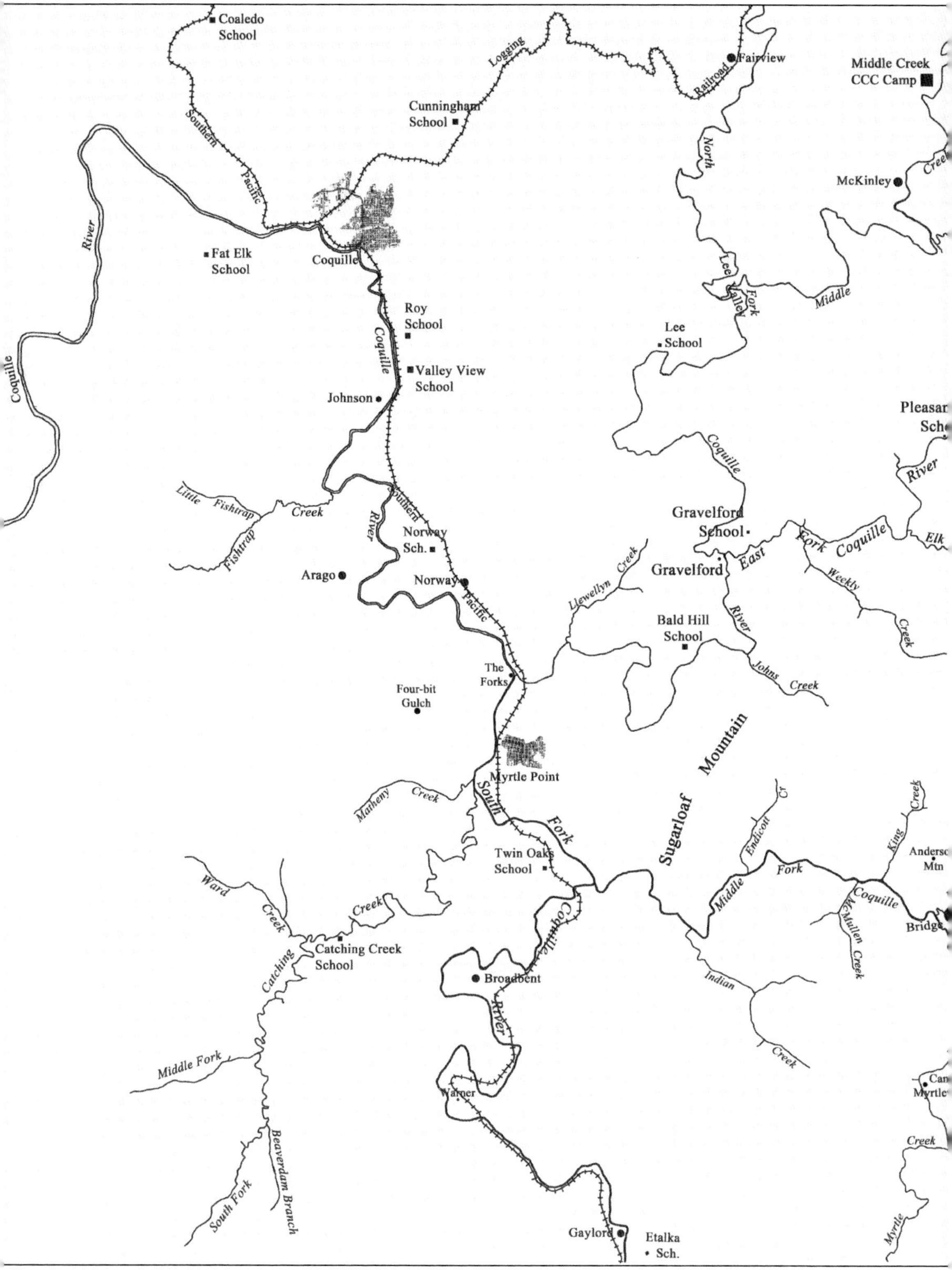
Coaledo School
Logging Railroad
Fairview
Middle Creek CCC Camp
Cunningham School
Southern Pacific
River
Coquille
North Fork
Creek
McKinley
Fat Elk School
Coquille
Lee Valley
Middle
Roy School
Lee School
Valley View School
Johnson
Pleasant Sch
Coquille
River
Little Fishtrap Creek
Fishtrap
Southern
River
Gravelford School
Norway Sch.
Arago
Gravelford
East Fork Coquille
Elk
Norway
Pacific
Llewellyn Creek
Weekly Creek
River
Bald Hill School
The Forks
Johns Creek
Four-bit Gulch
Sugarloaf Mountain
Myrtle Point
South Fork
Matheny Creek
Endicott Cr
King Creek
Twin Oaks School
Middle Fork Coquille
Anderson Mtn
Ward Creek
Creek
Coquille
McMullen Creek
Bridge
Catching Creek School
Catching
Broadbent
Indian Creek
River
Middle Fork
Warner
Myrtle
Creek
Beaverdam Branch
South Fork
Gaylord
Etalka Sch.
Myrtle

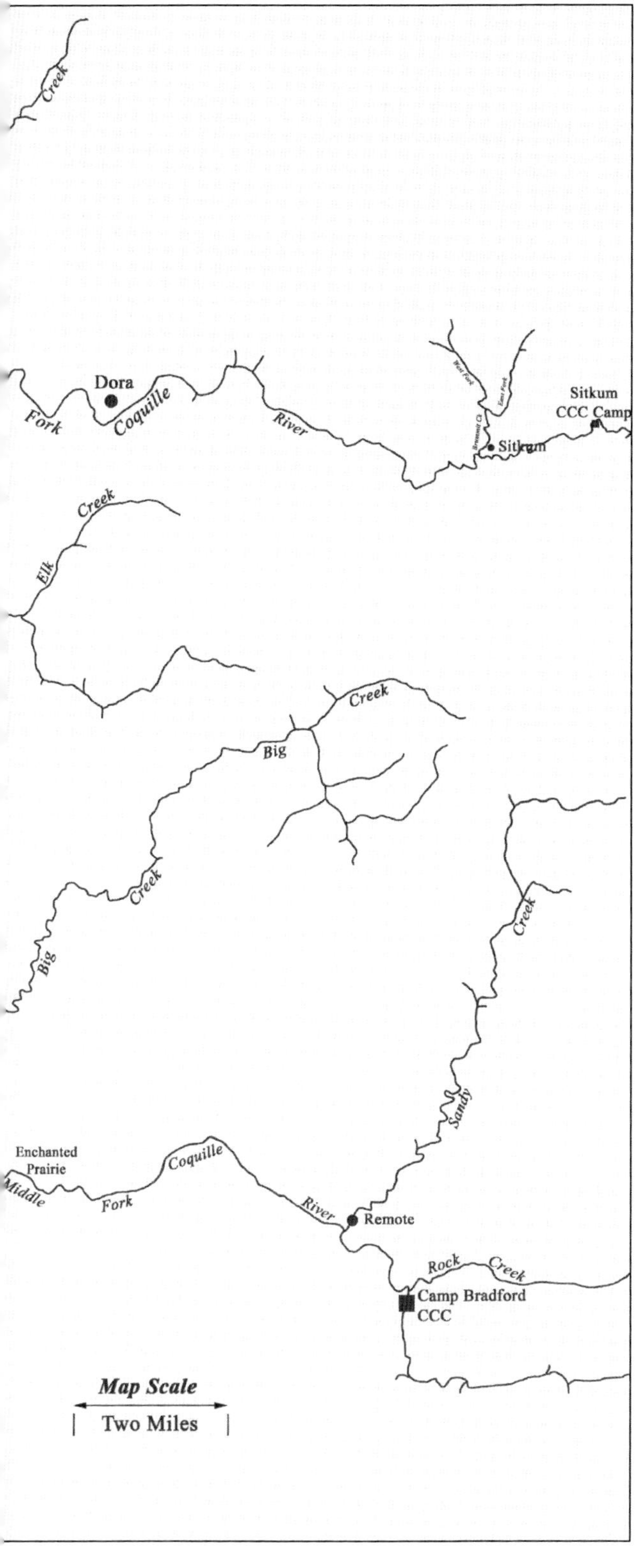

Waterways, communities, mountains, and railroad tracks—but no roads—are shown on this map. Locations of some of the area's country schools are designated, as are the four forks of the Coquille River—the South Fork, Middle Fork, East Fork, and North Fork. (DK.)

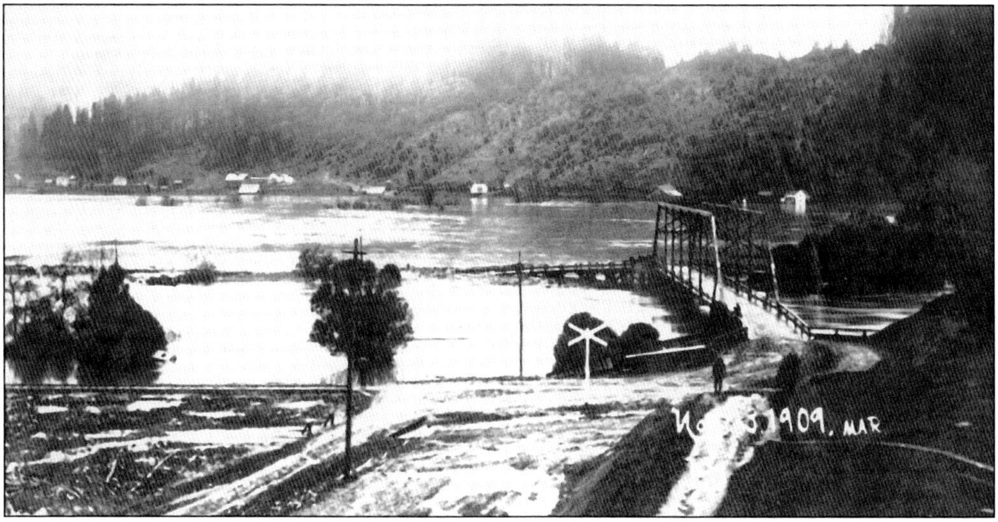

During a flood in 1909, men check for debris caught in the Stringtown approach at the west end of the Maple Street Bridge. This bridge over the South Fork of the Coquille River was replaced by the Spruce Street Bridge in 1917. Stringtown School, painted white, stands on high ground to the left of the cupola-topped barn owned by Daniel and Martha (Barklow) Root. (PD.)

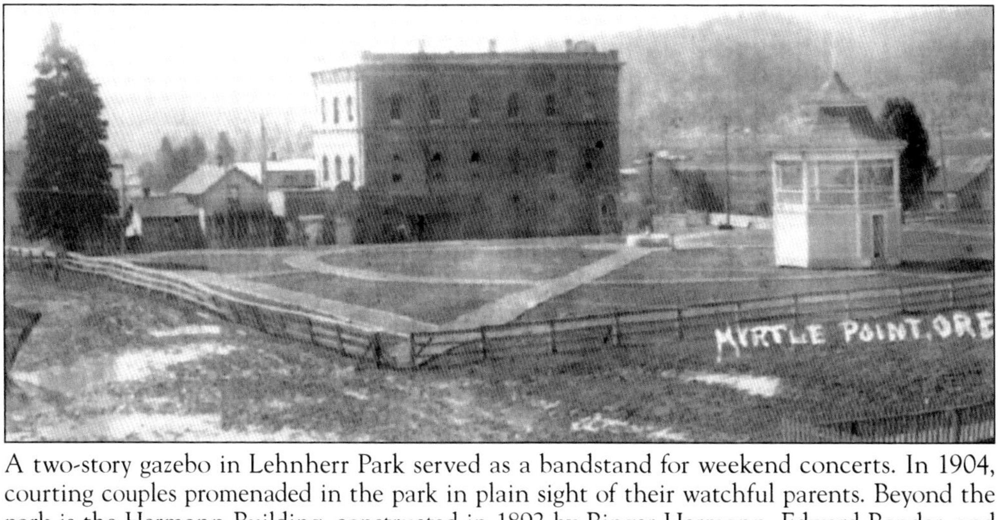

A two-story gazebo in Lehnherr Park served as a bandstand for weekend concerts. In 1904, courting couples promenaded in the park in plain sight of their watchful parents. Beyond the park is the Hermann Building, constructed in 1892 by Binger Hermann, Edward Bender, and Sol Wise. By 1904, Hermann's Bazaar, owned by Ernest and Emma Hermann, sold goods on the first floor. (CP.)

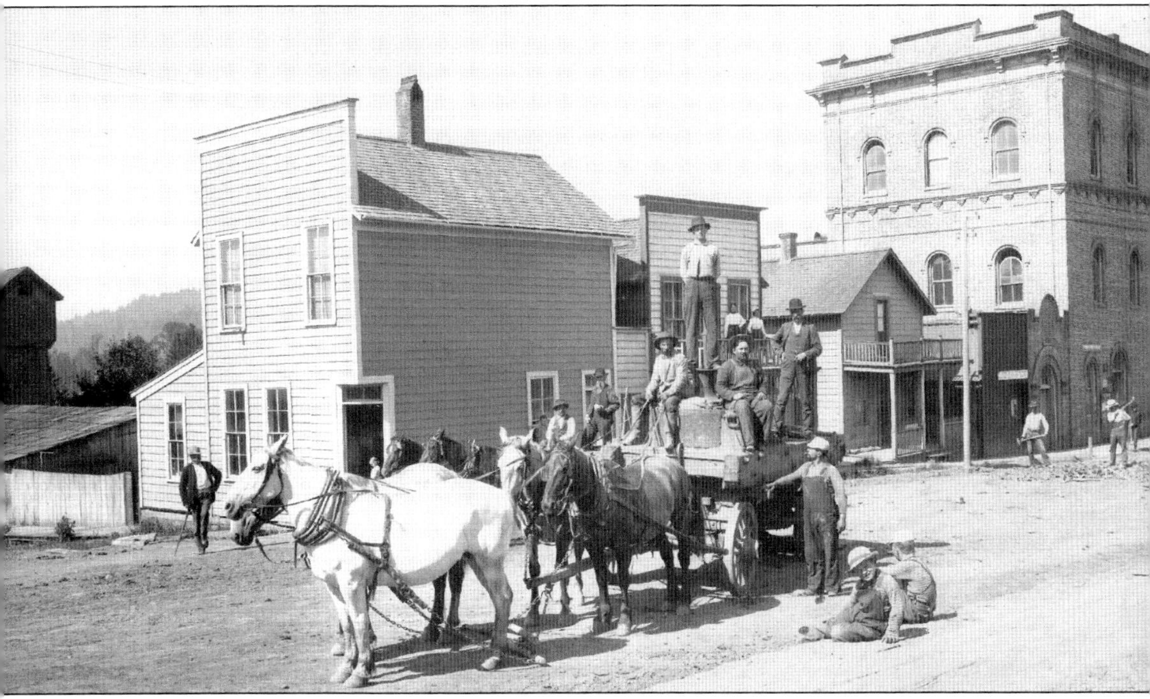

In 1903 or 1904, two teams stop at Spruce and Second Streets. On the near wagon are, from left to right, driver William Tell Lehnherr, George Langor, Charlie Adams, and Bill Page. The children in front are Elton Spires and Roy Spires. Bill Corbin, wearing a dark jacket, stands near the Widby home. The man in overalls next to the wagon is unidentified, and two unidentified women observe the scene from the balcony of the first newspaper office. Downstairs is Perkins' Drug Store, and next door is Dr. Henry Flentge's office. The post office is in the corner of the Hermann Building, the three-story brick building at right. (KL.)

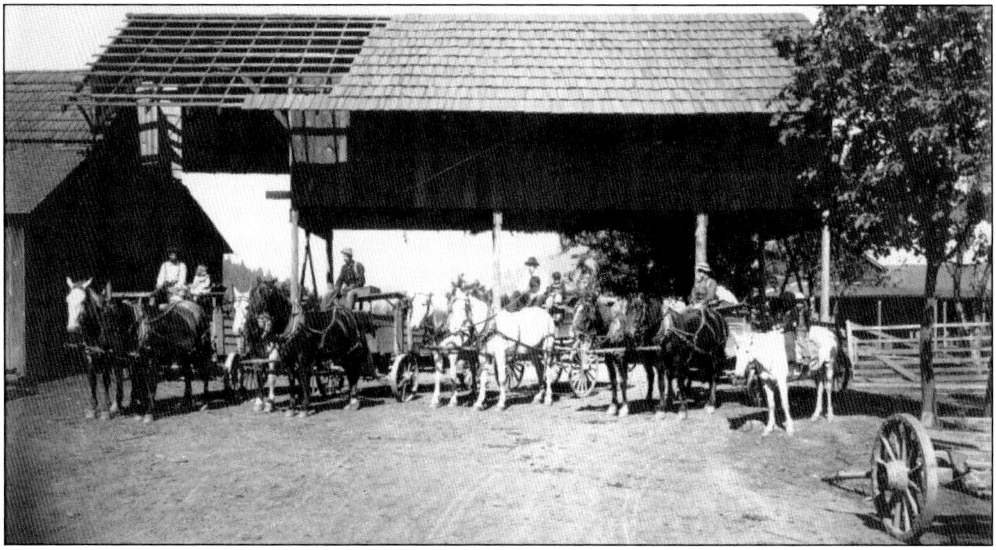

Lloyd Spires and his brother-in-law, William Tell Lehnherr, started a drayage business on Alder Street in 1888. Lined up in freight wagons in about 1903 are, from left to right, William Tell, Doris Lehnherr, Lloyd, Fred Spires, Elton Spires, and Oliver Spires. Bill Lehnherr Jr. and Roy Spires (right) ride double. The Lehnherr house (right), built in 1860 and later moved to 307 Alder Street, might be the oldest dwelling in Myrtle Point. (KL.)

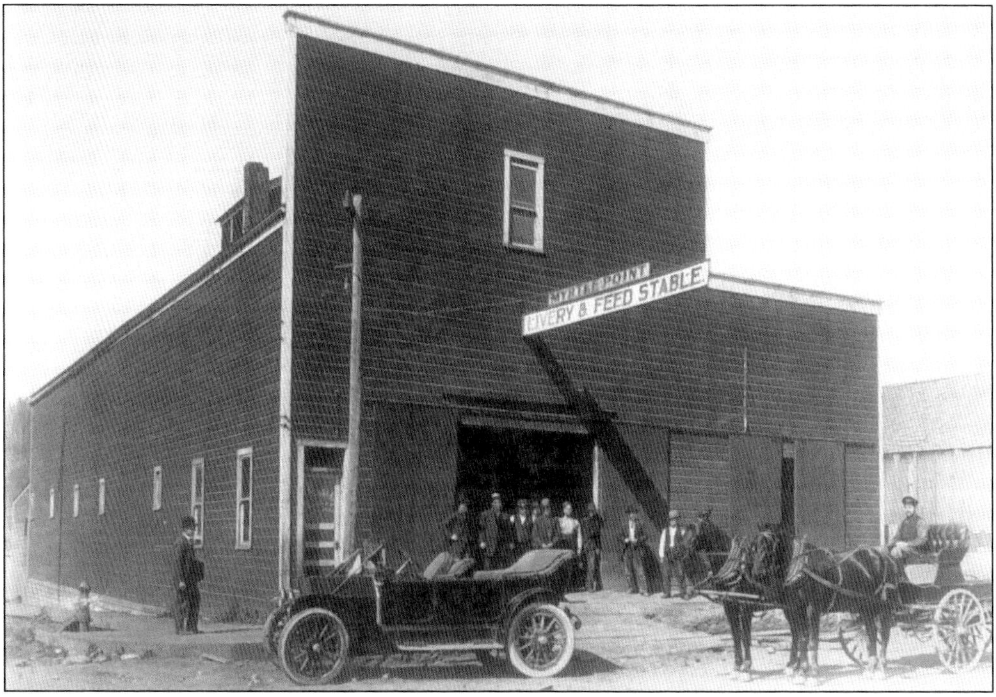

From about 1895 to 1915, Dan Barklow operated a Myrtle Point–to-Roseburg stage line from this livery stable located on Maple and First Streets near the river. Barklow's stages also hauled mail, passengers, and freight from Empire to Roseburg over the Coos Bay Wagon Road. This 1912 photograph shows the introduction of motor-driven stages. The door's sign at left reads, "Stable Office." (CL.)

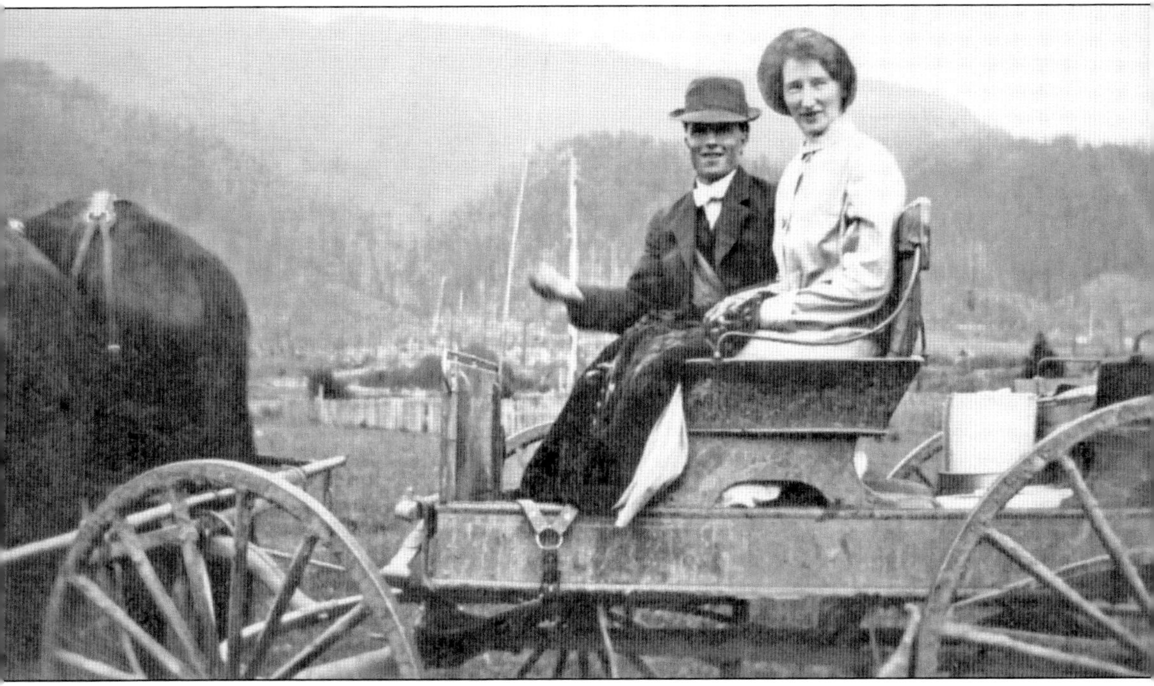

On their wedding day in 1913, Laurence B. Jennings and Eva Dolly (Gant) Jennings prepare to leave Powers to travel over the hill through Bancroft to Remote, where the groom was renting a place from his grandfather. The couple opened the Remote Store in 1924. The store was halfway between Coos Bay and Roseburg—42 miles either direction. (JLP.)

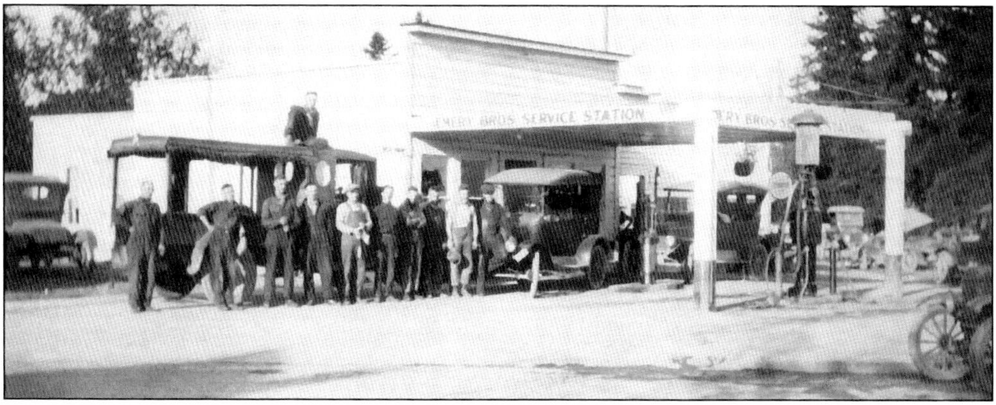

Emery Brothers Service Station opened in 1921 at the corner of Spruce and Seventh Streets. In addition to pumping gas, B.E. "Bud" Emery and his brother maintained a service car that was available night and day, and they sold Buick and Chevrolet cars, White trucks, and Sound and Federal tires. By 1924, Bud Emery and Claude Nosler were operating a service station. (CHMM 70 980-38x.)

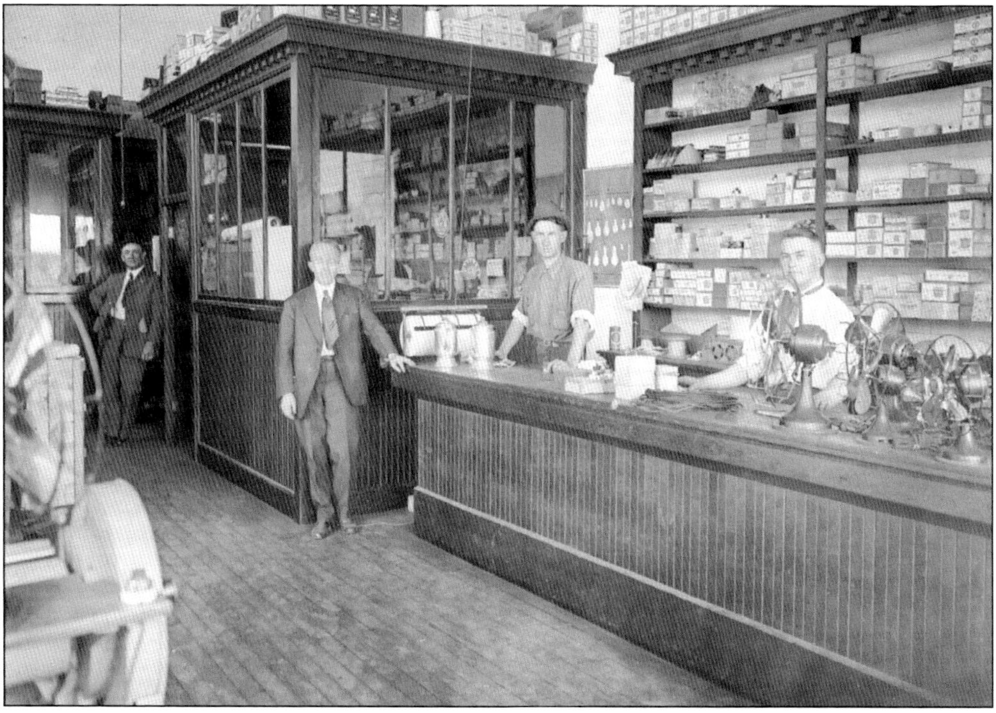

Electric fans line the counter of Brown Brothers Mercantile around 1910. The store's owners were Arthur Brown (left) and Louis Brown (second from left). Arthur later served as state Grange deputy and state chaplain. Another brother, Alva Brown, was a blacksmith in McKinley and had a stage stop on the Coos Bay Wagon Road. (CHMM 53 992-32.1.)

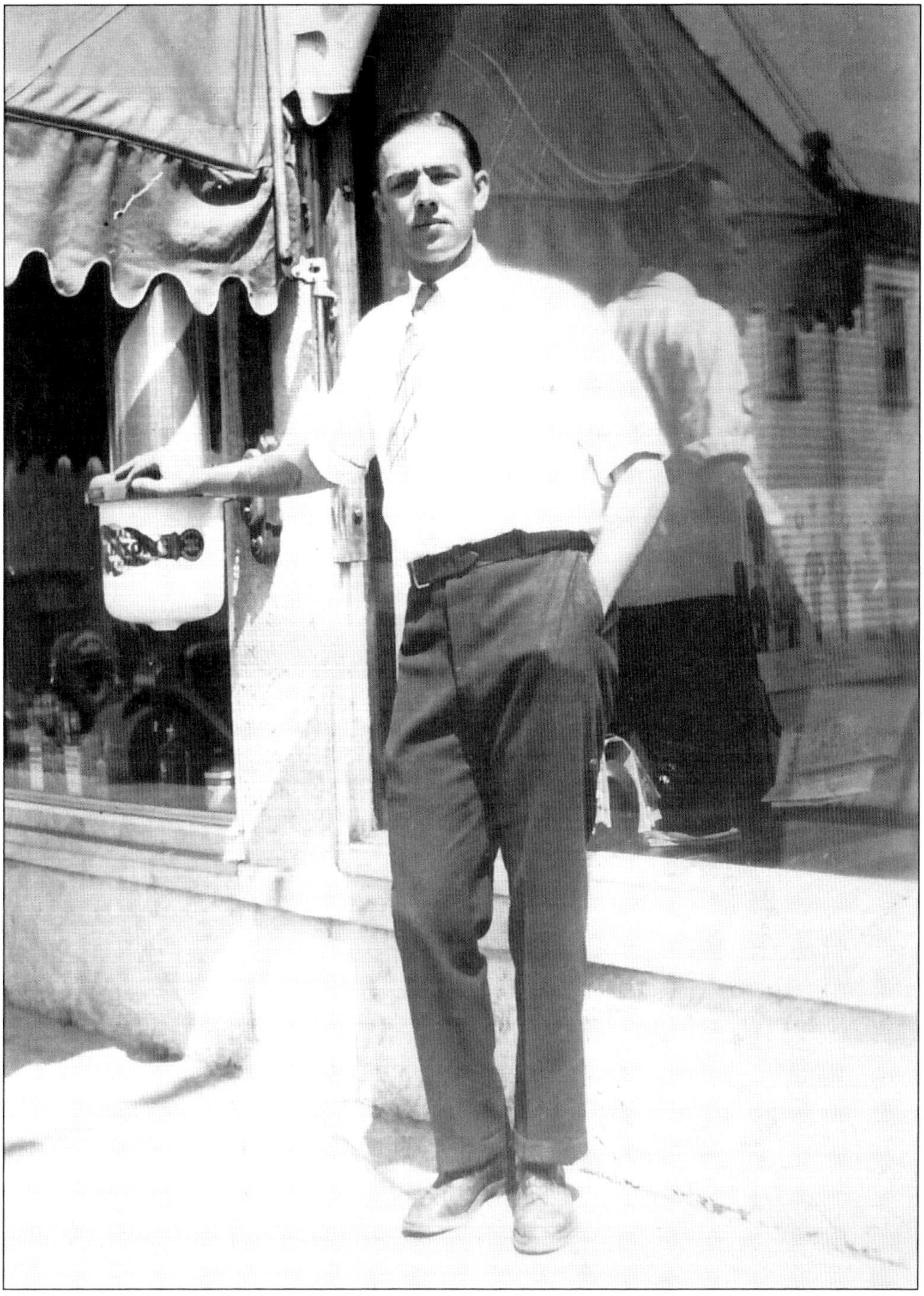

Ron Endicott stands outside his barbershop on Spruce Street in 1927. When the logging industry was booming, there were four barbershops in town. On Saturday nights, the shops were all busy when loggers with a week's beard came in for a shave and a haircut. Endicott's father, Walter Endicott, was also a barber in Myrtle Point. (CP.)

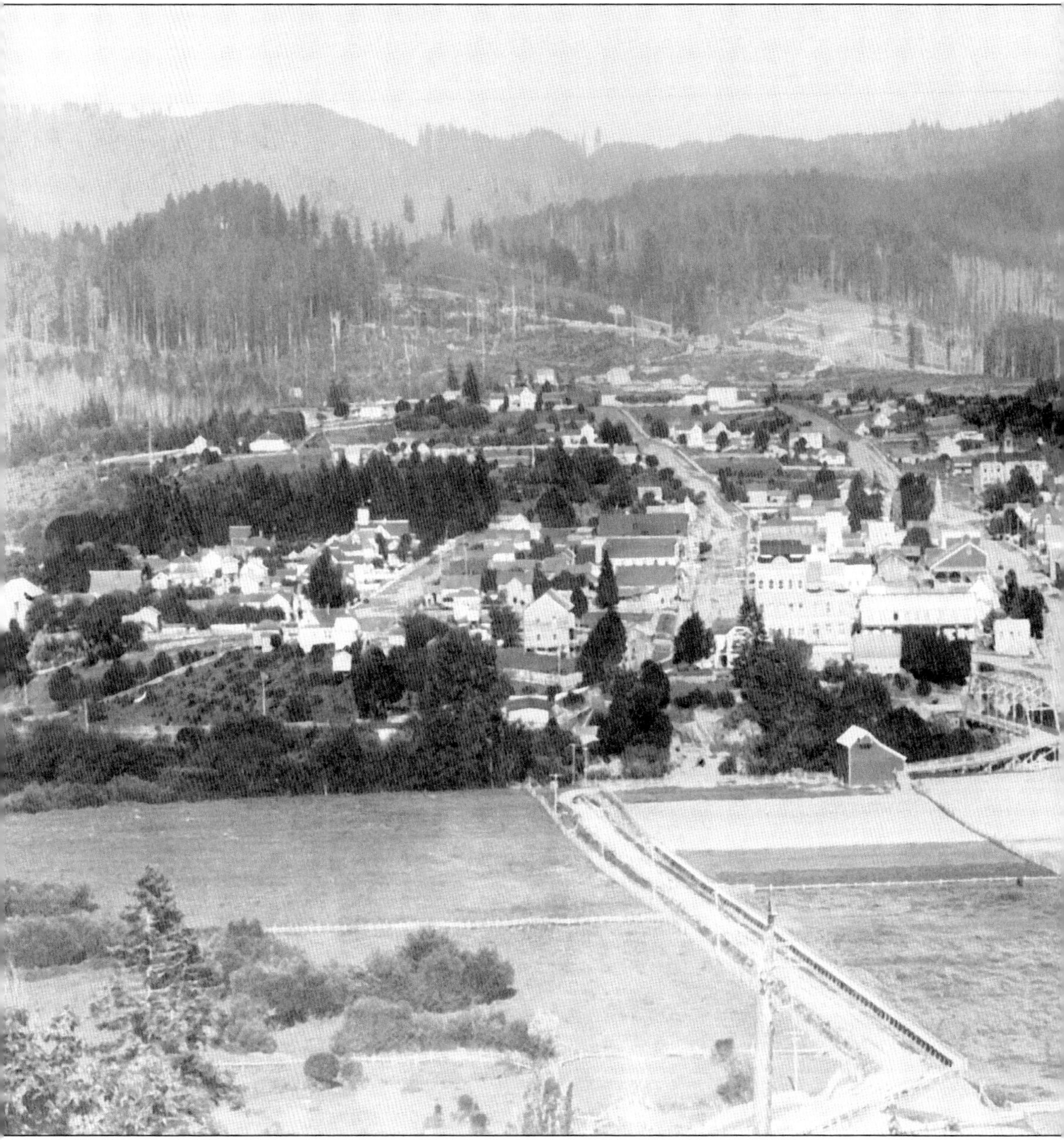

In this eastward view toward the town of Myrtle Point in the early 1900s, myrtle trees mark the river on both sides of the Maple Street Bridge. During winter floods, an elevated walkway served foot traffic from Stringtown. South of downtown, rows of fruit trees grow near today's Coos County

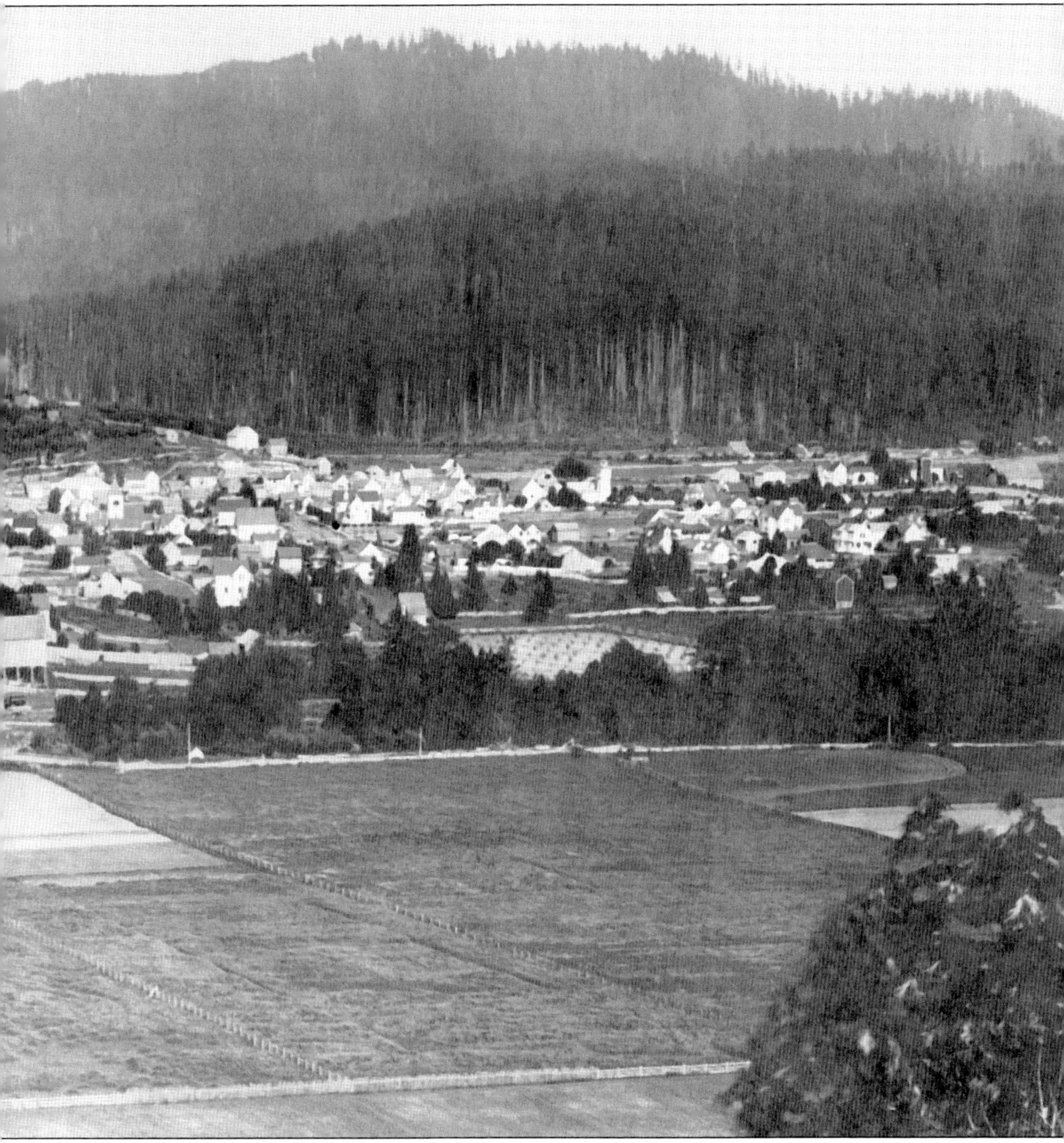

Fairgrounds. On Maple Hill is Edward Bender's house, the large white house between Maple and Spruce Streets. Douglas fir trees rise above the town on Sugarloaf Mountain. (PD.)

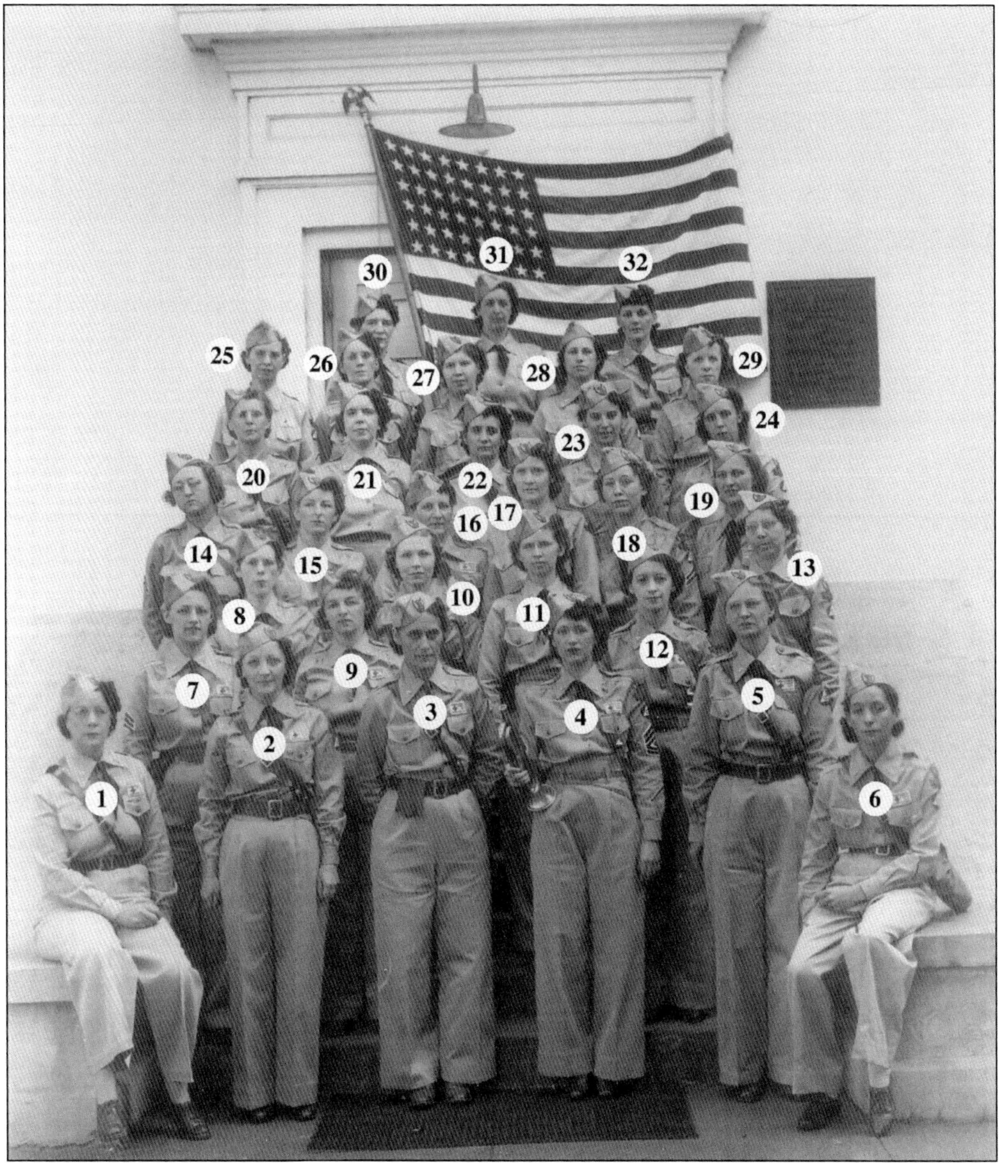

Volunteers from Coquille and Myrtle Point served in the Oregon Women's Ambulance Corps during World War II. Identified are Jackie Watzling (2), Kathryn Train (3), Ava Wicks (7), Dora (McMullen) Train (8), Jean McMullen (10), Lila (Davenport) Ocheltree (11), Polly Farmer (12), Adaline Farmer (13), Winona Farmer (15), Amelia Adams (16), Jean (Guerin) Davenport (17), Ann Watson (18), Norma Eggers (25), Willie Forrest (26), and Beth Baker (28). (SJ.)

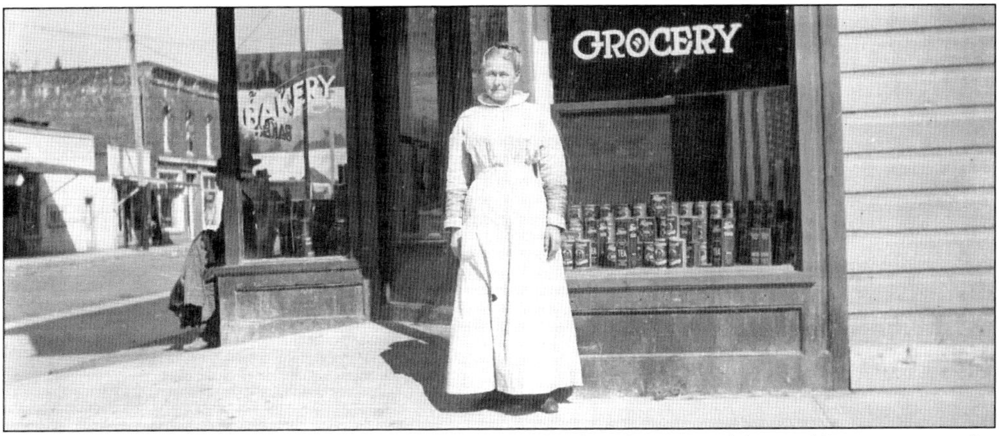

Mary Jane (Pullen) Barklow, shown in 1912, and her husband, Dan Barklow, sold groceries on the southeast corner of Spruce and Fifth Streets. Later, they cooked for the Myrtle Point Hotel and then opened a grocery store on the southeast corner of Spruce and Fourth Streets. They farmed in West Myrtle Point at the junction of Arago and Stringtown Roads. (MW.)

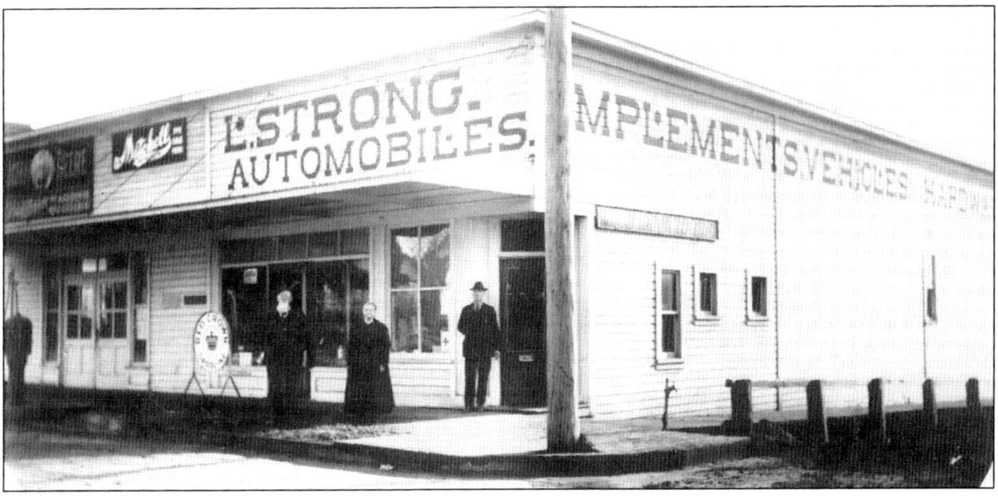

Lewis Strong sold automobiles in the early 1900s. Because some customers still used horses, he also sold Mitchell wagons and kept a hitching post at the side of his store. Lewis and Catherine (Wimer) Strong lived on the northeast corner of Maple and Railroad Streets. Lewis came in 1887, and the Wimer family before that. Catherine's brother James W. Wimer founded the Wimer & Huling Hardware Store. (CVM.)

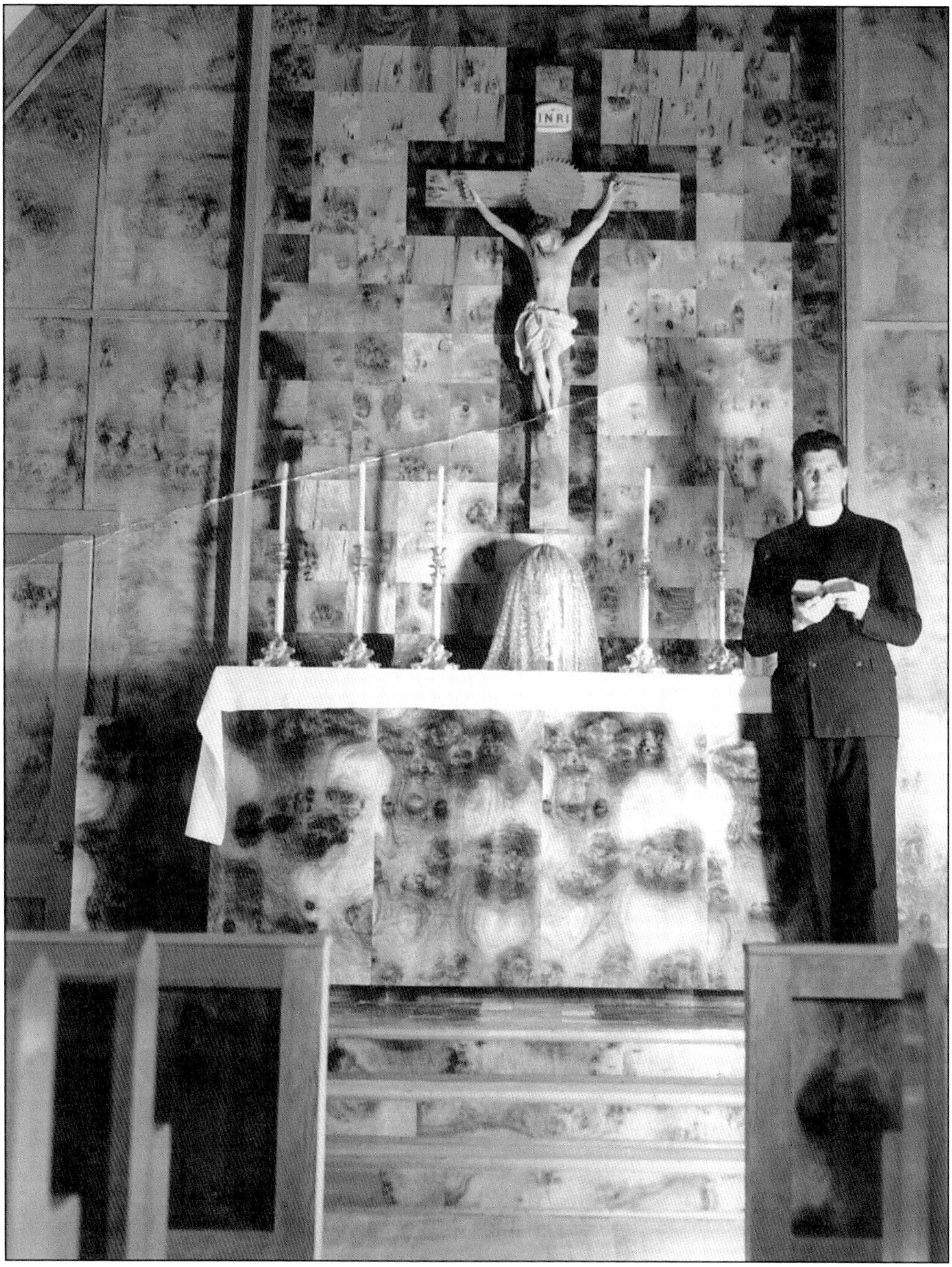

Three large myrtle trees supplied the veneer for the interior of SS Ann & Michael Catholic Church on Second Street between Spruce and Ash Streets. Fr. Daniel Kelly, shown inside the church, convinced Evans Wood Products in Coos Bay that myrtlewood could be made into veneer. Smith Wood Products then made the myrtlewood plywood paneling. The new church was dedicated in 1940, and a north wing was added in 1956. (AD.)

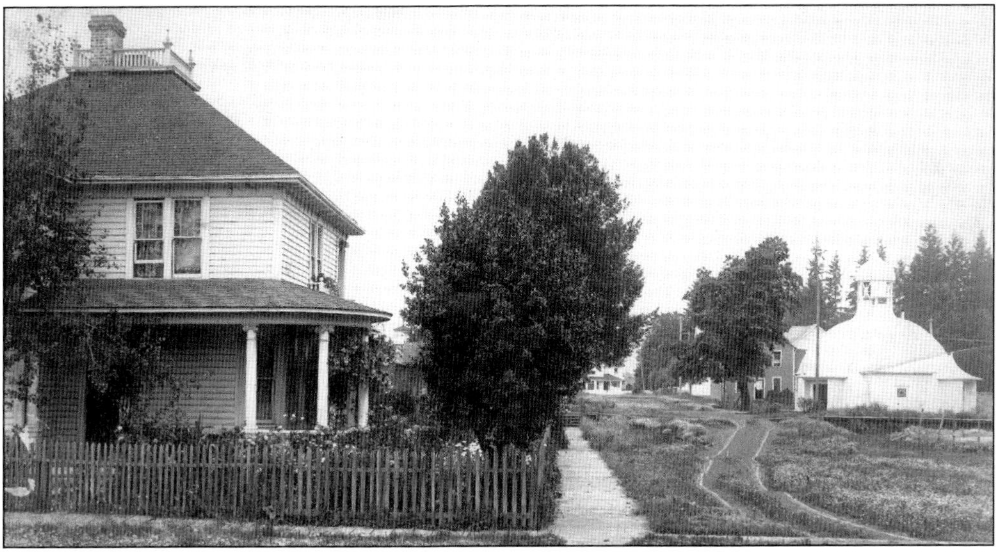

The first owners of this house on the corner of Willow and Seventh Streets were Wilhelm Fredrich Lange and his wife, Mathilde Lange, who built the residence in about 1905. Florence Felsher Evans lived here for many years. At the north end of Seventh Street is a home where Dr. Leslie Johnson once lived. Dr. Reuben R. Mast moved the house back and built a concrete hospital on the site in 1926. (CVM.)

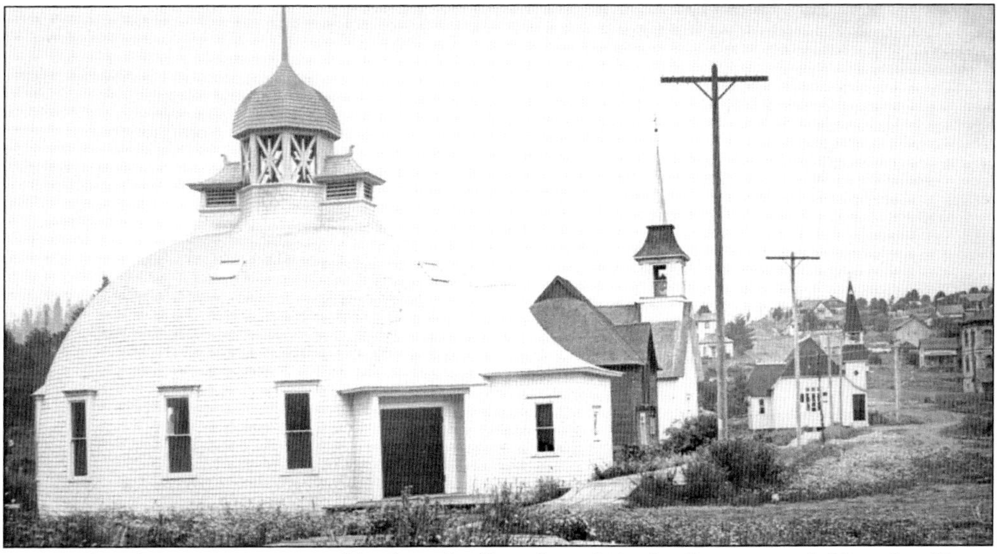

Three churches were connected by boardwalks after 1910: the Reorganized Church of Jesus Christ of Latter Day Saints building (left); the Methodist Episcopal Church, South structure, built about 1879 (middle); and the Presbyterian church (right, with steeple), built in 1891. Left of the Methodist Episcopal church is its parsonage. The multistory brick building to the far right is the high school, built in 1891 for $15,000. (MC.)

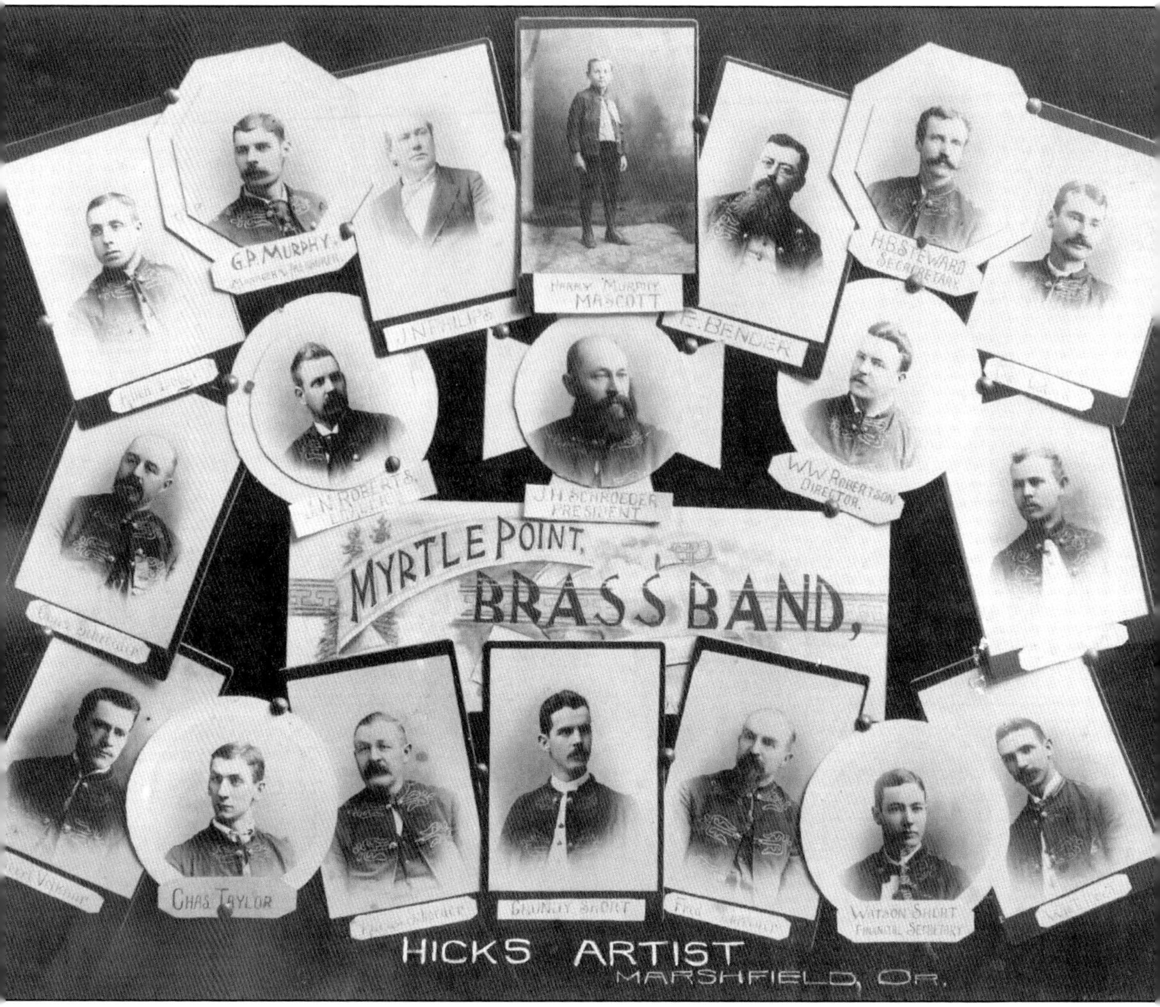

The Myrtle Point Brass Band, founded in 1880, performed widely, including at the Pioneer Reunion when the train first came to Myrtle Point in 1893. Band members included, from left to right, (bottom row) Albert Volknar, Chas Taylor, August Schroeder, Grundy Short, Fred Schroeder, Watson Short, and Wm. T. Reed; (middle row) Chas. Schroeder, J.N. Roberts, J.H. Schroeder, W.W. Robertson, and unidentified/illegible; (top row) Allen Dodge, G.P. Murphy, J.N. Philips, Harry Murphy, E. Bender, H.B. Steward, and Chas. Catlin. (KD.)

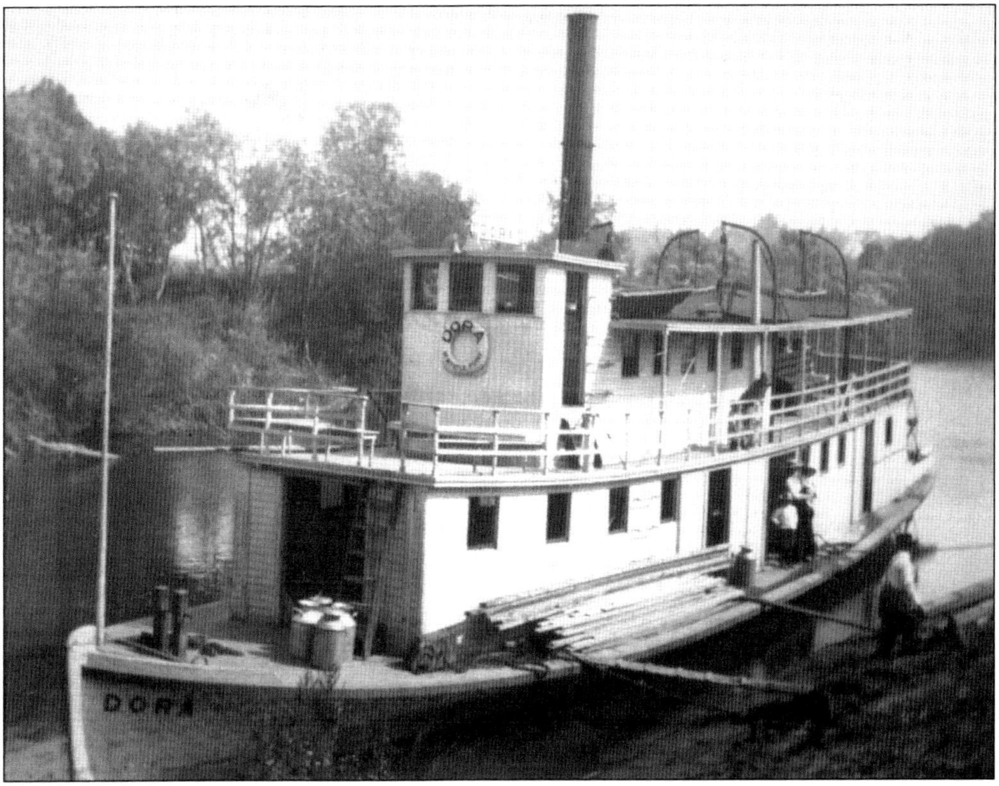

Capt. Russell Panter named this 70-foot stern-wheeler for his daughter Dora. In February 1921, the *Dora*, then under ownership of the Panter family's Myrtle Point Transportation Company, steamed to Myrtle Point on a mission to refloat the steamer *Myrtle*, which had sunk at its moorings behind Weedly Warehouse when loaded with most of a railroad carload of canned carrots from the Chase-Holt Cannery. (CHMM 992-8-1782.)

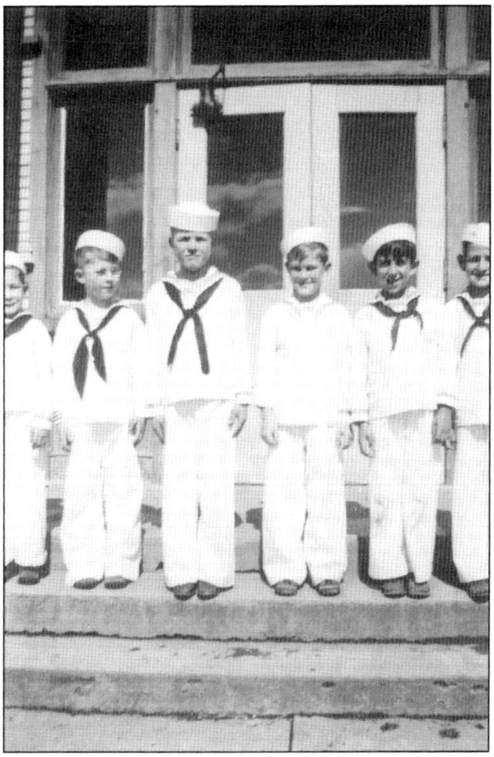

These young actors—ready to sing "Anchors Away" with swabbing-the-deck dance moves at Spruce Street School in 1942—are, from left to right, unidentified, Phillip Barker, Keith Hoffman, David Haberly, unidentified, and Bill Caffey. The Myrtle Point Grammar School, built in 1913 on Spruce Street, housed four grades in 1935. (DH.)

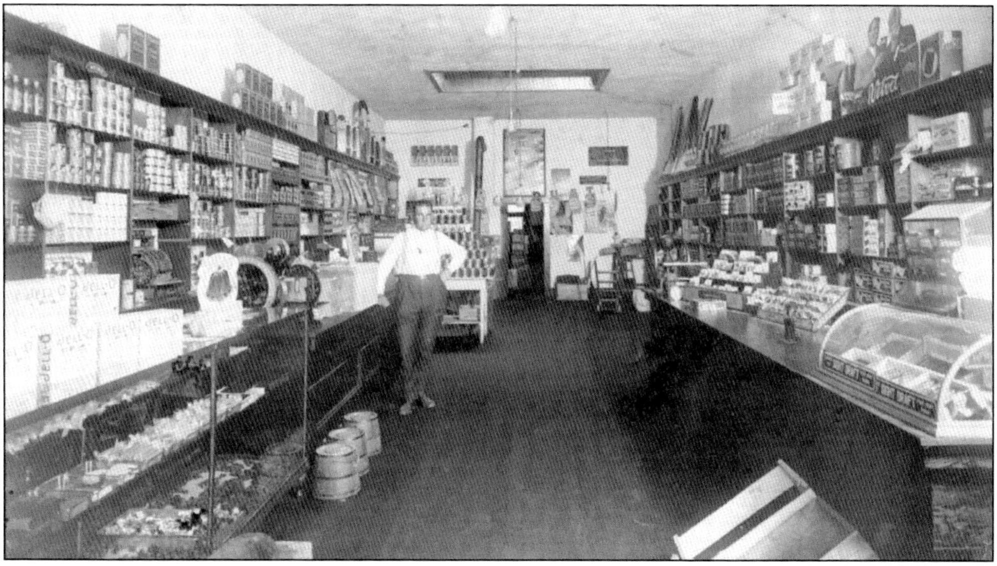

Earnie Barklow stands in his parents' mercantile store on Spruce Street in the early 1900s. Albert and Ora Barklow's store was two doors west of Ernest Davenport's butcher shop and one door east of the Hub. Four brothers—Homer C., Orvin Thomas, Elmer, and Ellis Gant—launched the Hub, a men's clothing store, in Myrtle Point, Coquille, and Bandon. The Hub advertised hole-proof hose and Hardeman hats. (HR.)

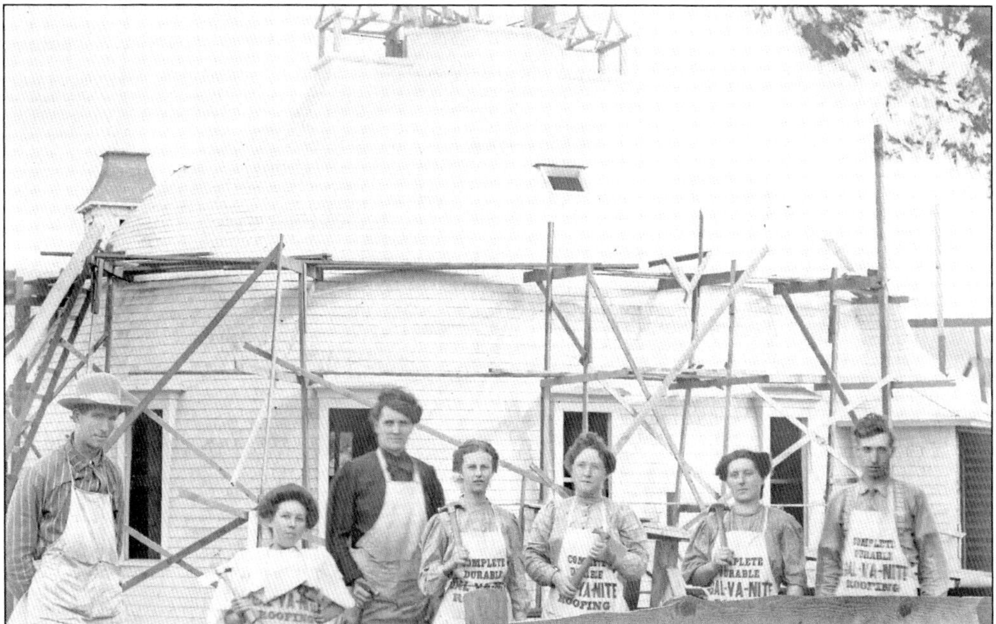

Members of the Reorganized Church of the Latter Day Saints helped their builders, Tom Dixon and Charles McCracken, construct a domed building in 1910 on the corner of Seventh and Maple Streets. Volunteers include, from left to right, Frank Dygert, Nellie Humes, Sara Hund, Zella Johnson, Ann Giles, Maude McCracken, and Ed Britton. Today, the building houses the Coquille Valley Logging Museum. (MC.)

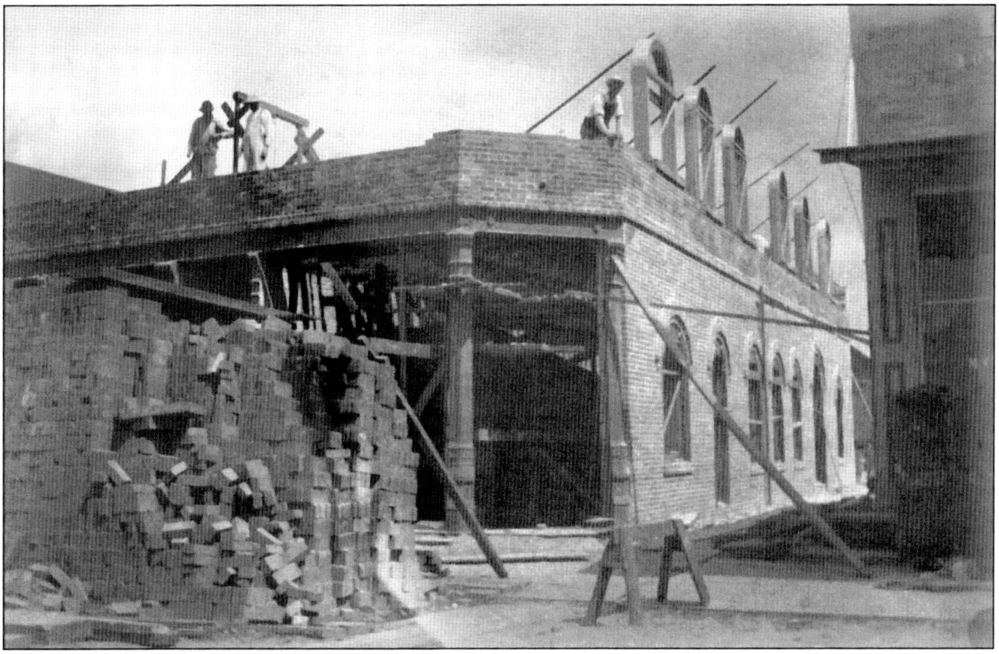

Bricks for construction of the Benson Bank in 1901 were supplied by Daniel Giles. Giles and his son Sam opened a brickyard in Myrtle Point in 1890 on Reedsford Road. They supplied bricks for many Myrtle Point buildings, including the high school on C Street, the Black Building, and the Hermann Building. (CHMM 49 967-137J.)

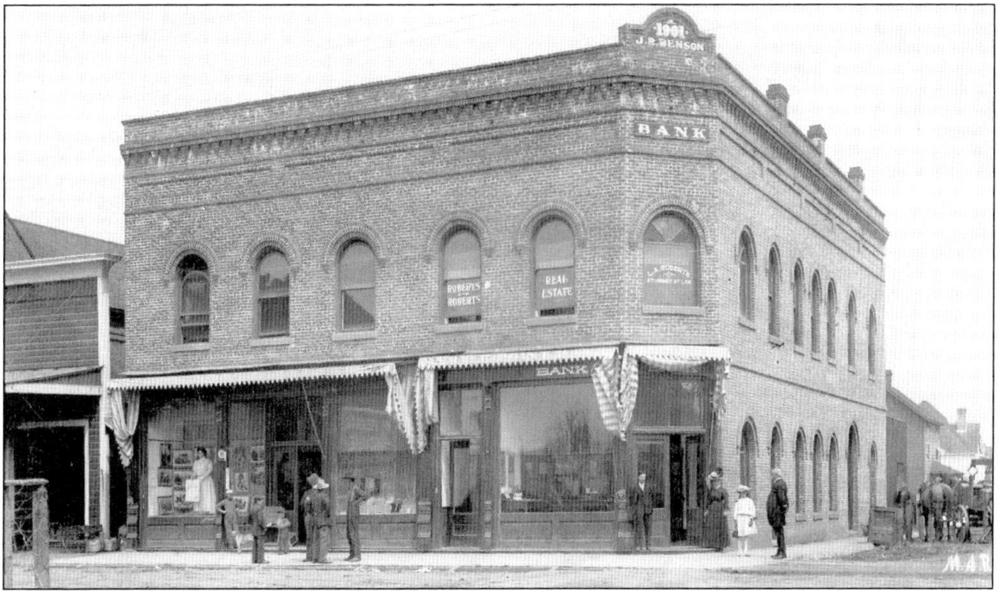

Standing at the corner of the Benson Bank in 1905 are, from left to right, unidentified, Mabel (Benson) Roberts, Vera Sherwood, and John R. Benson. Beside the building is a wagon loaded with milk cans. This structure on the corner of Spruce and Fourth Streets has also been the home of the Bank of Myrtle Point, post office, Nels P. Peterson Mercantile, and Myers & Myers Department Store; it today houses Hometown Hardware. (KL.)

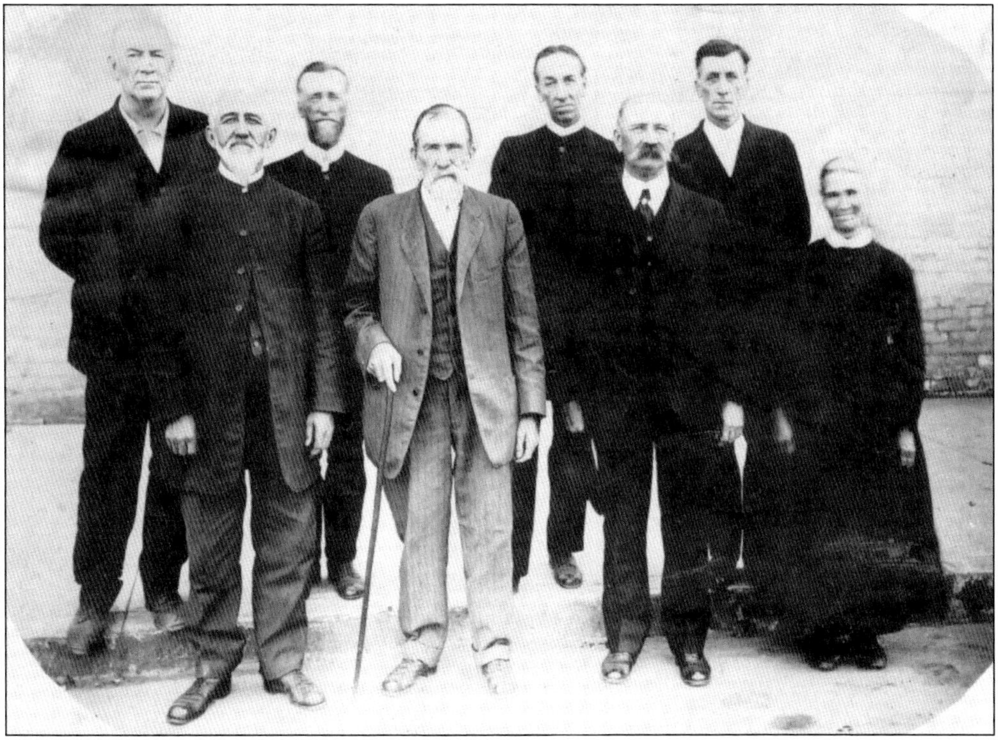

Children of John Barklow, arranged by age in 1910, are, from left to right, (first row) firstborn Thomas Barklow, Albert Barklow, Johnnie D. Barklow, and Martha Root; (second row) Daniel Barklow, Frank Barklow, Isaac Barklow, and Manley Barklow. Thomas was elected to the unpaid ministry of the Brethren Church in 1891. He farmed one mile south of Myrtle Point, clerked for Schiller B. Hermann, and worked at the Dixon store, where he received paid time off for church work. Another employer, storekeeper Nels P. Peterson, docked his pay. (HR.)

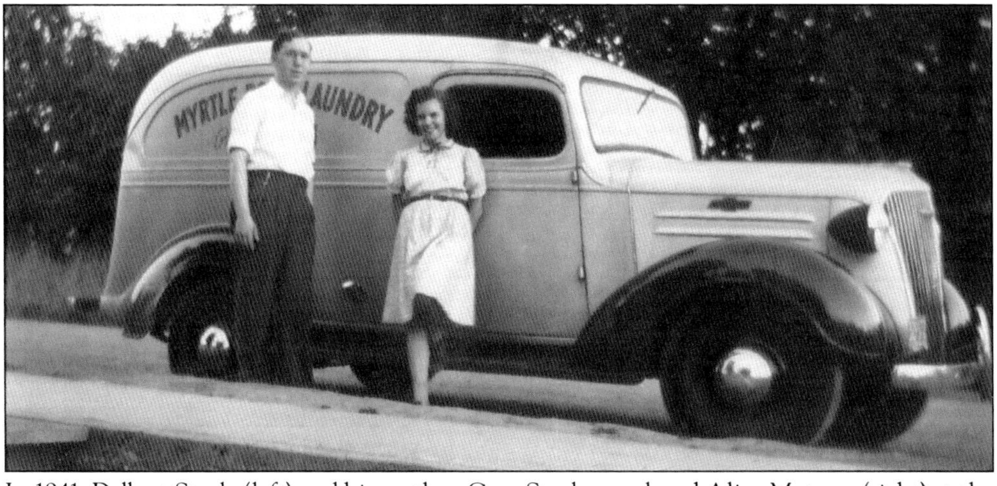

In 1941, Delbert Steele (left) and his mother, Cora Steele, employed Alice Metzgus (right) at the Myrtle Point Laundry, located near the corner of Spruce and Eighth Streets. Machines in a back room washed items collected from Mast Hospital and other customers. After line drying, linens were fed through a mangle, while shirts were starched and ironed. During World War II, Delbert was an Army corporal on Africa's Gold Coast. (AD.)

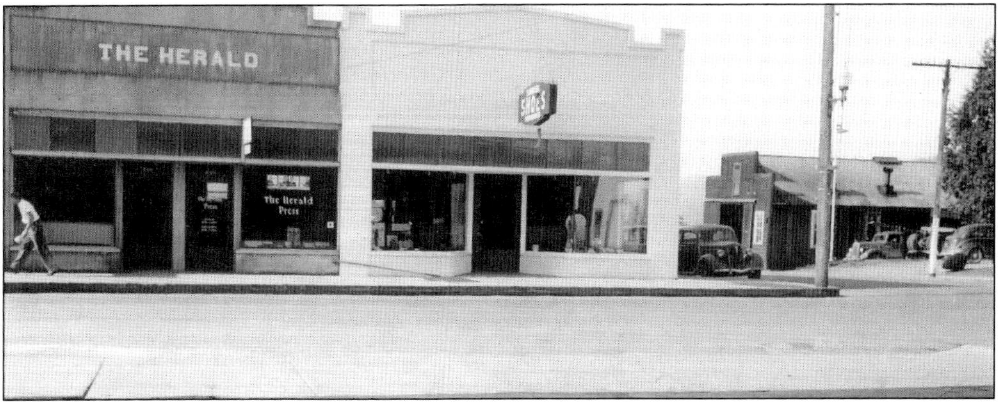

Vehicles from the 1930s park near the Herald Press and Breuer's Shoes. W.L. Dixon published Myrtle Point's first newspaper, the *West Oregonian,* in 1889. George B. Hamilton owned the city's newspaper from 1925 to 1935. He named the newspaper the *Herald* and bought this building on Spruce Street. To the right, on Fourth Street, is Henry Hermann's blacksmith shop. Hermann opened his shop in 1907 and worked there for 47 years. (KD.)

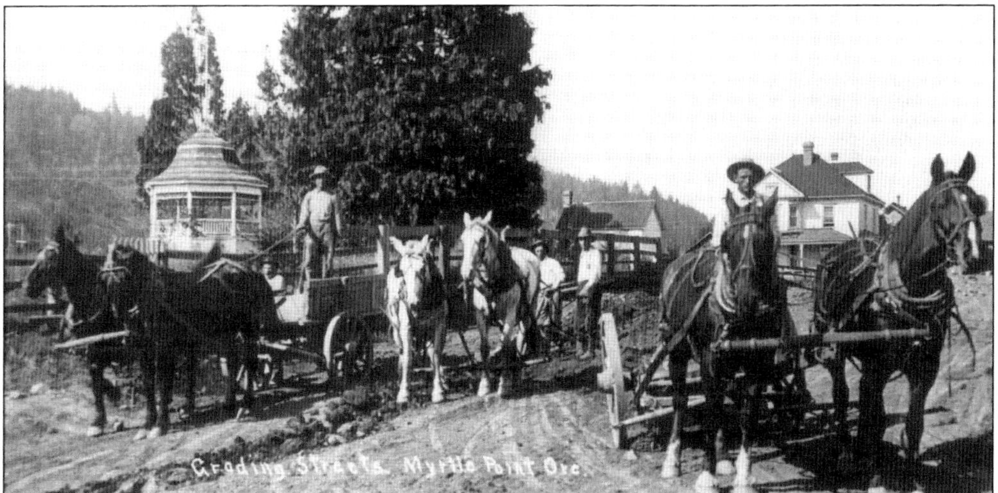

Horses and men grade Second Street near the gazebo in Lehnherr Park in the early 1900s. Behind them is a three-story house on Ash Street owned by Benjamin and Olive Shull. Early residents of Ash Street included Christian Lehnherr, Peter Wise, and William W. Crumley, who was a captain of the *Dora*, a steamer on the Coquille River. The Catholic church is located east of the grading. (PD.)

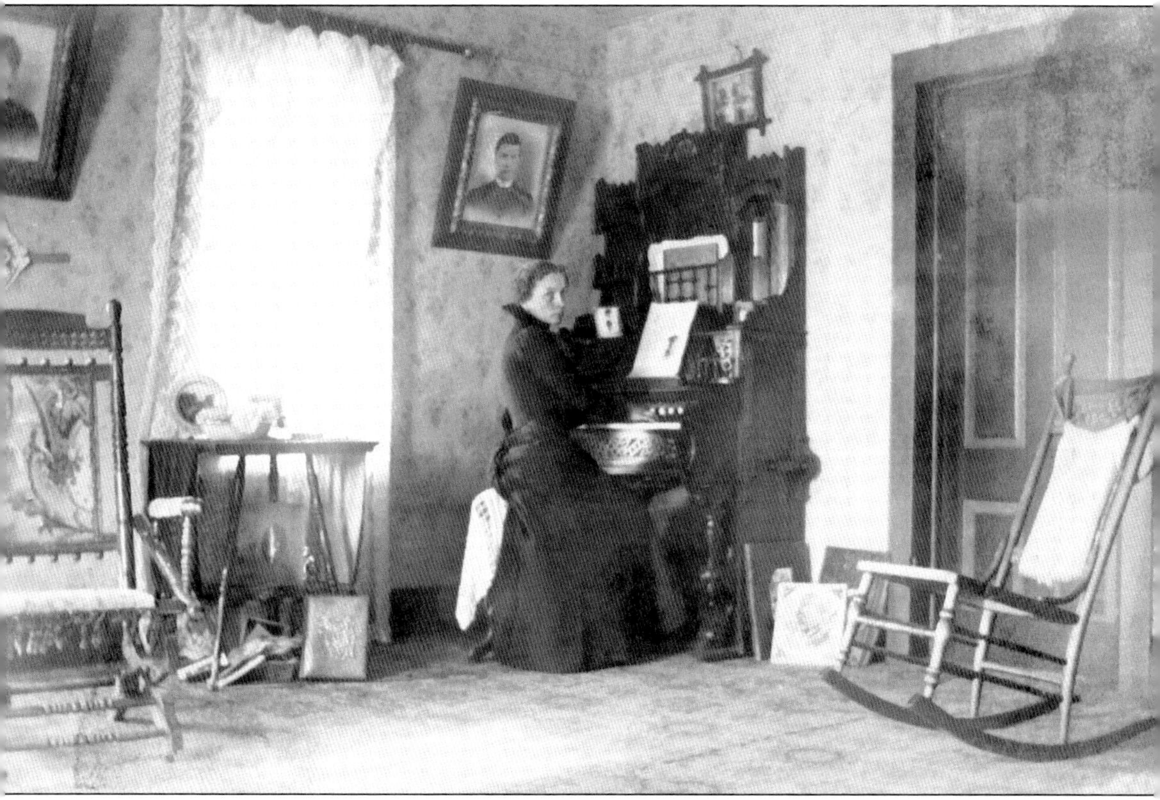

After Lollie Marsters married Edwin Sherwood, they lived at 822 Cedar Street. She is pictured here playing the pump organ in her parlor in 1898. Earlier, the home was occupied by Oscar O. Reed and his wife, Mary (Lehnherr) Reed. This house, which still stands, was a funeral chapel for a time. Today, the Lutheran church is across the street. (KL.)

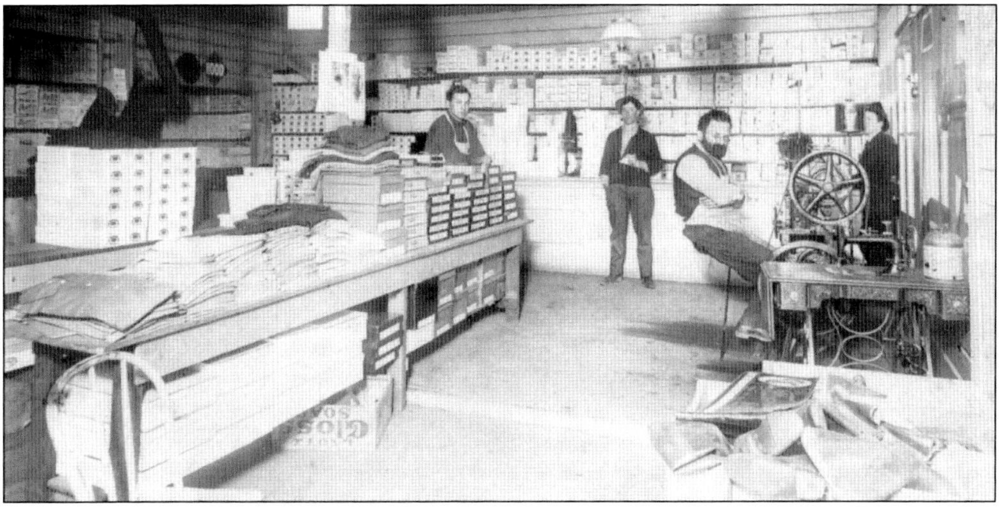

Sam Breuer, seated, began repairing and selling shoes in Myrtle Point in 1891. In the early years, he walked to town from his Indian Creek farm. Sam's son Paul (left) was the second generation to operate Breuer's Shoes. In the 1920s, Breuer's Shoes was located in a two-story building on Spruce Street near Third Street. By 1936, the store had moved to Spruce and Fourth Streets. (KD.)

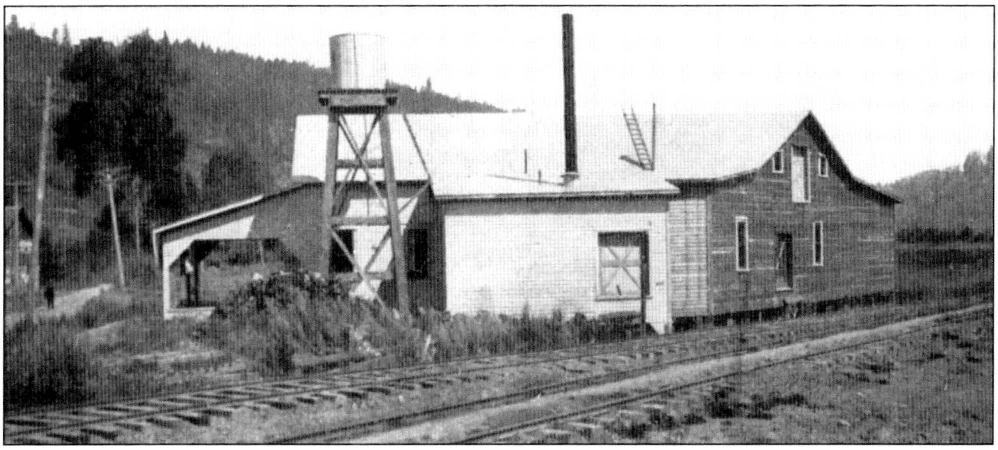

Located near today's Port of Coquille River office, the Holt-Chase Cannery shipped canned fruits and vegetables by boat and train in the 1920s. In the 1940s, the Myrtle Point Union High School Community Cannery, at the corner of Fourth and Maple Streets, canned meat, fruit, and vegetables by appointment. Cannery leaders included Ted Kirsch, Dorothy Gurney, Mabel Barklow, and Paul Davis. In 1897, Myrtle Point had a commercial fruit dryer. (CHMM 76 009-16.5645.)

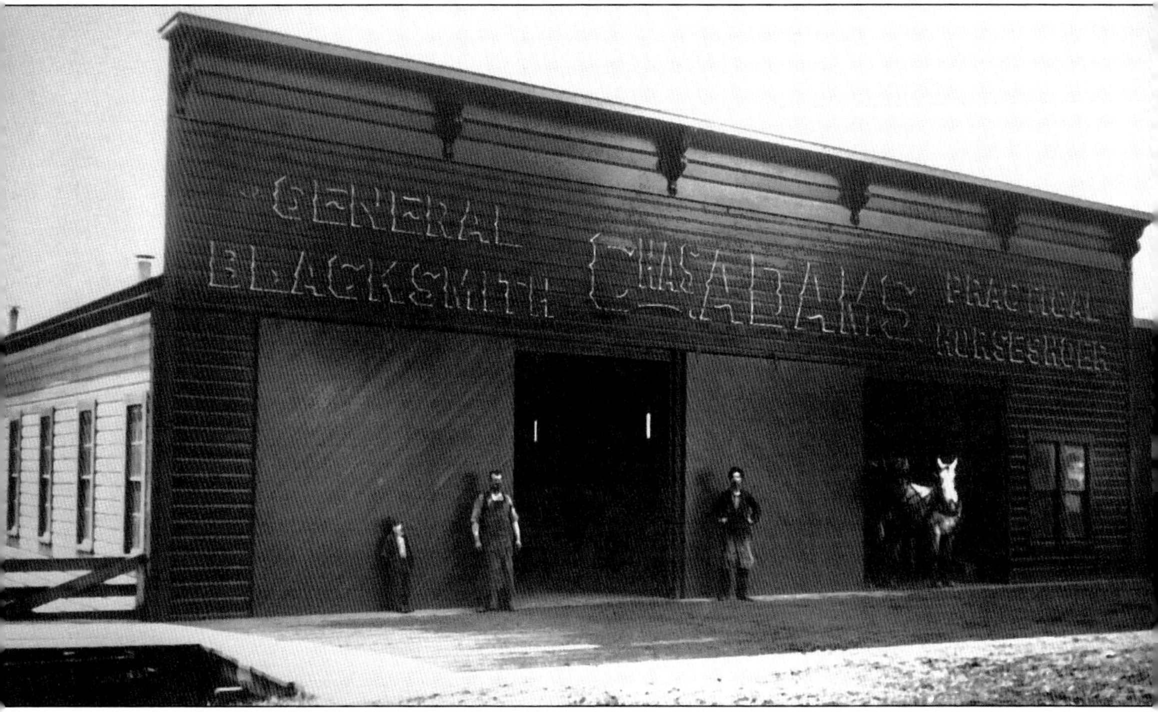

Repairing mill machinery, fabricating wagon parts, and custom shaping horseshoes kept blacksmiths busy in Myrtle Point. Pictured in 1904, the Charles Adams blacksmith shop, located on Maple Street, supplied shoes for all types of horses, including the large draft horses that worked on farms and in the logging industry. (CHMM 54 992-8-1966.)

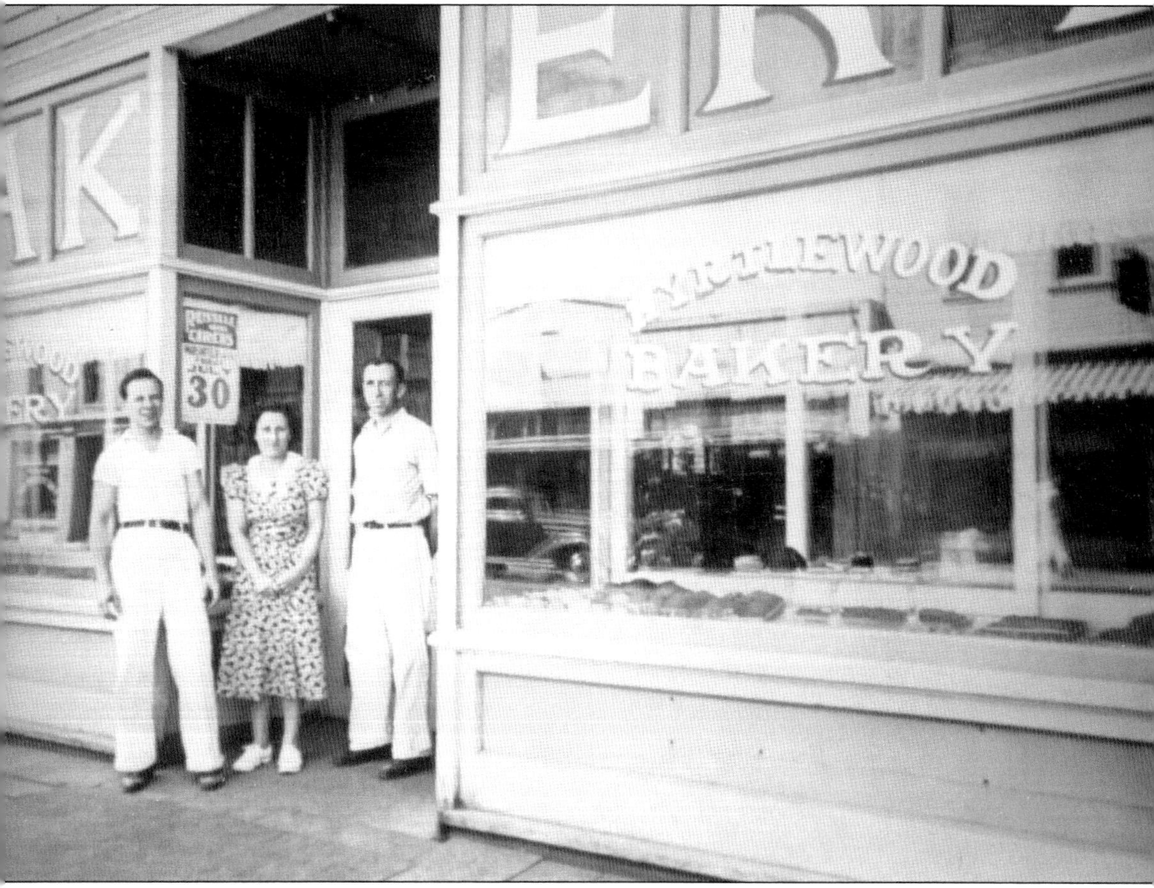

Beginning in the 1930s, Ralph Whitaker (left) and his brother, Howard Whitaker (right), built wood fires in their bakery's Dutch oven every night except Friday. Pauline Strong (center) worked in the bakery in about 1948, around the time when a propane oven replaced the oven that burned slab wood. During fair week, Howard's wife, Frances, and Ralph's wife, Ruth, helped roll piecrust. In a single day, the Whitakers baked 66 pies and sold them all. The bakers' wives, who were sisters, both taught in Myrtle Point schools. The bakery, located across Spruce Street from the Schroeder furniture store, was between Western Auto and Barker's Jewelry. (BW.)

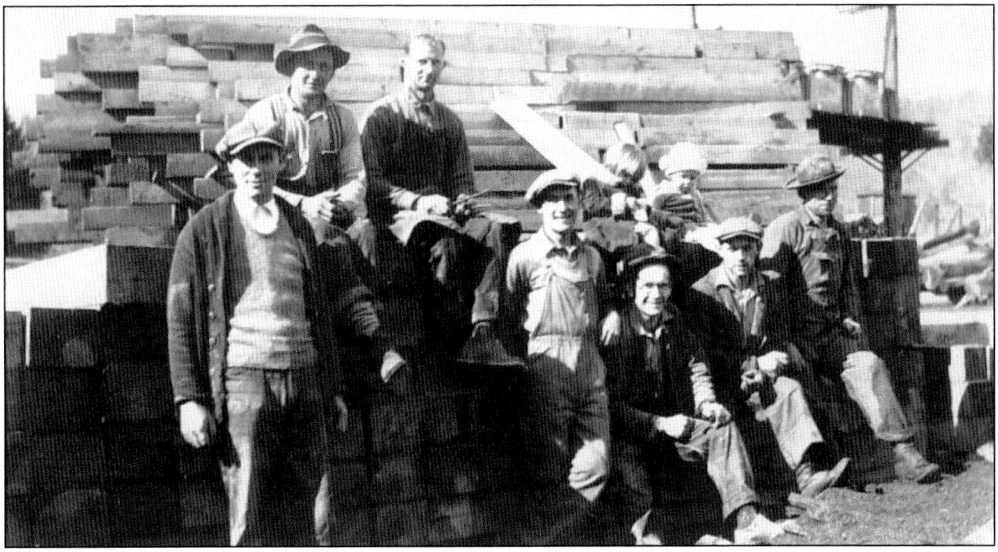

Frank Sander owned Myrtle Point Mill & Lumber Company at the foot of Maple Street. The mill produced railroad ties and dimension lumber. The mill employees pictured here in 1931 are, from left to right, Giles Harris, unidentified, Frank Sander, Gus Metzgus, unidentified, Fred Zumwalt, and John Rissberger. The children are Alice (left) and Helen Metzgus. (AD.)

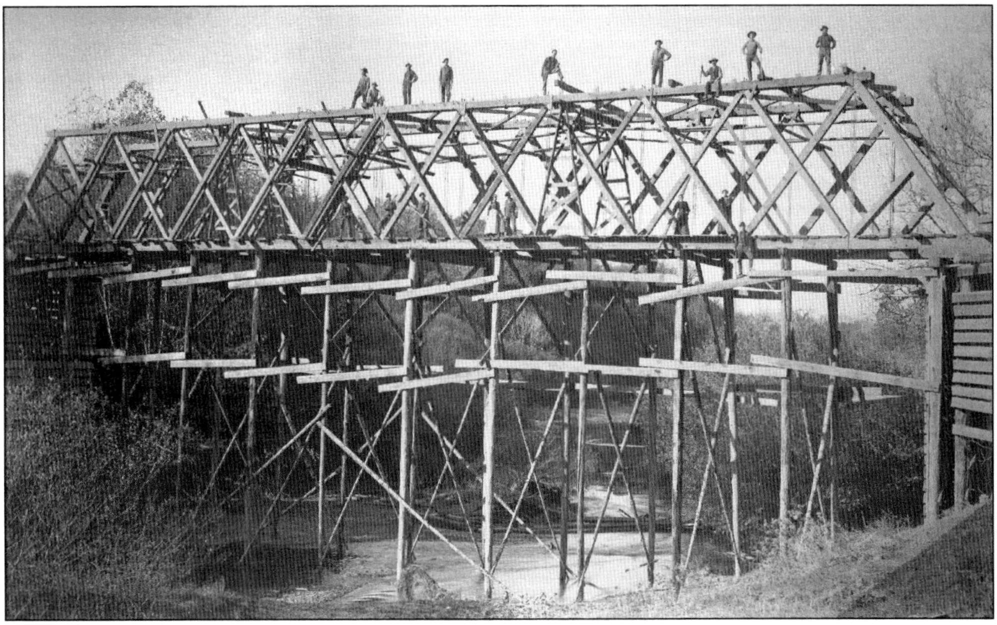

More elevated than the Maple Street Bridge that it replaced in 1917 was the Spruce Street Bridge. In this image, three women join the men on the partially constructed bridge high above the South Fork of the Coquille River. The span connected Myrtle Point with West Myrtle Point. Seventeen years earlier, John Giles had fallen 30 feet while working on a bridge over the South Fork. He was shaken up, but not hurt. (CHMM 66 992-8-1963.)

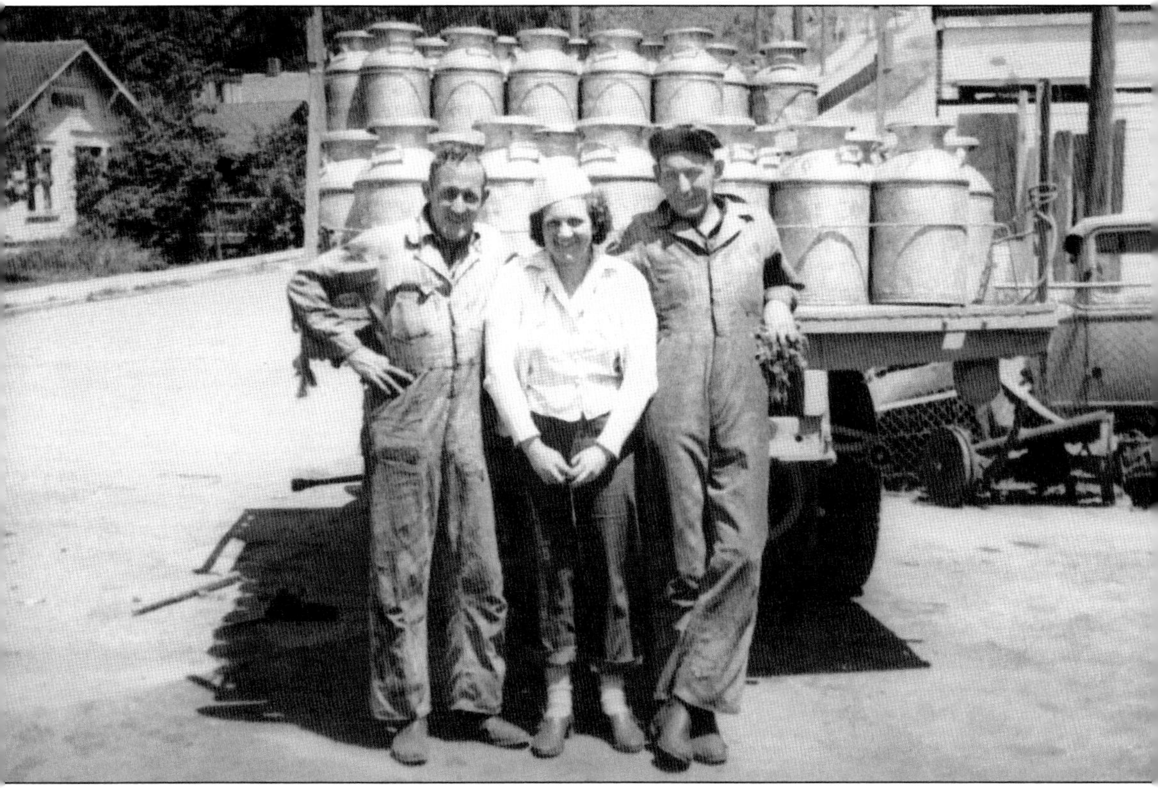

Located beside Highway 42 in the late 1940s, B&R Service Station had mechanic bays, a gas pump, and a coffee shop. Earl Roush (left) managed Thornton's Tire Shop but often helped out at B&R. Later, Thornton's Tire Shop became a bowling alley. Phyllis Roush (center) waited tables for her father, Ambrose "Am" Roush (right), who owned B&R with Harry Beal. (WL.)

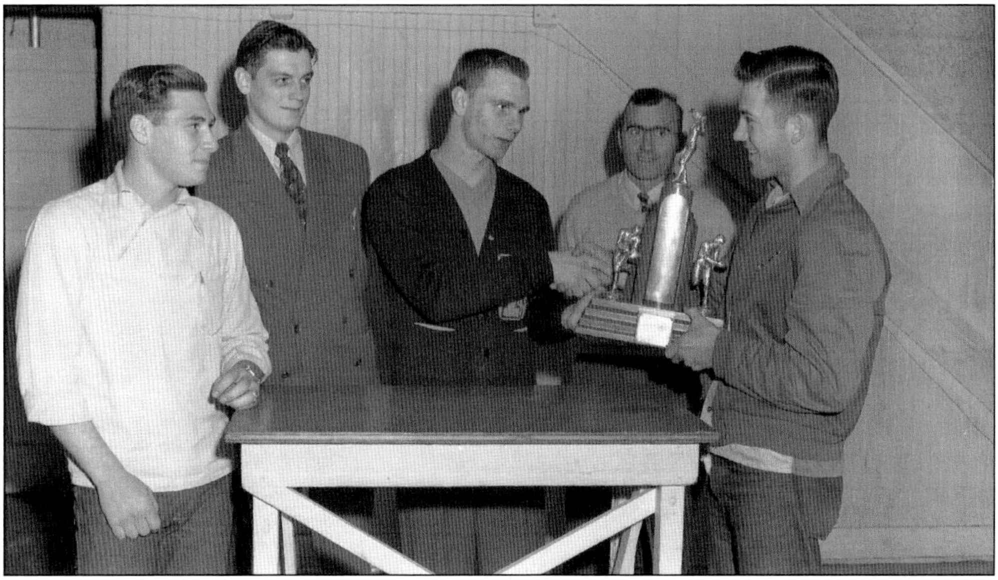

Myrtle Point High School football players and coaches admiring the Coos Trophy that the team won in the fall of 1948 are, from left to right, cocaptain Ed Gilkison, coach Dale Bunnell, Marvin Fliteroff, coach Curt Beckham, and cocaptain Tinker Hatfield. The team won the football championship three years in a row. Gilkison was student body president during his senior year, 1948–1949. (CHMM 134 995-1.4989.)

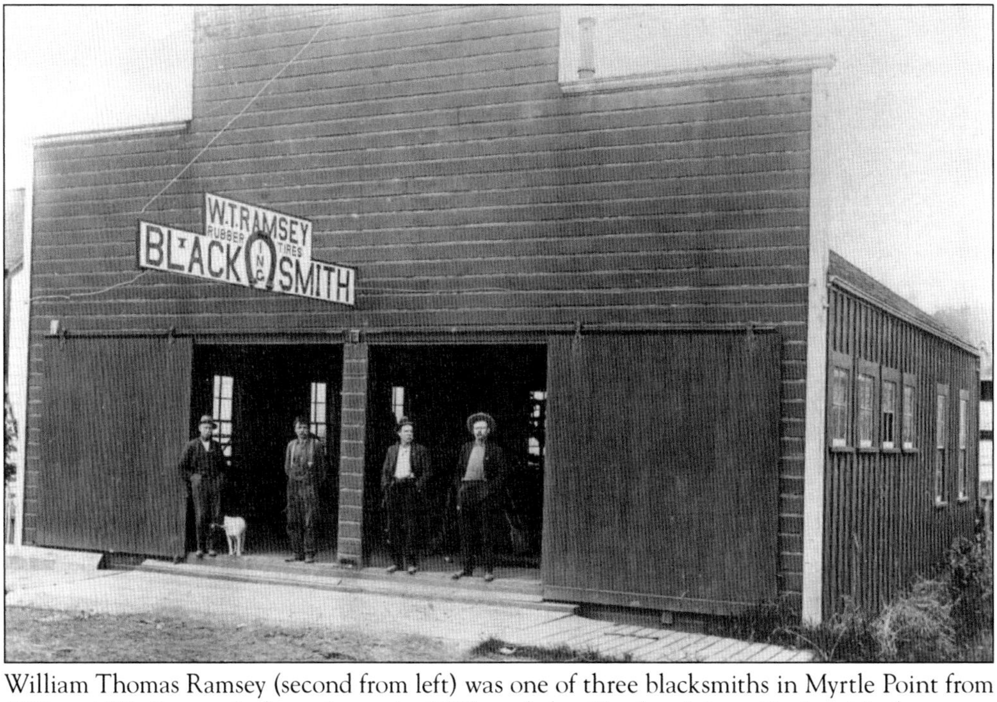

William Thomas Ramsey (second from left) was one of three blacksmiths in Myrtle Point from 1918 to 1921. Ramsey's shop, shown in 1920, and the Charles Adams blacksmith shop were located on Maple Street. Henry Hermann owned the third shop. Ramsey, who operated his shop for about 20 years, had four sons and a daughter who attended Myrtle Point's grammar school. (CHMM 157-989-NA2.)

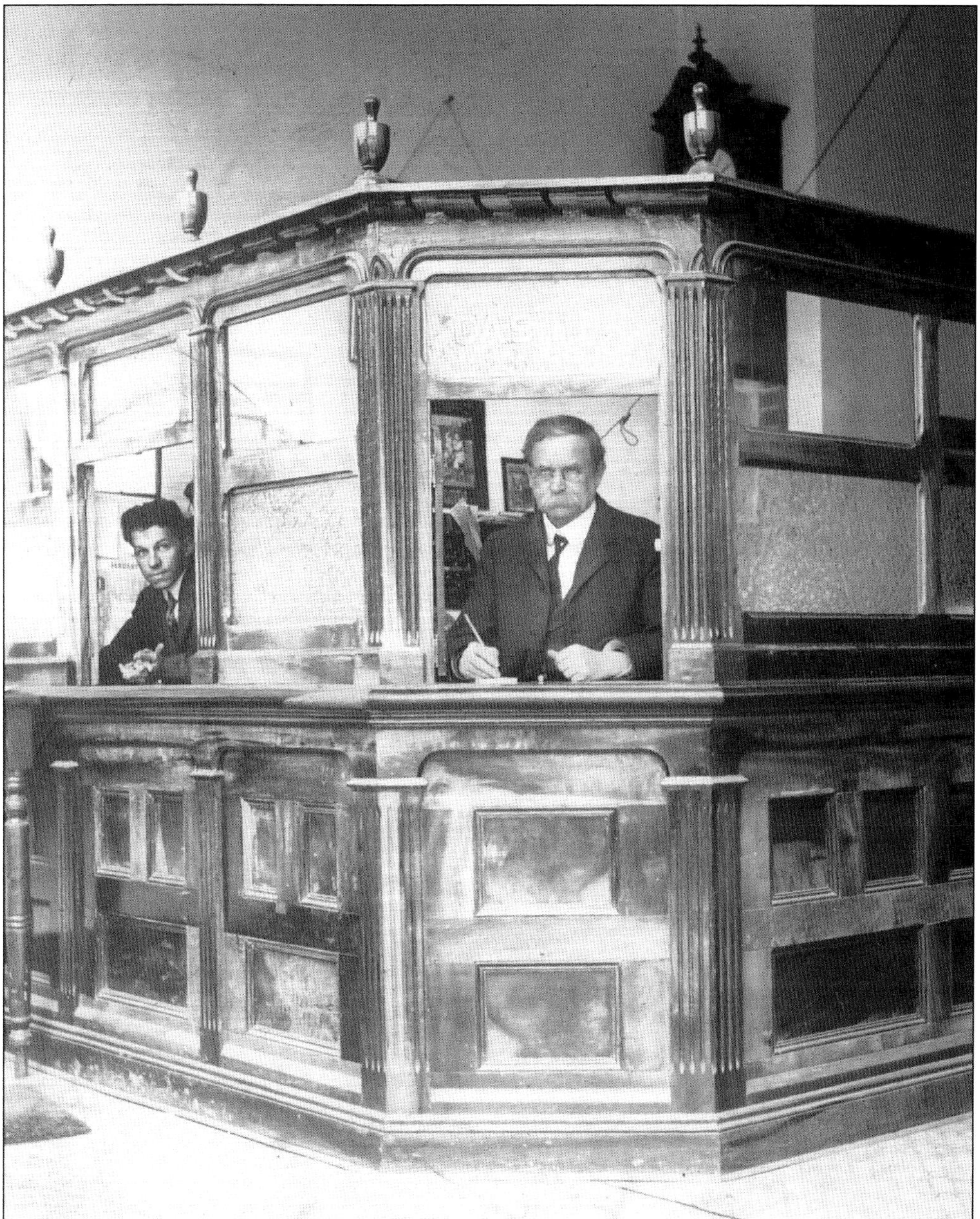

John R. Benson (right) and W.F. Hendricks, Benson's brother-in-law, founded a private bank around 1901 that became the Bank of Myrtle Point in 1912. William Hendricks (left), probably Benson's nephew, is ready to count out coins on the bank's myrtlewood counter. In 1913, a robber cut a hole in the floor of Ed Roberts's law office above the bank, dropped to the vault, blew open the strongbox with nitroglycerin, and made off with about $10,000. (CHMM 50 967-137T.)

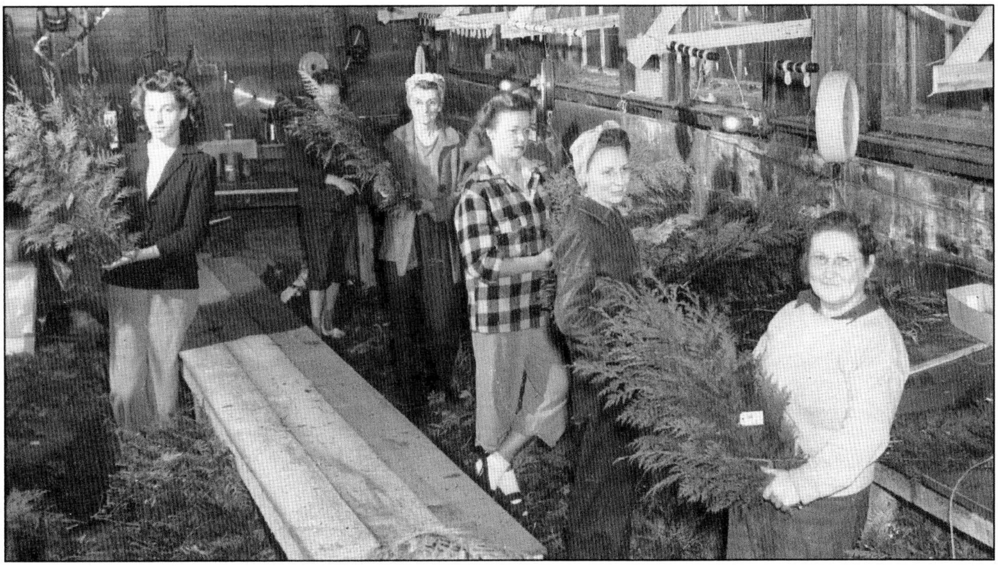

Cedar, salal, huckleberry, and sword ferns were processed at Kirk's fern plant on Maple Street between Fourth and Fifth Streets. Pictured here around 1947, Ethel (Robinson) Hollenbeck (third from left) and unidentified coworkers are bunching cedar. In earlier days, the building provided space for roller-skating parties and dances sponsored by the Veterans of Foreign Wars. (LW.)

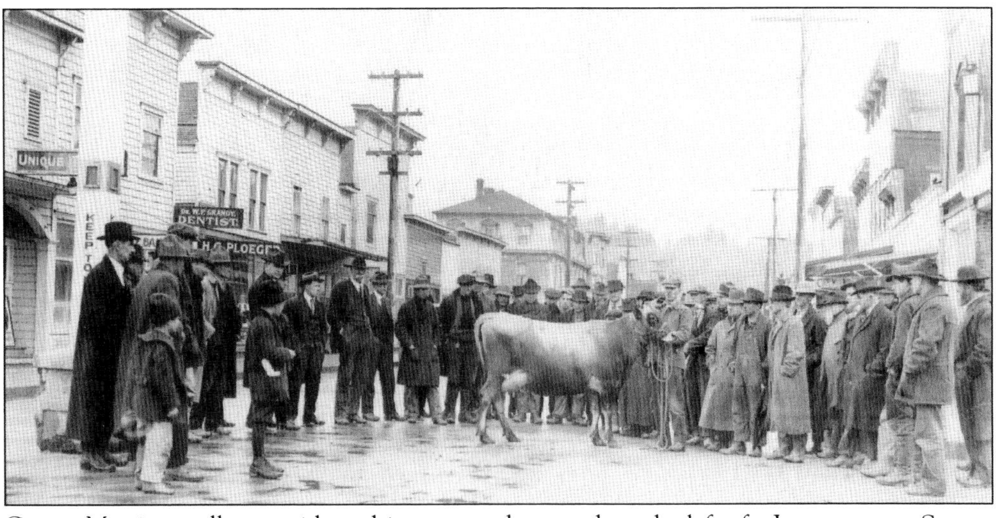

George Martin, a tall man with a white moustache, stands to the left of a Jersey cow on Spruce Street around 1920. Farmers wanted to improve their dairy herds for increased production. On the north side of Spruce are the Unique Theatre, Dr. W.P. Grandy's office, and the Henry G. Ploeger men's clothing store. Robert's Grocery is one door past Ploeger's. On the next block is the Guerin Hotel. (MER.)

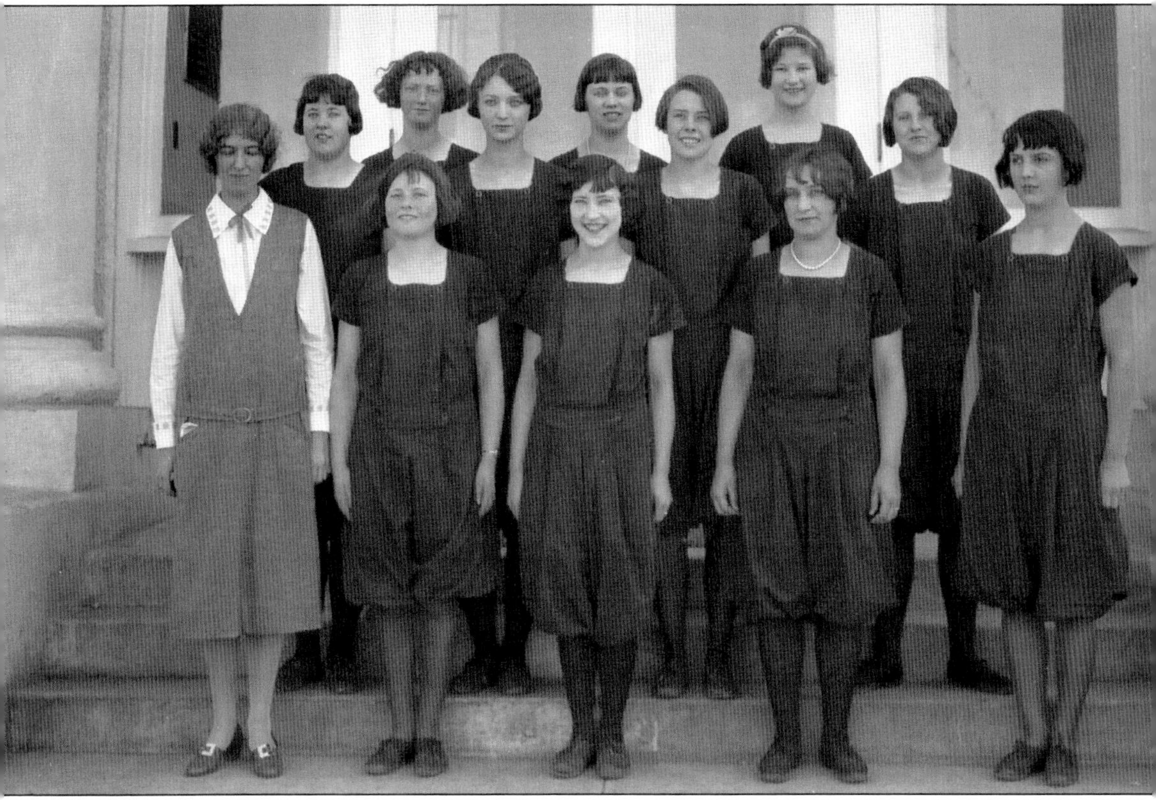

The 1926 girls' basketball team photograph for Myrtle Point High School includes, from left to right, (first row) coach Wilna Manly, Thelma Snyder, Florence Felsher, Dena Mast, and Avolia Baker; (second row) Isabelle Bryant, Zona Kelly, Hilda Fredenburg, and Gladys Tripp; (third row) Vera McCulloch, Bernice Davenport, and unidentified. The team defeated Riverton and North Bend but lost two games to Coquille. (Photograph by John Stadden, CHMM 119 987-S1203.)

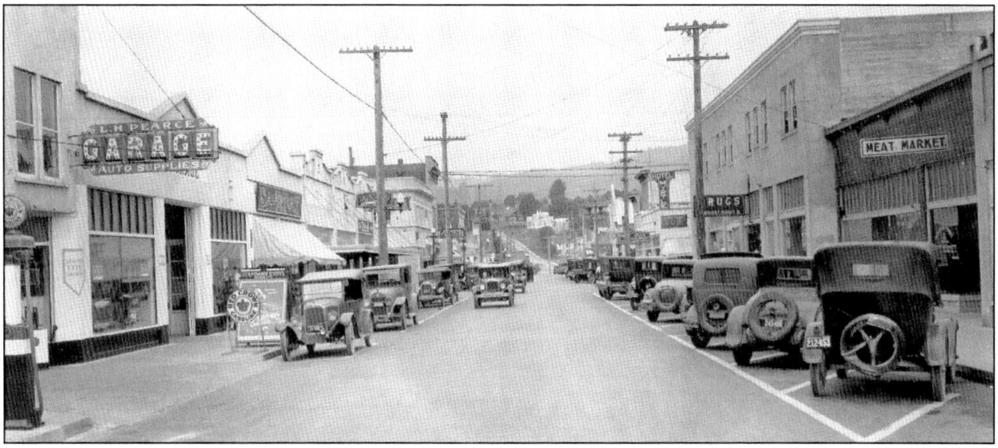

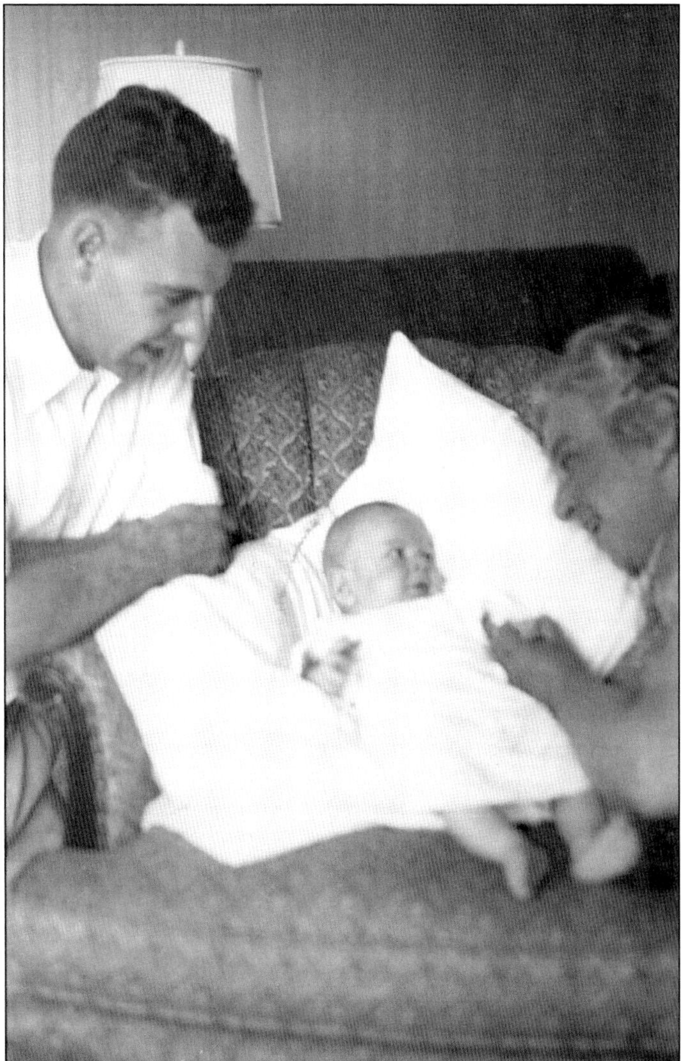

L.H. Pearce opened a harness shop in 1903. Gradually, he changed to selling automobile tires and then added a garage, pictured here in the 1920s on the north side of Spruce Street. East of Pearce's garage is the Safeway grocery store. At the end of the block, Perkins' (later Flentge) Drug Store faces Sempert's Drug Store on the south side of Spruce. (MER.)

After graduating from medical school in 1935, Dr. Herbert Hall Thomas (left) treated patients at Mast Hospital. In 1942, Laura Thomas (right) traveled from Iowa to meet her infant grandson Hall Herbert Thomas (center). The first twins Dr. Thomas delivered were Harold and Howard Neideigh. Doctors at Mast Hospital included Dr. Ernest Frank Beber and Dr. Edmund Reed Gurney. (AD.)

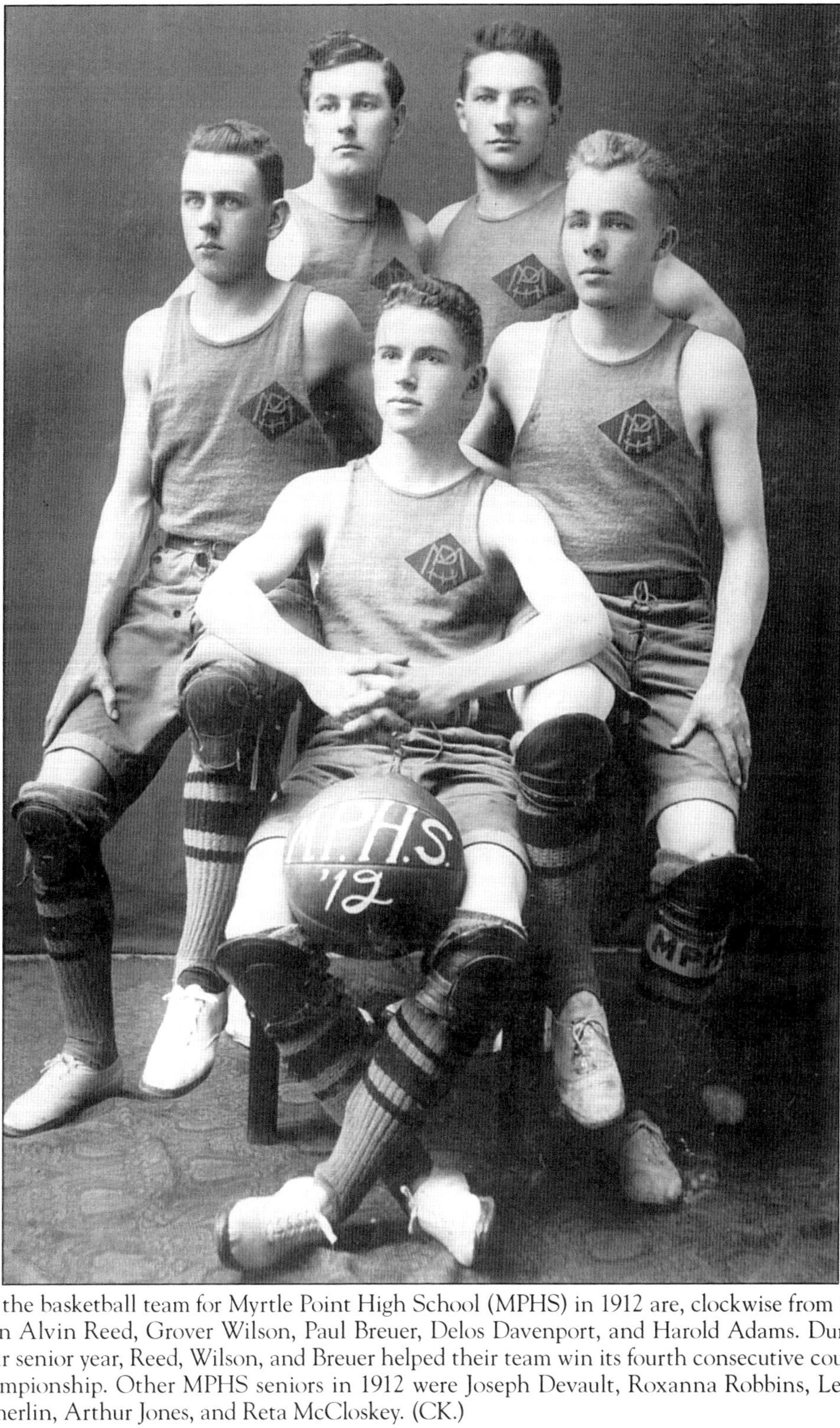

On the basketball team for Myrtle Point High School (MPHS) in 1912 are, clockwise from left, Orin Alvin Reed, Grover Wilson, Paul Breuer, Delos Davenport, and Harold Adams. During their senior year, Reed, Wilson, and Breuer helped their team win its fourth consecutive county championship. Other MPHS seniors in 1912 were Joseph Devault, Roxanna Robbins, Lester Sumerlin, Arthur Jones, and Reta McCloskey. (CK.)

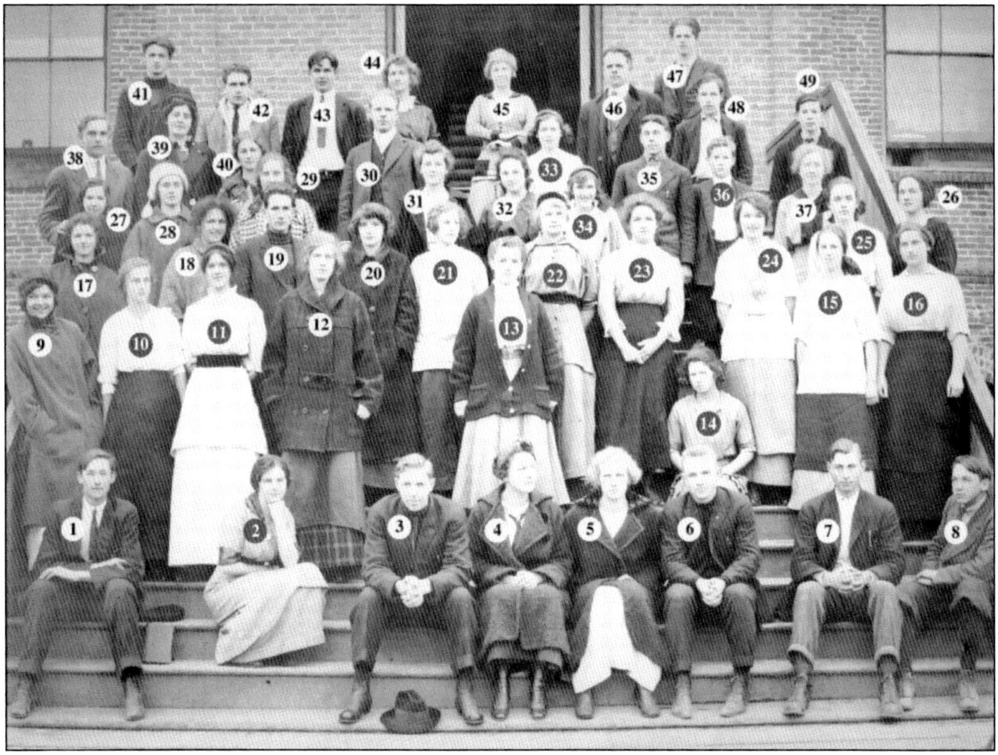

The students and teachers of Myrtle Point High School fill the steps of their school on the corner of Maple and C Streets in 1915. They are, as numbered, Arthur Widby (1), Annie Johnson (2), Victor Stevens (3), Mabel Eggers (4), Grace Hall (5), Floyd Wimberly (6), ? Miller (7), and Harold Gourley (8), Hazel Neal (9), Rowena Roberts (10), Lola Greene (11), Chesta Chandler (12), unidentified (13), Lula Ray Jarvis (14), Fairy Davis (15), and Mary Smalley (16), Nita Hayes (17), Jo Hayes (18), Ervin Barklow (19), Nola DeArmond (20), Elfreida Barklow (21), Florence Hall (22), Stella Barklow (23), Helen Whitaker (24), Lila Smith (25), and Gladys Krantz (26) Grace Summerlin (27), Grace Krantz (28), Zella Summerlin (29), Floyd Walker (30), Hazel Lee (31), Ira Harmon (32), Ruth Wade (33), Elva Greene (34), Chester Root (35), Lorin Guerin (36), and Emma Guerin (37), John Hall (38), Audrey Bryant (39), Abby Elwood (40), Larry Miller (41), Roy Spires (42), Nick ? (43), Zella Walker (44), Devore (45), ? Wimberly (46), Sam Carter (47), Harry Stewart (48), and Dewey King (49). (KL.)

Two

Coos County Fair
Bucking Broncs, Prize Pickles, and Cotton Candy

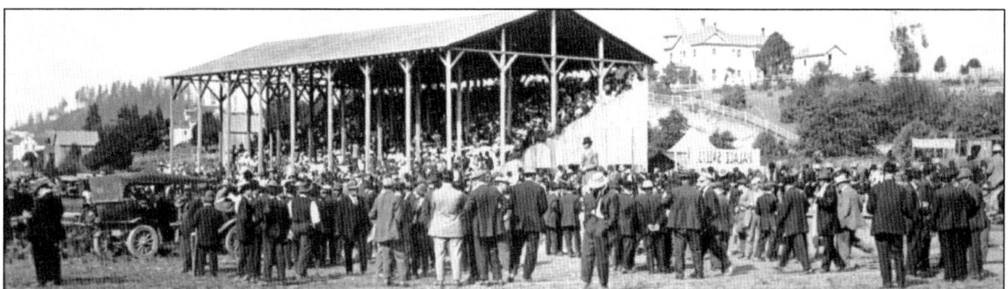

While women and children fill the grandstands, men wait in the September sun in 1913. In 1914, women could sit in the stands for free, but men had to pay 10¢. Overlooking the fairgrounds is the home of Russell Cooke "R.C." Dement and Lucy (Norris) Dement, who had nine children. R.C., along with P.M. Cole, sold property to use as a fairgrounds. (CVM.)

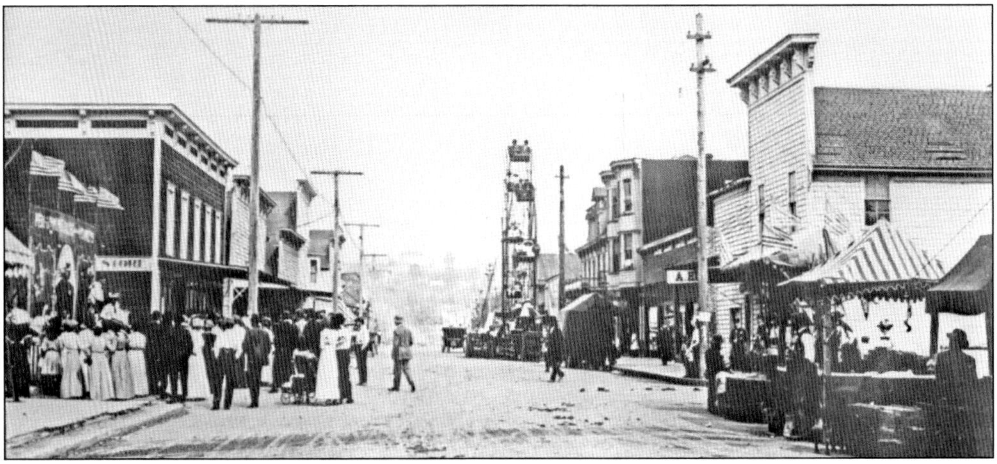

A Ferris wheel on Spruce Street in 1912 rises higher than the nearby Guerin Hotel. The Coos and Curry County Fair Association was incorporated on April 19, 1912. Within a few months, the association chose a site on the southwestern edge of Myrtle Point, bought land, and began constructing buildings. Horse races were held at the fairgrounds that first year, while booths and carnival rides were erected in downtown Myrtle Point. (CHMM 143 992-8-1952.)

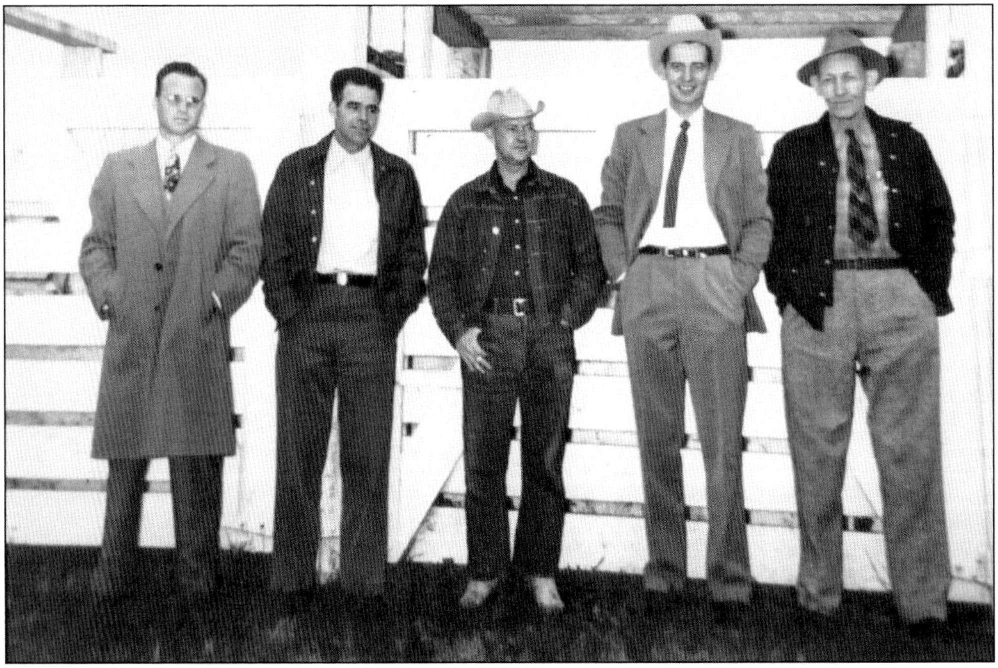

Serving on the fair board in about 1950 are, from left to right, Tom Guerin, Leland Barklow, Harold Clarno, Sam Dement, and Ambrose "Am" Roush. In 1912, the officers of the first fair board were R.C. Dement, president; J.L. Knight, vice president; L.A. Roberts, secretary; and Thomas D. Guerin, treasurer. Board members were A.E. Adlesperger, Coos Bay; Robert L. Wagner, Port Orford; and O.J. Seeley, Coquille. (CCFM.)

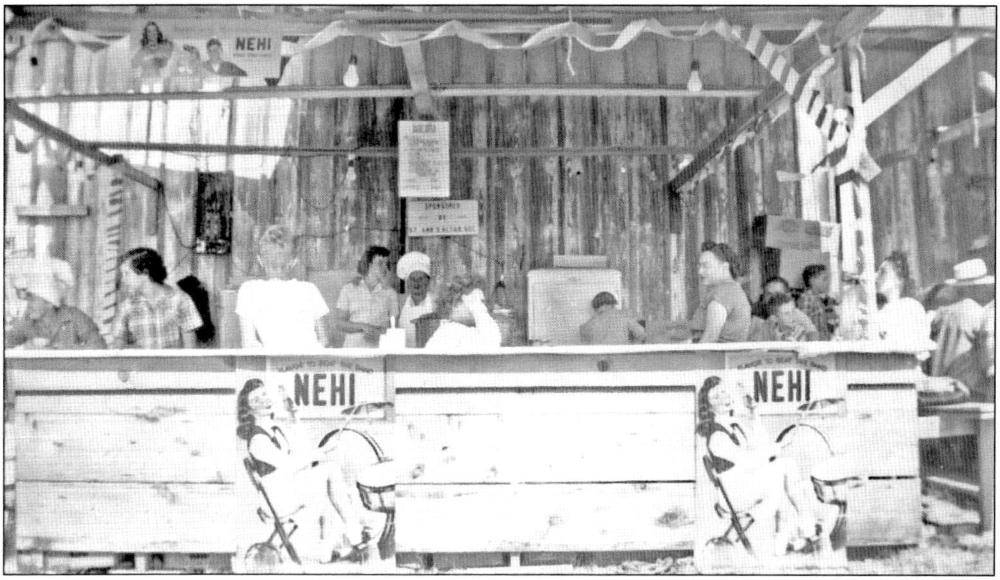

Nehi soda pop advertisements decorate the food booth that St. Ann's Altar Society opened at the fair in 1949. A committee representing the Catholic congregation in Myrtle Point, likely including Agnes Metzgus (far left), cleared $863.71 that year serving hamburgers, sandwiches, and slices of cake and pie. Kathryn Lawson found workspace near the refrigerator; she might be cutting a blackberry pie. (AD.)

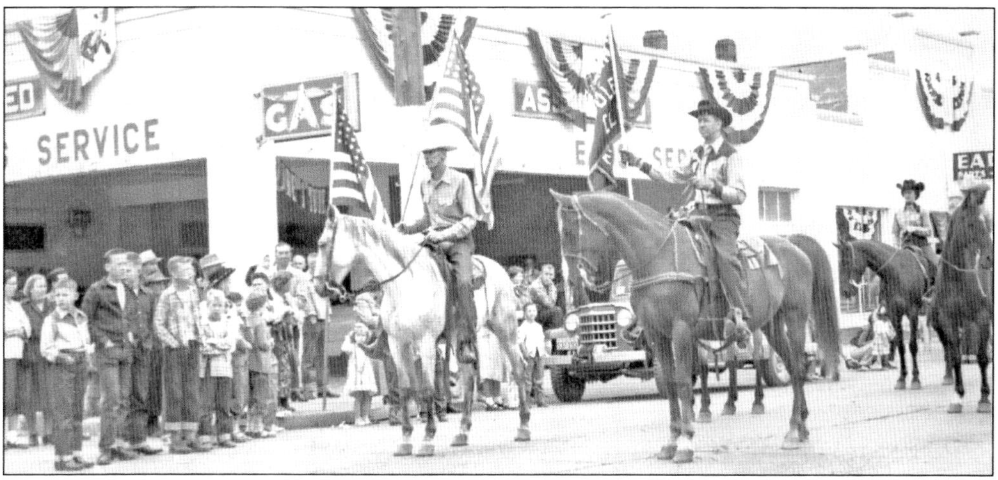

Leading the fair parade in 1952 are George King (with the Stars and Stripes) and V.B. "Tex" Billingsly (with the saddle club flag). The parade passed in front of Ead's Service Station on Spruce Street. King ranched on Ward Creek, and Billingsly operated the Billingsly Huggins Insurance office in Myrtle Point. Both men were members of the Myrtle Point Saddle Club. (CP.)

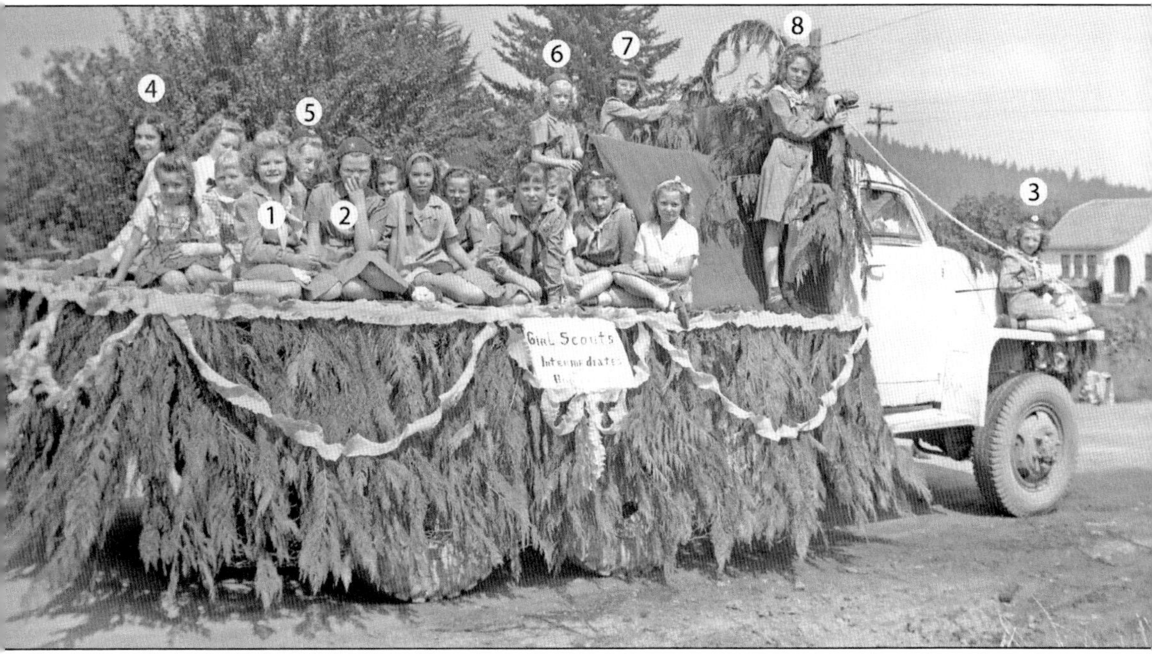

Girl Scouts decorated their float with cedar boughs and a pup tent in 1949. Identified in this image are Arlene Aasen (1), Mary Jo Schroeder (2), Betty Bartles (3), June Brewster (4), Evelyn Crook (5), Christine Shields (6), Shirley Toby (7), and Eleanor Barklow (8). Other members of the troop, led by Frances Whitaker, were Karin Train, Rochelle Noyes, Miriam Train, Anabel Baron, Carolyn Barklow, and Charlotte Train. (CHMM 47 95-1.1940.)

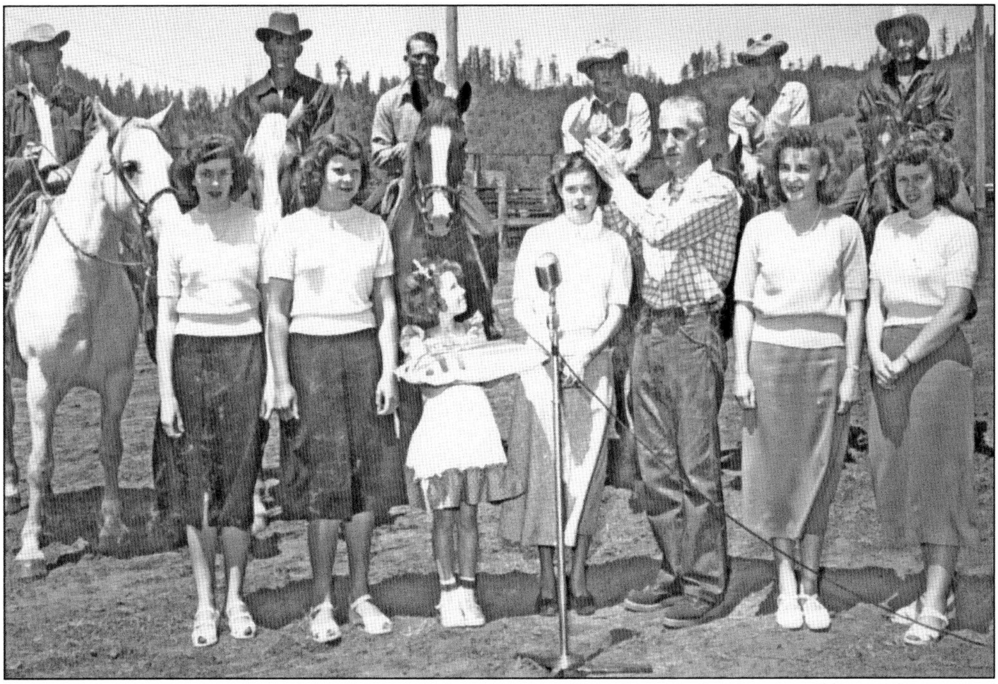

The shodeo at the fairgrounds on July 4, 1949, sponsored by the Myrtle Point Saddle Club, opened with the crowning of the Goddess of Liberty, Barbara Clarno. Mitch Myers, mayor, holds the crown while crown-bearer Beverly Bartles looks on. Runners-up in the essay contest are, from left to right, Margueritte (Lakey) Morris, Suzanne Krueger, Maureen Evans, and Amy Marie Davenport. Observing from their horses are, from left to right, Harold Clarno, Jiggs King, Kenneth Barkdoll, Bill Roush, Ralph Clarno, and Am Roush. (CK.)

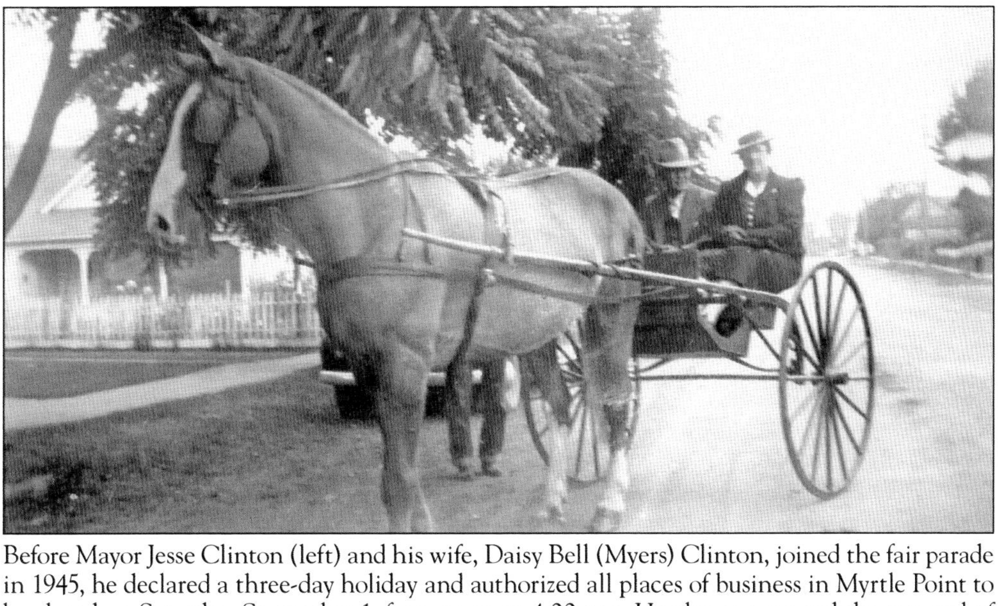

Before Mayor Jesse Clinton (left) and his wife, Daisy Bell (Myers) Clinton, joined the fair parade in 1945, he declared a three-day holiday and authorized all places of business in Myrtle Point to be closed on Saturday, September 1, from noon to 4:00 p.m. He also announced the removal of wartime restrictions and predicted a record crowd at the fair. (CK.)

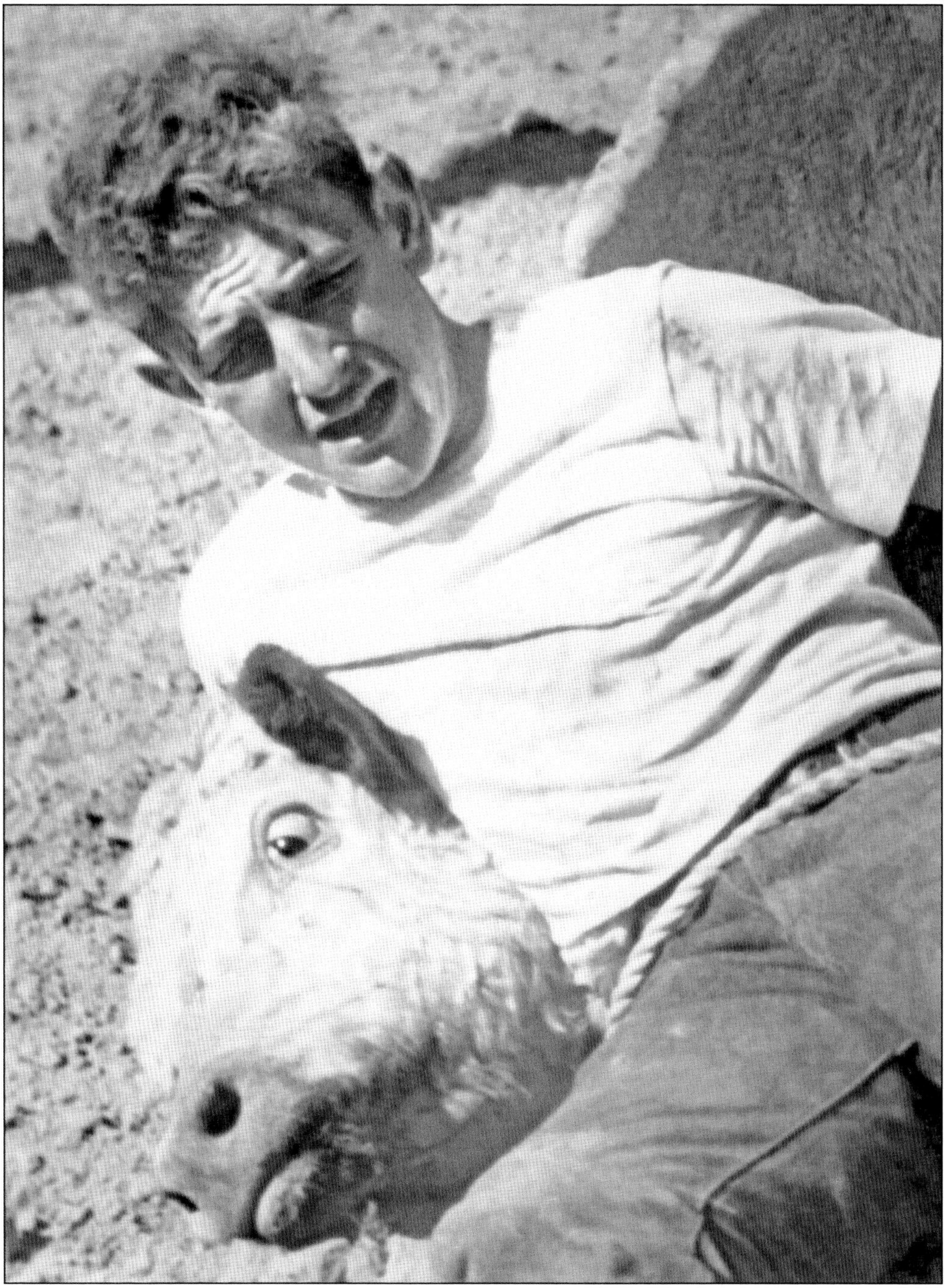

The goal of the calf scramble was to catch a donated animal, take it home to raise and train, bring it back to the fair to exhibit, and then keep it or sell it at the annual youth auction. Harvey "Buck" McCall wrestled this calf to the ground in 1950. Next, he had to keep the calf pinned down, grab the rope halter that was tied around his waist, and slip it over the calf's head. This was no easy task. Sometimes the calf wrangler got a little help with the halter from rodeo clowns or bystanders. (CCFM.)

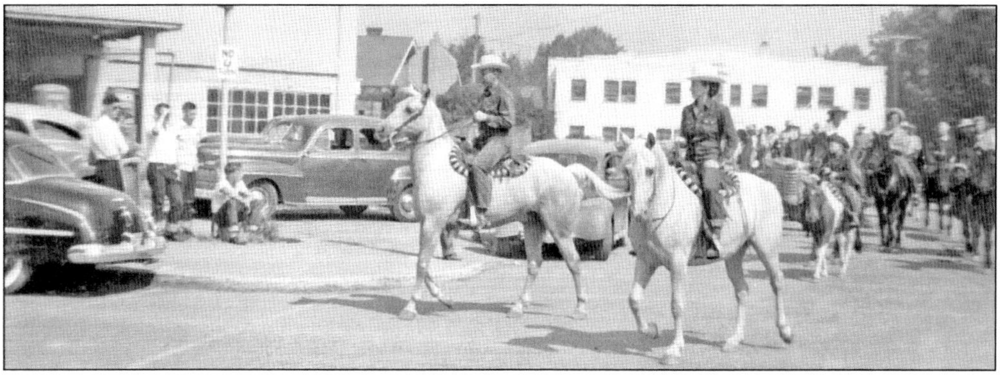

At a fair parade in the late 1940s, a matched pair leaving Seventh Street rounds the corner at Bud Emery's service station. Mast Hospital is in the background. A few years later, Ruth (Stonecypher) Barklow and her daughter, Karen Barklow, led the Grand Entry at the start of the rodeo. Ruth's mount, a former circus horse, heard familiar music. It reared up, sidestepped, and tried to roll over with Barklow. She had a battle on her hands. (SD.)

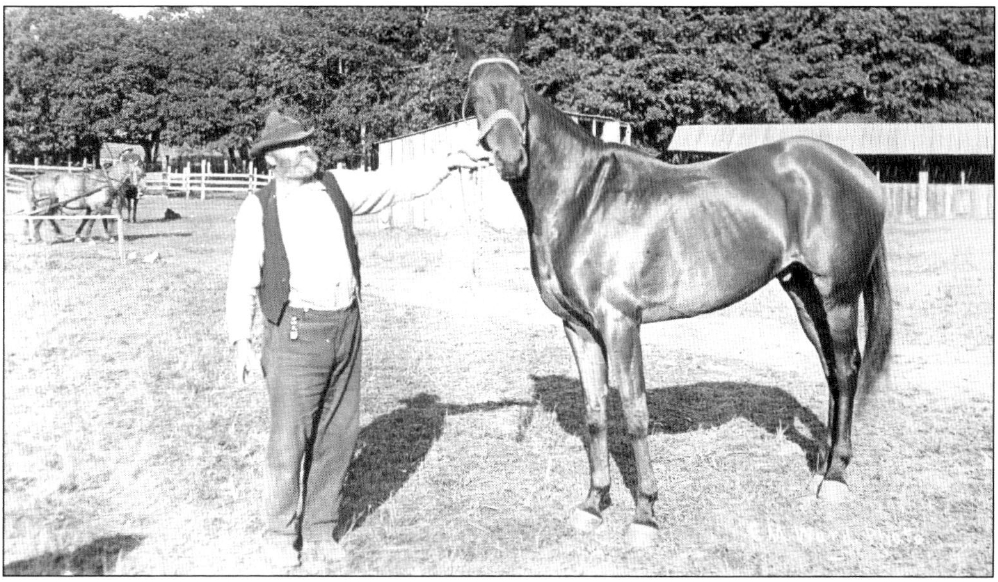

Hiram Hatcher shows a racing quarter horse at the fair in 1920. Hatcher, a Civil War veteran and a former Texas Ranger, competed with Cecil Carter, Wallace Martin, Fred Hobson, and Joe Knight on the horse-racing circuit. In 1918, his horses won the three-eighths dash and the half-mile dash. The 1920 fair featured ball games, boxing matches, aeroplane exhibitions, and Ford Model Ts racing backwards around a half-mile track—a contest won by Amzy Mintoyne. (CCFM.)

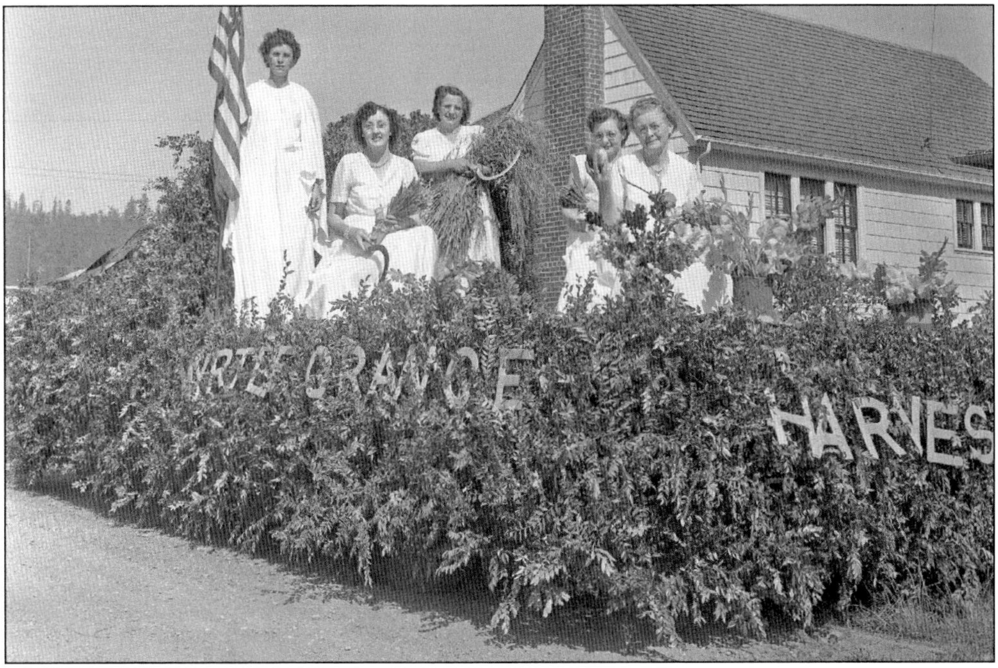

Myrtle Grange members riding their float in the late 1940s are, from left to right, Opal (Southmayd) Davis, Leona Lewis, unidentified, Leila Rochek, and Golda Caudle (Leila's mother). Granges began actively participating in the fair in 1931. Myrtle Grange, which won the trophy for community exhibits in 1946, was organized in 1898 at Giles Hall. (CHMM 13 995-1.10976.2.)

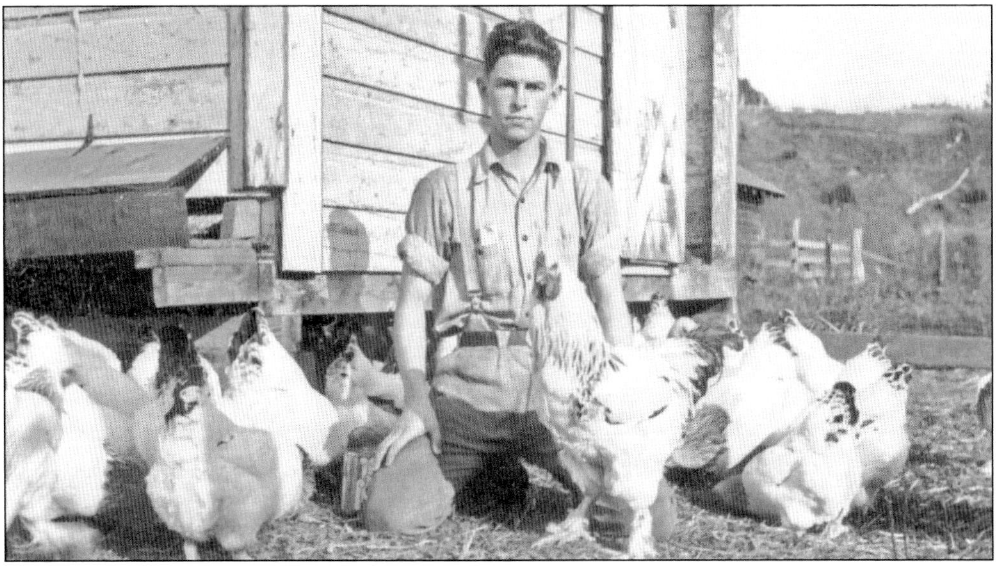

When Howard Leatherman was in high school in the early 1930s, he raised Brahma chickens on his family's farm in Lee Valley. He farmed in Coos County all his life, owning a dairy farm, a sheep ranch, and a beef spread. In 1939, Glenn "Junior" Gulstrom, Gerald Woodward, and Fred Watson earned a trip to Cleveland by winning the poultry-judging contest at Oregon State College summer school. (HL.)

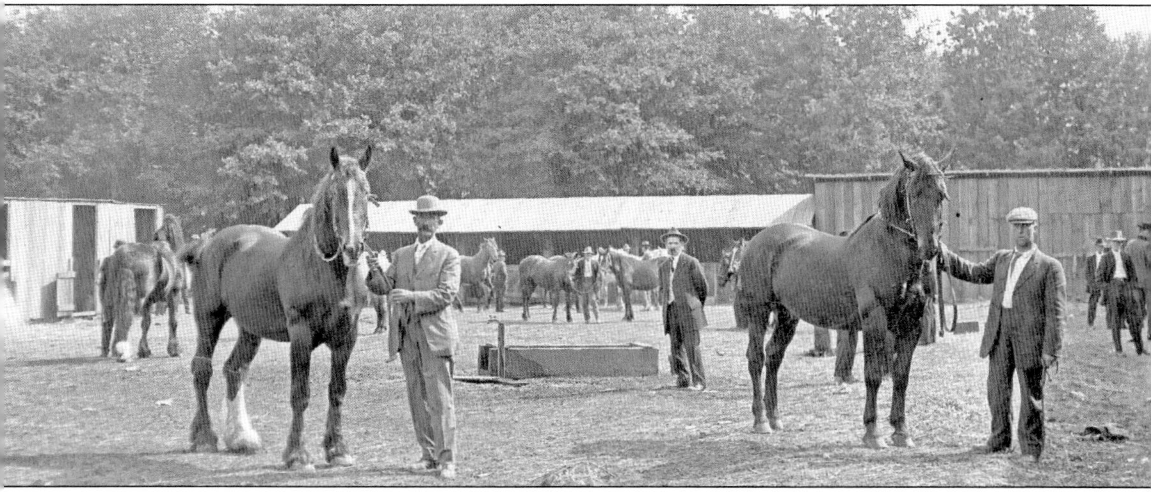

At a draft-horse competition at the 1913 Coos Curry County Fair, Walter Laird (right) shows a Percheron possibly owned by his half brother, James D. Laird, who stands in the background to the left of the horse. Both men drove teams of horses over the Coos Bay Wagon Road. The man showing the Clydesdale at left is unidentified. Later in the day, draft horses competed in pulling contests. (CL.)

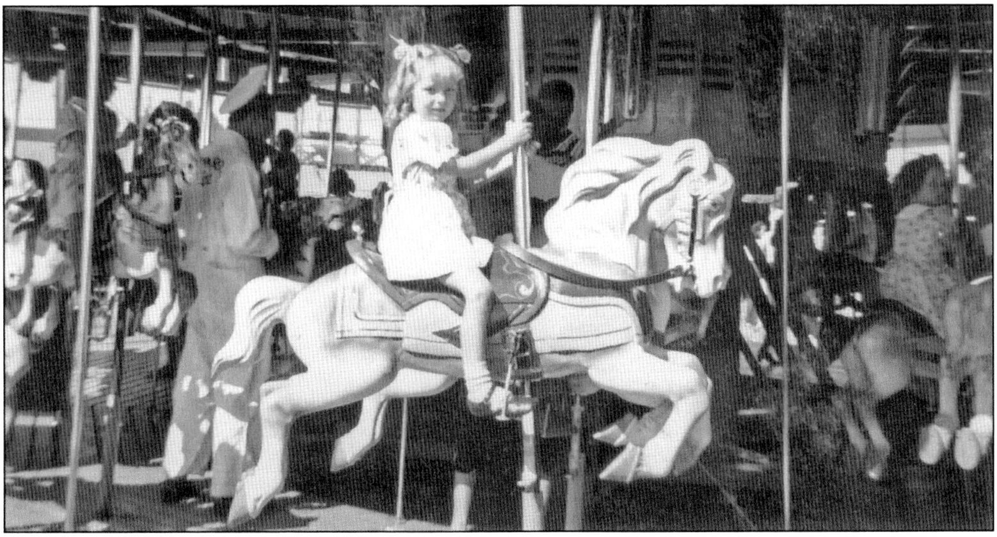

From the carousel, Kathy Spires has a good view of other carnival rides at the fair in about 1945. She may also have ridden one of the Shetland ponies fitted with saddles and bridles that walked circles in the spokes of a giant wheel. In 1944, during World War II, the Browning Brothers Amusement Company provided carnival rides at the fair. (KL.)

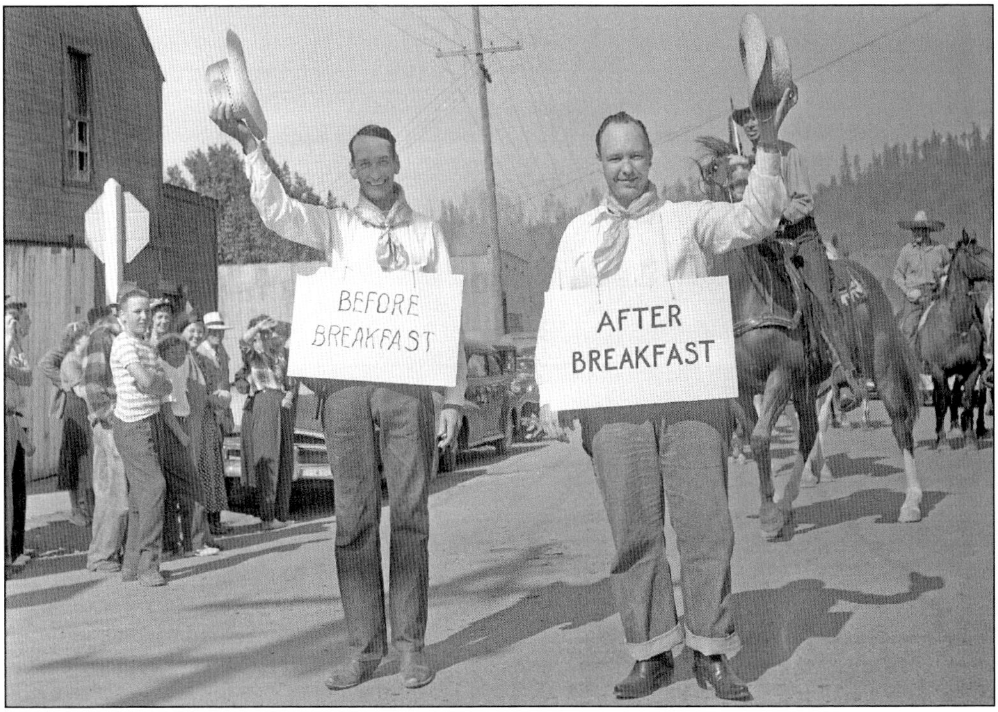

Attorneys Wallace Dement (left) and Frank Meldrum advertise the Cowboy Breakfast, an annual fundraiser for the Myrtle Point Saddle Club. V.B. "Tex" Billingsly rides his horse in the parade behind Meldrum in the late 1940s. Breakfast cooks included Mildred (Payne) King, Minnie (Wilson) King, Ruth (Stonecypher) Barklow, Lilas (Clinton) Ellis, Ardyce (Clinton) Billingsly, Grace (Culbertson) Wilberger, Gladys (St. John) Labart, Verona (Clinton) Brewster, and Genevieve (Clark) Preston. (CHMM 11 995-1.10983.2.)

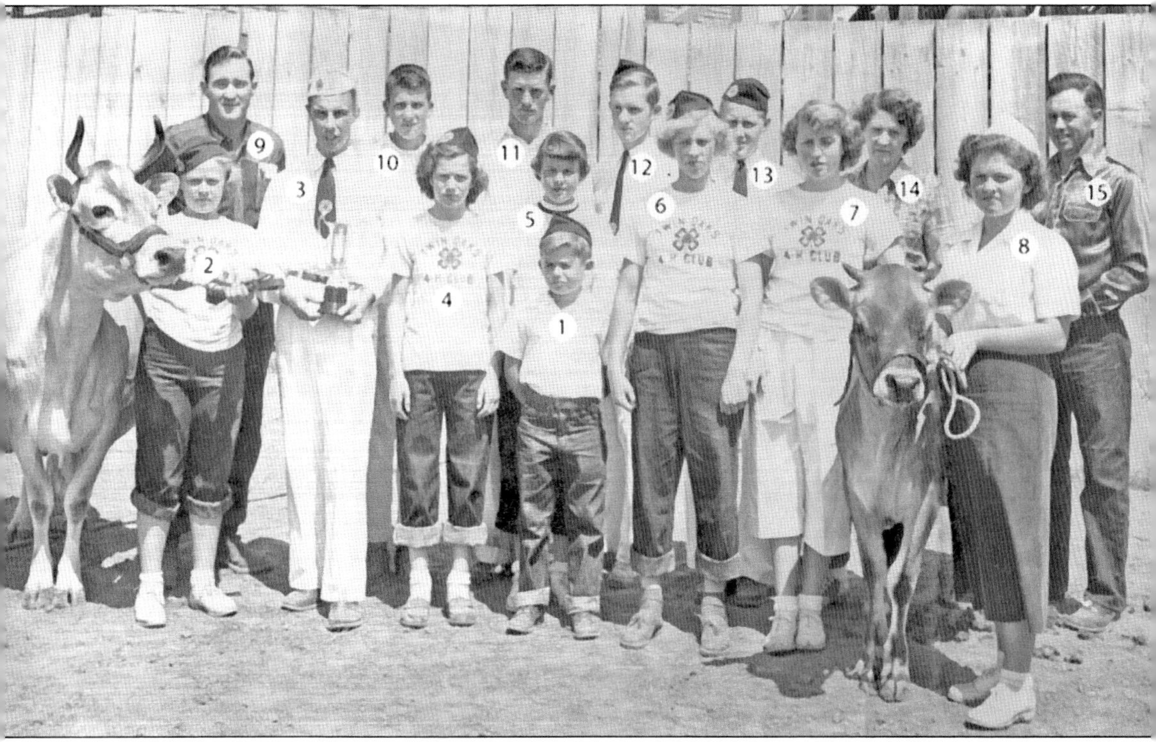

A Jersey cow named Rosie (left) lines up at the fairgrounds in the late 1940s with members of the Twin Oaks 4-H Dairy Club. Jean Davenport led the 4-H club for 51 years. Her husband, Lloyd C. "Duke" Davenport, was coleader for 44 years. Twin Oaks club members at the time include, from left to right, (first row) Jeanne Davenport (2), Bill Evans (3), unidentified (4), Gary Larsen (1), Carol Kay Hall (5; behind Gary Larsen), Joanne Davenport (6), Shirley Davenport (7), and Linda Larsen (8); (second row) unidentified (9), Larry Stevens (10), Dick Evans (11), John Trigg (12), Jim Trigg (13), Jean (14), and Duke (15). (CCFM.)

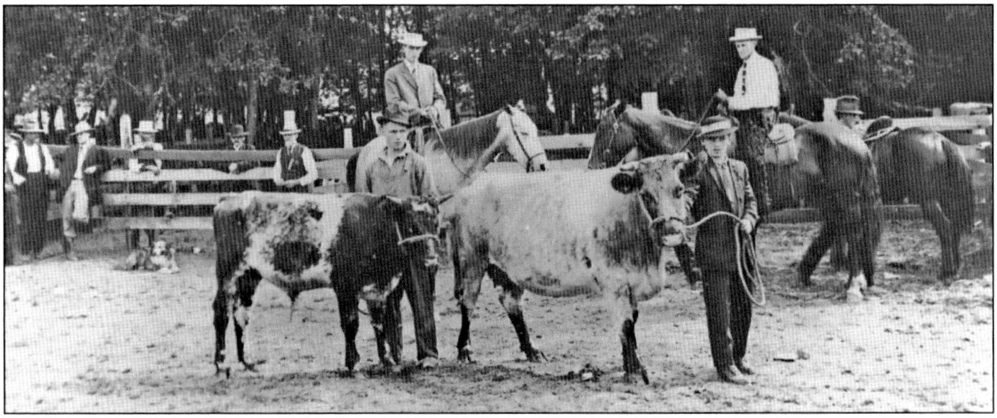

From his saddle, Russell Cooke "R.C." Dement (right), watches his son Clair Dement (front, right) show a shorthorn cow at the 1912 fair. R.C. owned a dairy farm at Norway for 40 years. He helped organize Security Bank in Myrtle Point and was its president for 15 years. As a young man, in about 1868, he filed on a homestead on upper Dement Creek. (CCFM.)

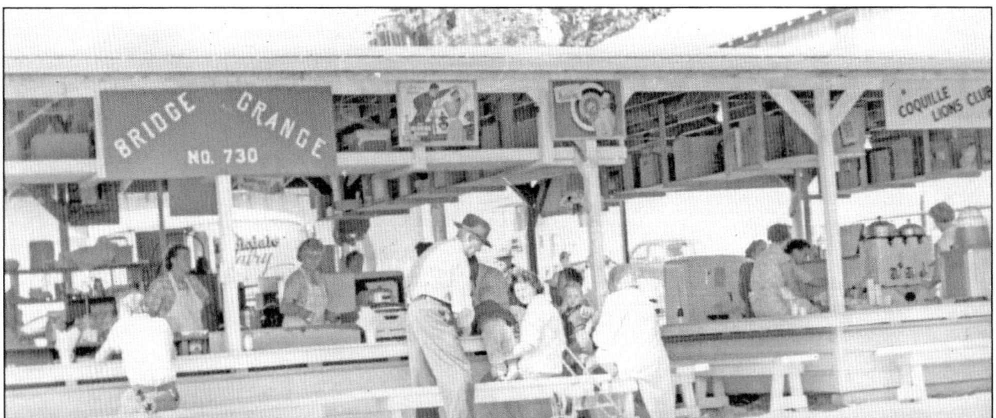

The Bridge Grange advertised its hamburgers with the slogan "A loaf of bread, a pound of meat, and all the mustard you can eat!" This food booth continued a tradition that began in 1912 when F.G. Hermann and Ida W. Hansen opened a confectionery stand on the fairgrounds. At the early fairs, the Palace of Sweets had a large sign above its booth. (CCFM.)

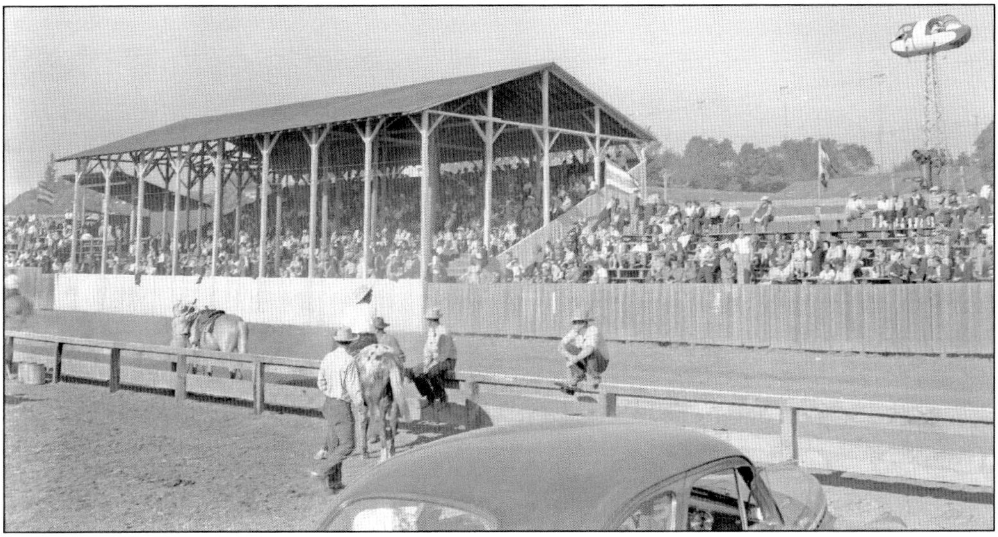

A crowd waits for the next horse race in the east grandstand in the late 1940s. Carnival attractions included the Hammer, shown here in the background above the spectators, the Rock-O-Plane, the Octopus, and games of skill. Contestants with good aim could take home a teddy bear, a live goldfish, or a live duck. The Hammer swung riders into the air over and over. In a booth beneath the grandstand, facing the carnival, Boy Scouts sold hot dogs and carbonated drinks, including Lemmy, Squirt, Grapette, and Orangette. (CHMM 05 995.1-1667.)

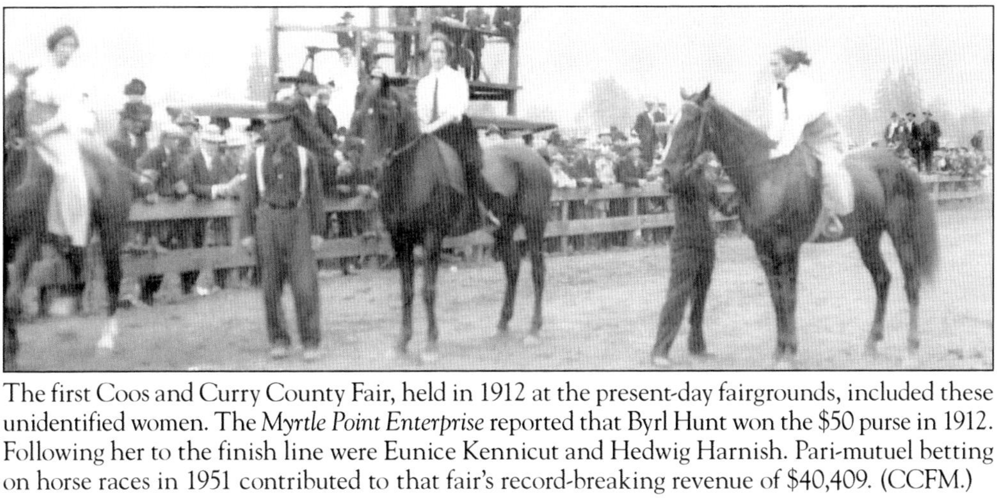

The first Coos and Curry County Fair, held in 1912 at the present-day fairgrounds, included these unidentified women. The *Myrtle Point Enterprise* reported that Byrl Hunt won the $50 purse in 1912. Following her to the finish line were Eunice Kennicut and Hedwig Harnish. Pari-mutuel betting on horse races in 1951 contributed to that fair's record-breaking revenue of $40,409. (CCFM.)

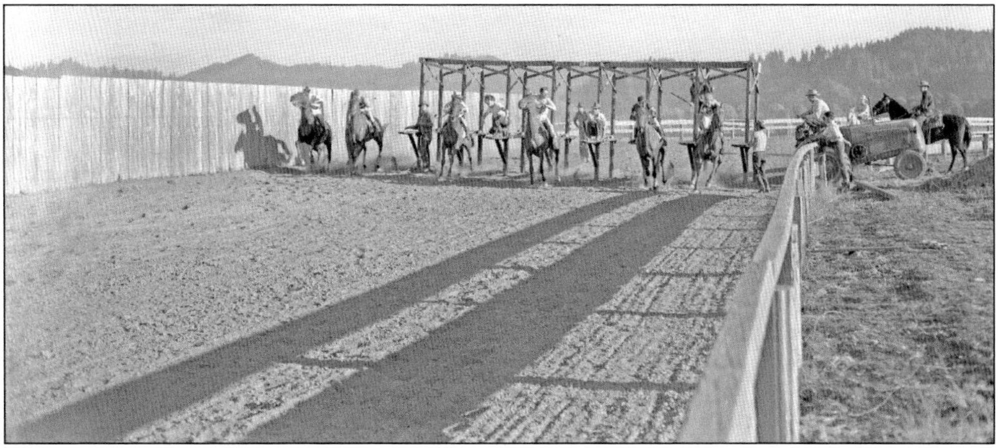

Flat ground for a half-mile racetrack was the top goal when the newly organized fair association looked for a fairgrounds site in 1912. Horse racing at the fair ended in 1947. An early version of the fair was held near Arago in 1885 with horse races, exhibits, and a restaurant. The event was named the Southwest Oregon Agricultural Society's Fair at Hall's Prairie. (CHMM 04 995-1.1669.)

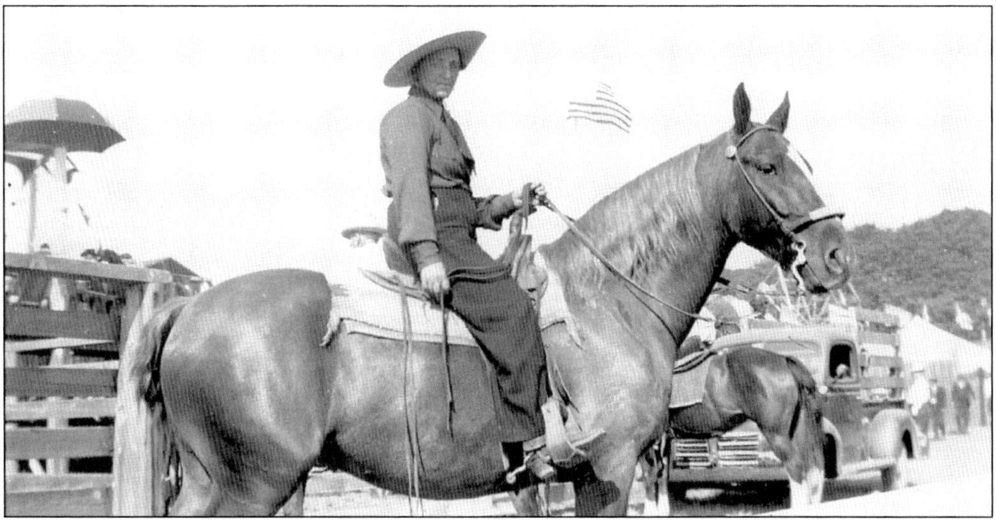

Lena (Whitney) Thomas, pictured in the rodeo arena in 1944, learned to ride on her grandparents' ranch on Sugarloaf Mountain, just east of Myrtle Point. Her grandfather George Martin was a stagecoach driver for Dan Barklow on the Myrtle Point–to-Roseburg route. Lena worked for Coos Bay Lumber Company as a waitress in logging camps near Powers in the 1920s. (CP.)

Three

Country Life
The Plow, the Axe, and the School Bell

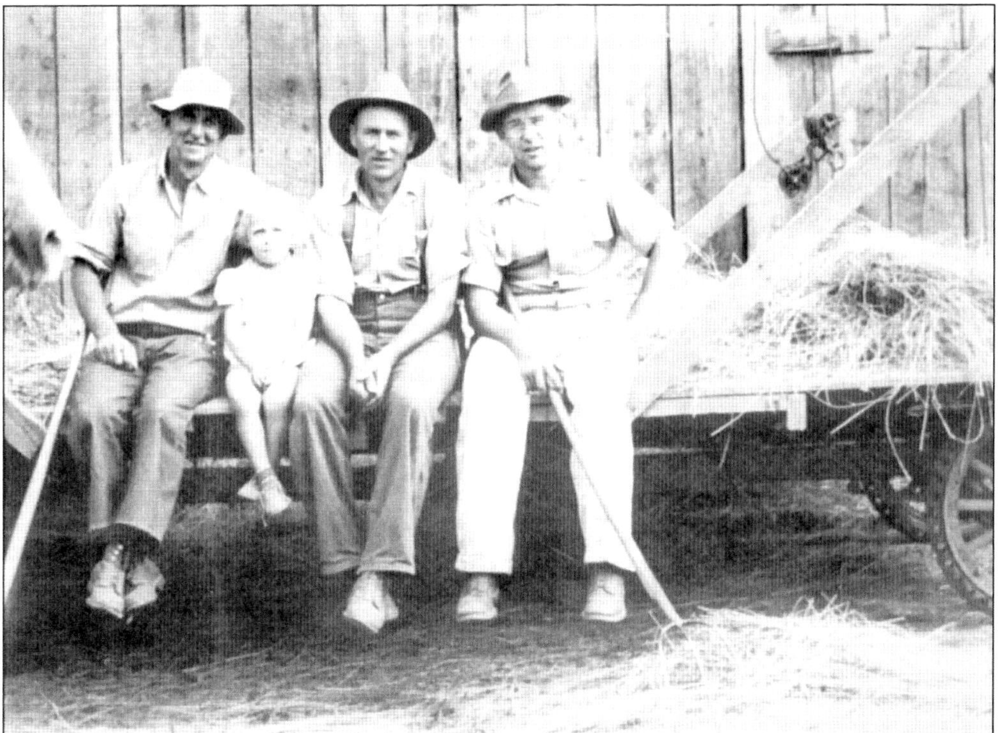

Hauling loads of loose hay to the Davenport barn on Catching Creek in 1945 are, from left to right, unidentified, Jeanne Davenport, Joseph Albert Davenport, and Ernie Davenport. Ernie was on leave from flight training during World War II. Later, while Ernie was waiting at an airfield to take off in his B-17, his commanding officer announced that there would be no more flying that night—the war was over. (MER.)

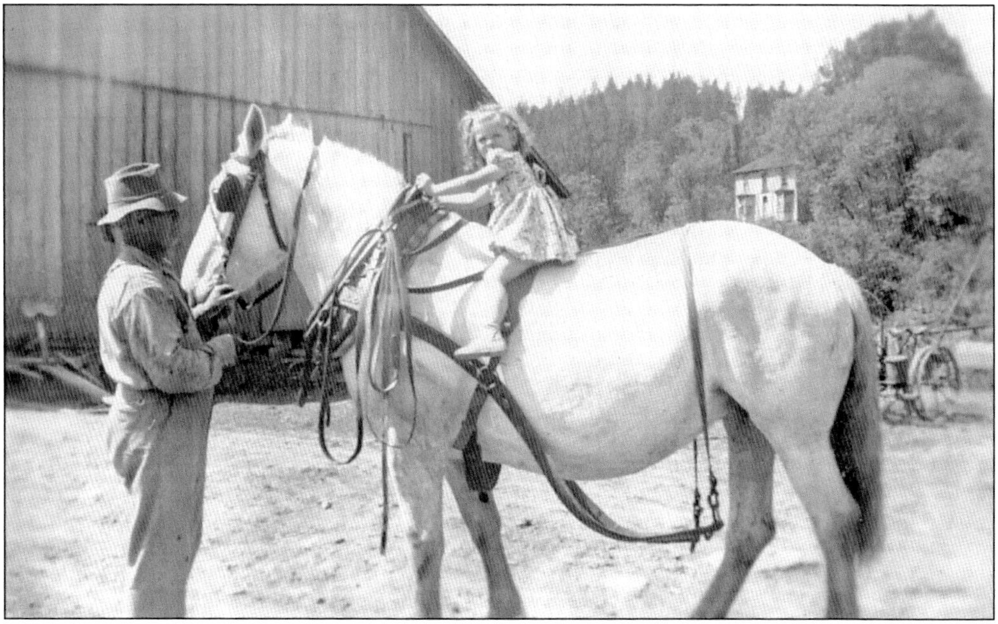

Albert "Bert" Davenport lets his granddaughter Beverly Holt take a ride in 1941. She was visiting her grandparents along with her mother, Audrey (Davenport) Holt. Joseph Albert Davenport was Bert's son. In the background is Joseph Albert's house, built by Daniel Giles in the early 1890s. Giles's first brickyard was located behind the barn. The Davenport family began farming on Catching Creek in 1900. (BB.)

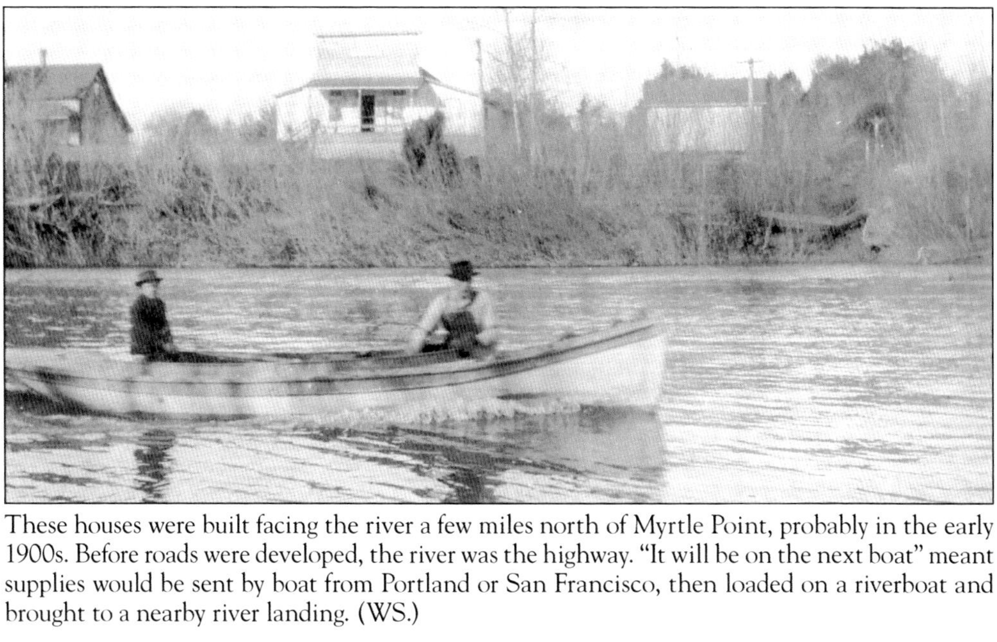

These houses were built facing the river a few miles north of Myrtle Point, probably in the early 1900s. Before roads were developed, the river was the highway. "It will be on the next boat" meant supplies would be sent by boat from Portland or San Francisco, then loaded on a riverboat and brought to a nearby river landing. (WS.)

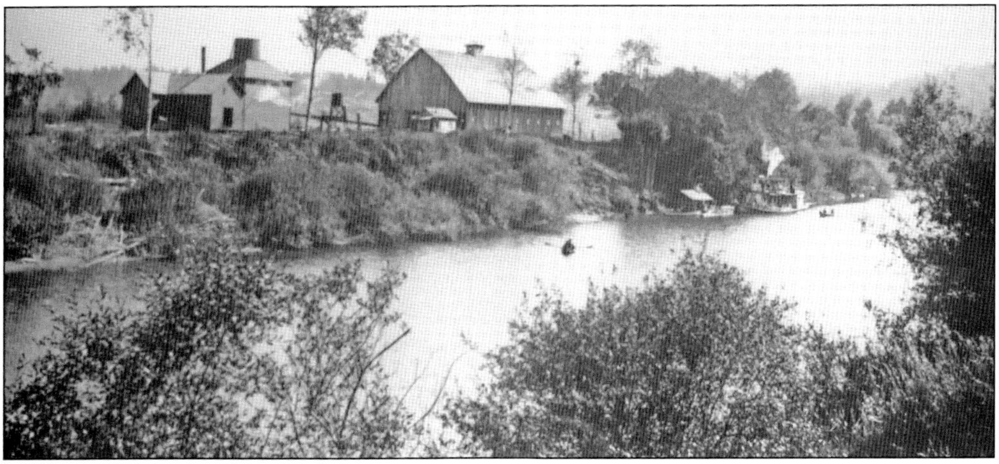

Around 1900, George Davis, Sam Kelley, and Claudie Martini built this creamery in Norway. Early butter makers were Sam Kelley, H.B. Quain, Finley Schroeder, and Clarence Barklow. James Hilderbert "Bertie" McCloskey purchased it in 1905 and added a cheese factory with a community hall upstairs. He sold to Swift & Company in about 1928. Carl Brothers Creamery, owned by Herman L. and John D. Carl, was also located in Norway. (CHMM 26 009-16.5611.)

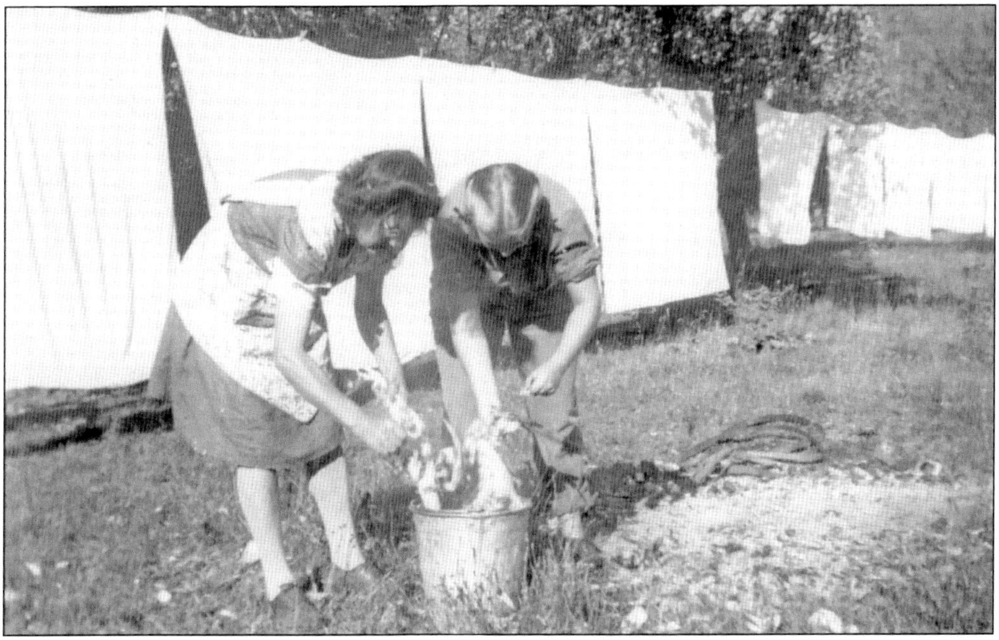

After washing sheets and hanging them on the line, Beunice (Robison) Lillie (left) and her daughter Laura pluck chickens in about 1940. Beunice and her husband, Albert E. Lillie, farmed near Arago. Beunice and her identical twin sister, Bernice (Robison) Gulstrom, were the daughters of Price and Laura (Hoover) Robison. Beginning when they were young, the twins sang duets. (WS.)

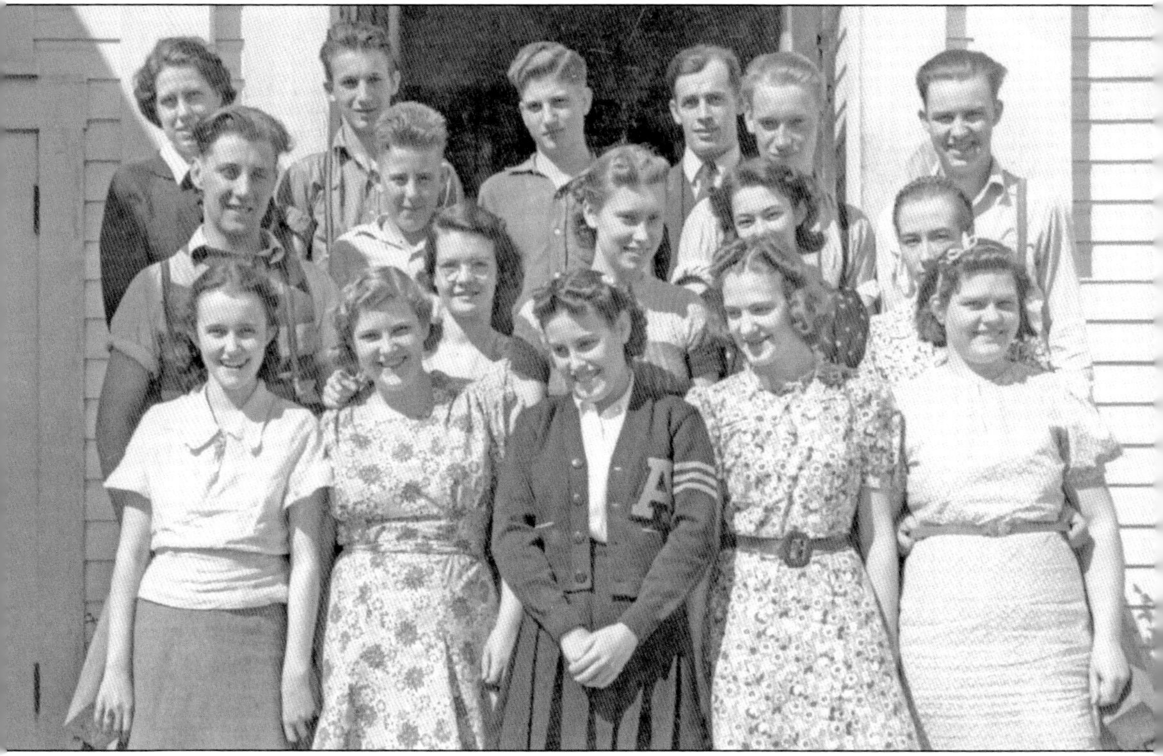

Lois Robison, front and center, wears a letter sweater for Arago High School in the early 1940s. Students and teachers are, from left to right, (first row) Anne Watkins, Laura Bernice Lillie, Robison, Mary Jean McAllister, and unidentified; (second row) Leon Garrone, Glenn "Junior" Gulstrom, Betty Doyle, Virginia King, Maxine Rackleff, and Gladys Miller; (third row) assistant high school teacher Esther Davidson, J. Rodin, Gerald Woodward, principal Reginald Menegat, Robert "Bob" King, and John Pettinger. (WS.)

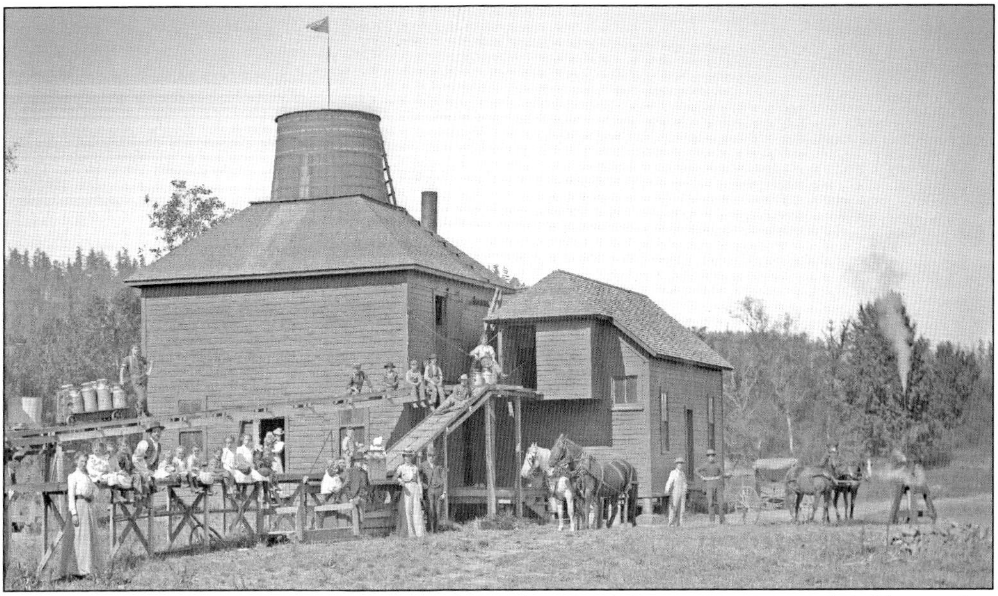

A trolley loaded with milk cans stops on its elevated track while men, women, and children gather in 1902 at the Norway Creamery. Many farmers milked fewer than 10 cows in 1902, although the farming operations of Ernest Davenport and Barklow Brothers each milked 50 cows. Later, from about 1915 to 1939, Myrtle Gold Creamery received milk at the corner of First and Spruce Streets in Myrtle Point. (CHMM 36 992-8-3440.)

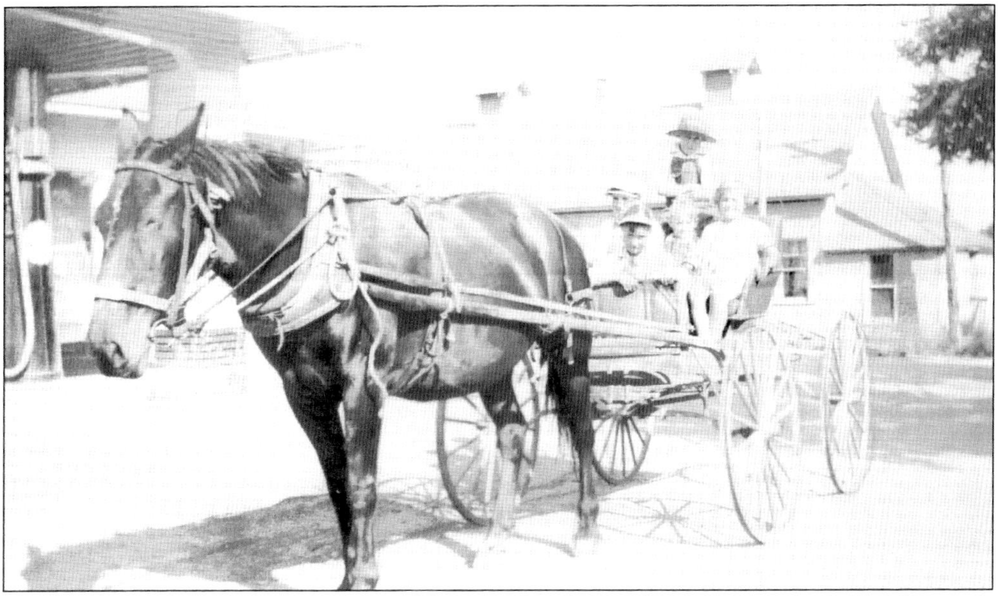

A family pauses in front of the Arago Store's gas pump, possibly in the 1930s. The building with two cupolas is the Arago Cheese Factory, which burned in 1946 or 1947. In 1920, J.D. Carl sold the Arago Cheese factory, which he had operated for four years, to 22 dairymen. Previously, in 1915, C.E. Broadbent had managed the Arago Cheese Factory. (WS.)

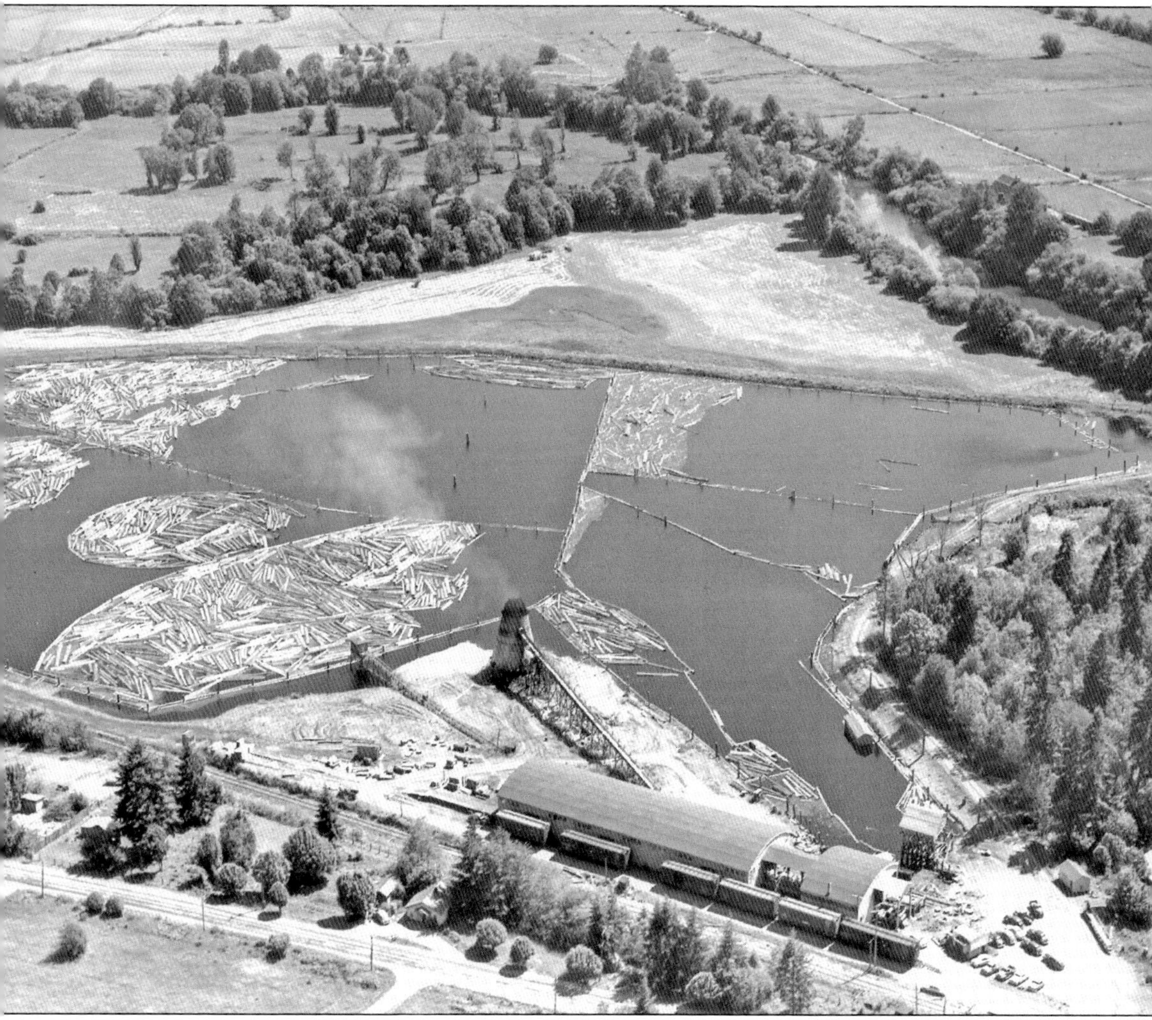

A wigwam burner burns waste wood at the Myrtle Point Veneer plant. Edged by myrtle trees, the Coquille River curves through fields behind the millpond. In 1948, mill manager O.C. Davenport gave a tour to 60 visitors, including Myrtle Point mayor Elton Schroeder. Herman Tedson, owner of the Norway Store, provided refreshments. (CHMM 991-2.19.)

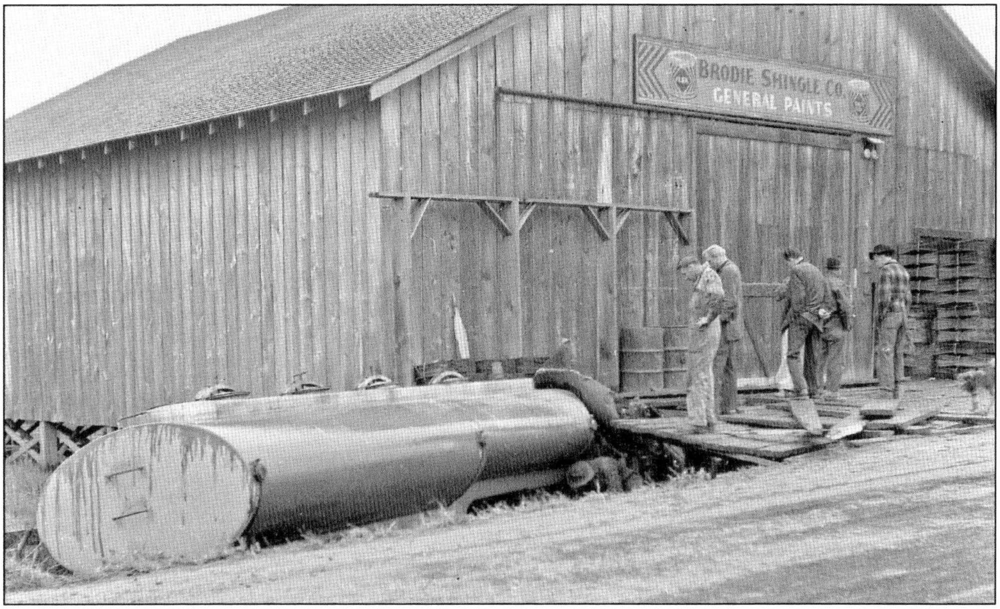

One man climbed into the ditch to take a closer look at a the tank from a Western Condensing Company truck that overturned near the front door of Brodie Shingle Company in Norway in 1948. Edmond Brodie started the business in about 1933, and his sons, Darrell and Eldon "Scoop" Brodie, had joined the business by 1949, when the company erected a two-story building in Myrtle Point at the corner of Third and Spruce Streets. (CHMM 161 995-1.2510.2.)

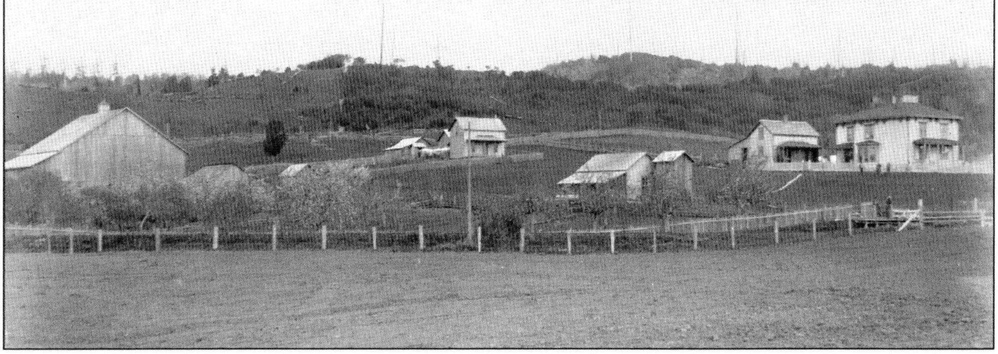

Snags appear on the hills behind the J. Fredrick Schroeder homestead near Norway in 1890. Mary (Perry) (Grant) Schroeder, wife of Fredrick Schroeder, was said to be the first female child born in Oregon. Two of Mary's sisters married two of her husband's brothers. In 1903, the Schroeders sold the farm to their two sons, C. Albert and Frank E. Schroeder. (CHMM 110 989-P312.)

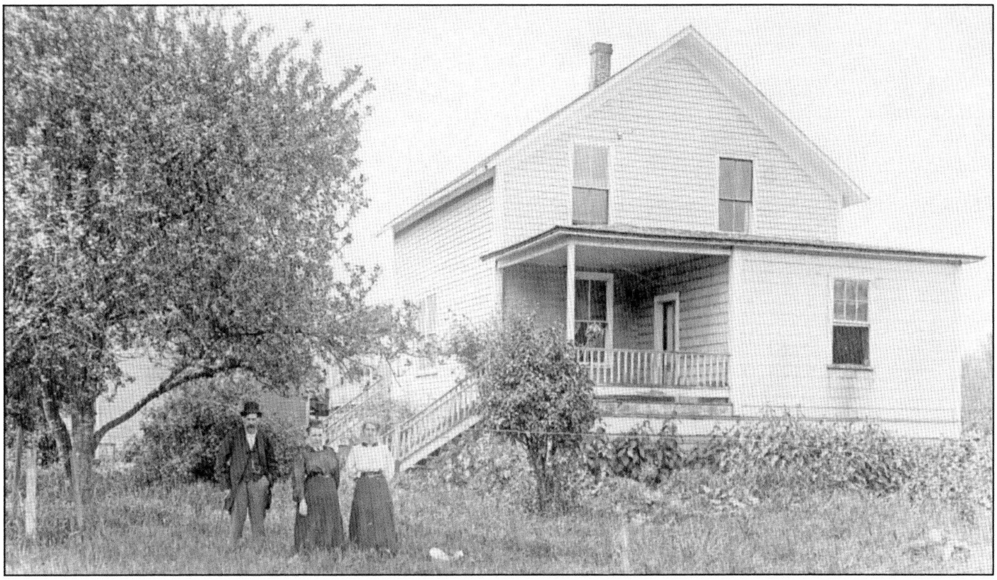

Glenn Robison (left) lived in this house in West Norway with his wife, Aletha (Barklow) Robison (center) and their children. Also shown is Glenn's sister-in-law Naomi (Root) Robison (right). For a time, Glenn's grandmother Christiana Hoover lived here too, occupying the ground-floor room with the open window. Hoover, who refused to have electricity installed in her room, spat tobacco juice out the window, staining the exterior paint. (HR.)

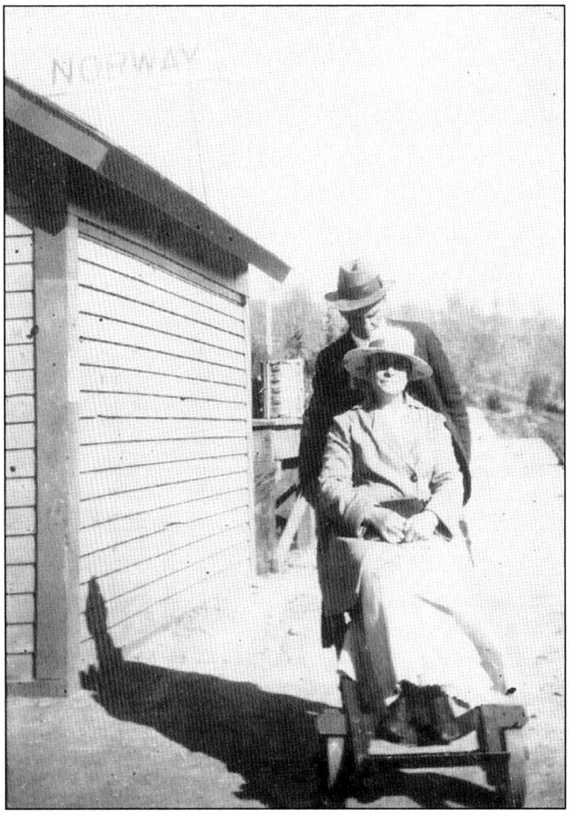

With a hand truck, John Albert Hart wheels his wife, Alice (Wantland) (Phillips) Hart, on a raised platform between the Norway train depot and the tracks, probably in the 1920s. Both of the couple's daughters became teachers. Estella Hart taught at Upper Catching Creek School and then married Frank Porter, a logger and high-climber. Verna Hart taught at Twin Oaks School and then married Joseph Albert Davenport, a dairy farmer. (MER.)

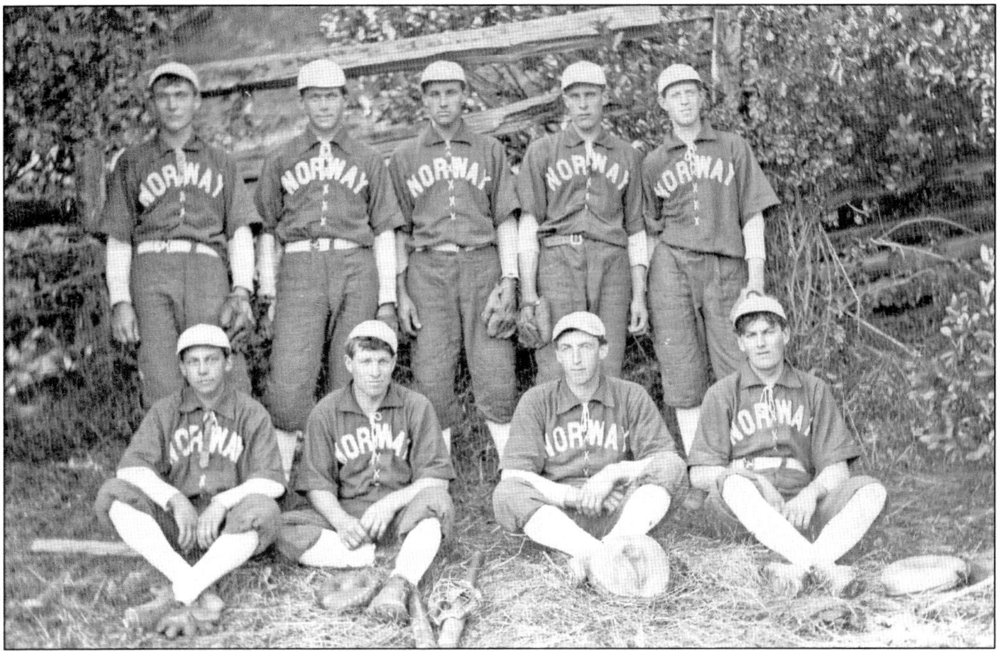

This Norway baseball team played in about 1898. The players are not specifically identified. Known Norway players were Gene Cole, Percy Dean, Lyman Rackleff, Walter Johnson, Chester Schroeder, Grover Wilson, John Carl, Theodore "Dutch" Clinton, Walter Barklow, Ray Clinton, Walter "Corbett" Robison, Percy Schroeder, Ray Lewis, Lee Ray, Maurice Ray and J. Hilderbert "Bertie" McCloskey, who was also manager. Norway's opponents included Marshfield, Lee Valley, Gravelford, and Myrtle Point. (CHMM 984-16.15.)

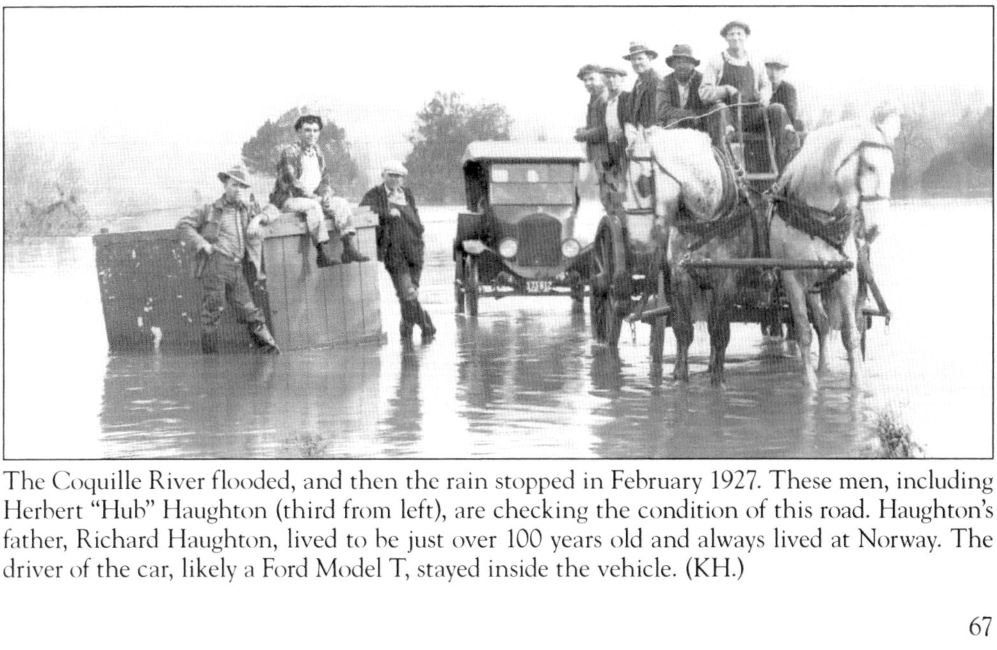

The Coquille River flooded, and then the rain stopped in February 1927. These men, including Herbert "Hub" Haughton (third from left), are checking the condition of this road. Haughton's father, Richard Haughton, lived to be just over 100 years old and always lived at Norway. The driver of the car, likely a Ford Model T, stayed inside the vehicle. (KH.)

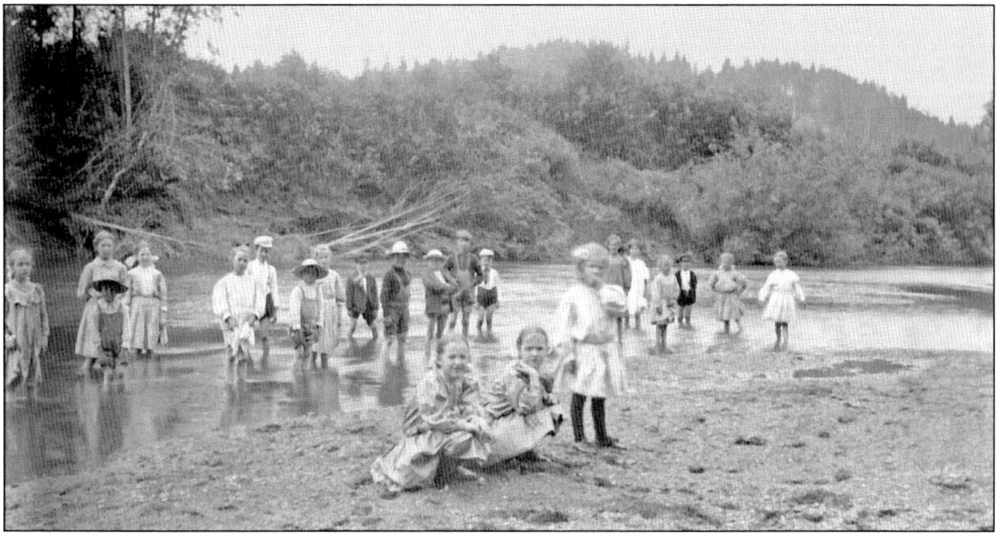

Children play in the South Fork of the Coquille River at Reed's Ford, near today's Reedsford Road, in the early 1900s. Horses used this crossing when traveling the early mail route that went from Myrtle Point to Port Orford by way of Catching Creek and Eckley. Oscar Oran Reed was an early settler at Reed's Ford. His first wife was Mary Lehnherr. After her death, he married Margaret "Maggie" Britton. (CHMM 64 967-137P.)

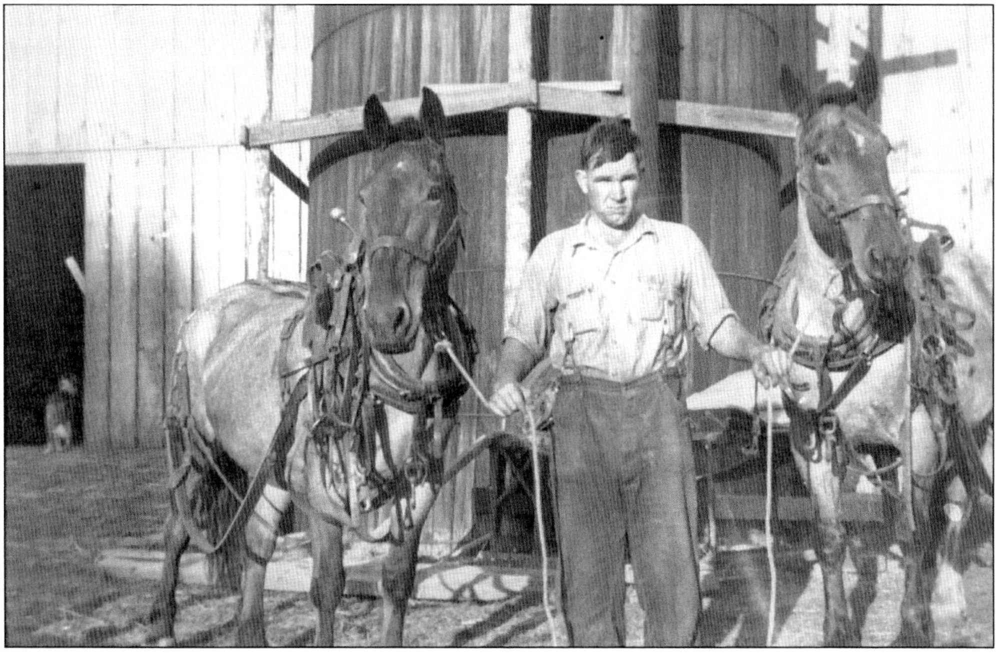

In harness and ready to work, King (left) and Prince stand with a ranch hand named Ralph in front of a silo at the Hoffman ranch near Powers Junction in 1936. "The strength is in the horse's shoulders," wrote Ernest Davenport. A harness connected the padded leather collar to hames, and leather straps over the horse's back connected the harness to the britchen, the straps around the back end that helped to hold the load when going downhill. (DH.)

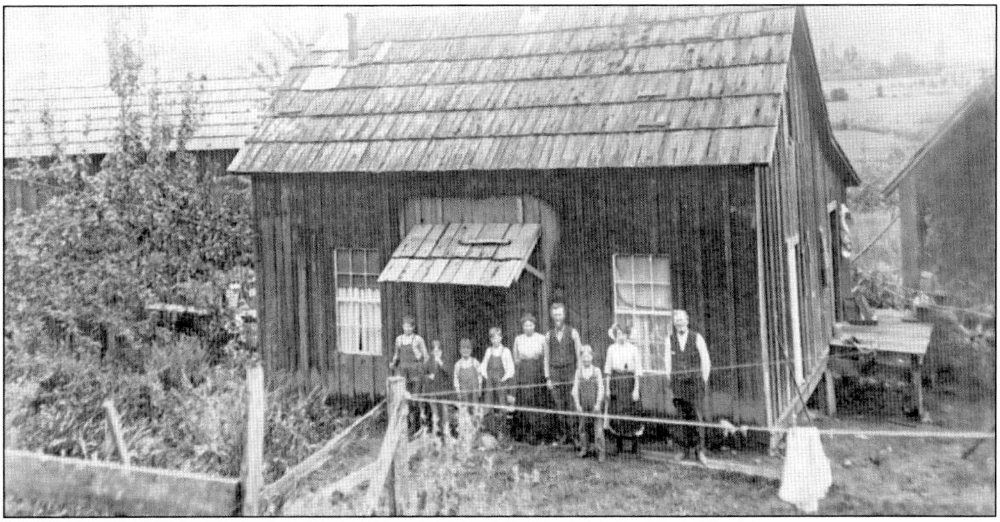

"At one time or another—everyone in the family lived here," said Harold Robison about this house in Stringtown. Stringtown, also called West Myrtle Point, was across the river from Myrtle Point. Frank Barklow (far right) lived in Stringtown in 1904. In later years, a woodshed and porch were added to the right. (HR.)

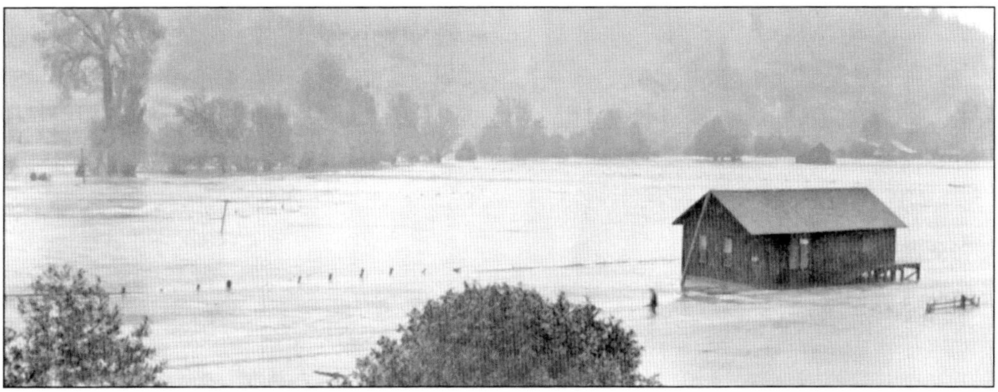

Train tracks that run on the near side of Myrtle Point's first train depot are covered by floodwaters on November 23, 1909. Barns and possibly William Rackleff's sawmill are visible in the distance. Later, the depot was located at the foot of Maple Street. Although floods were common, it was rare for the river to freeze over as it did in 1932. (RG.)

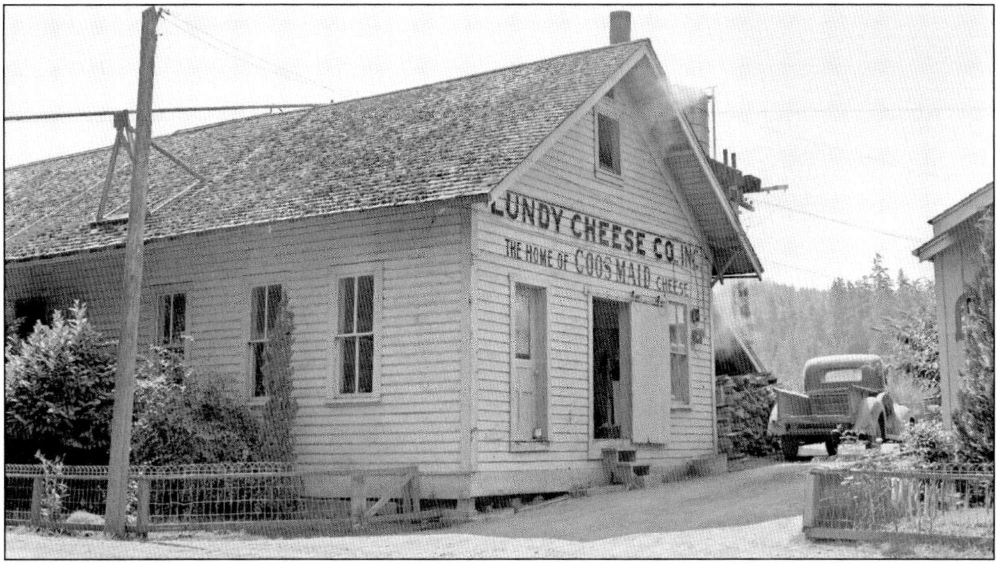

Lundy Cheese Factory, incorporated in 1920 and still making cheese in 1933, was located on Lundy property northwest of the junction of South Fork Road and Catching Creek. Ernest Davenport remembered the cheese maker emptying his father's milk cans into the vat. "We drove the horses and wagon on around, ran scalding water to clean the cans, and then took warm water home to clean the milk equipment," Davenport said. (CHMM 29 989-N4.10.)

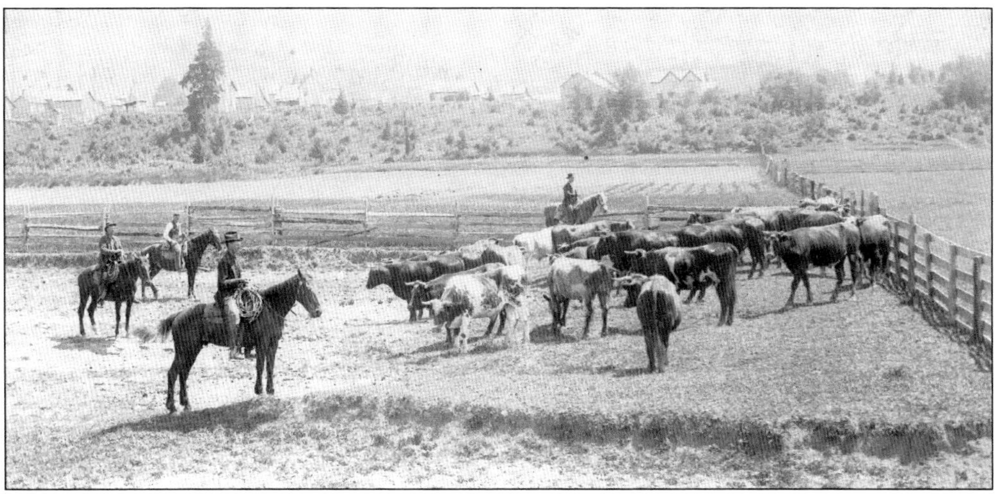

Russell C. Dement, likely the rider in the foreground, shipped cattle by rail from Myrtle Point in 1896. He sent two carloads of beef to the Beaver Hill Coal Mines that January. Overlooking this field is the city of Myrtle Point. (SD.)

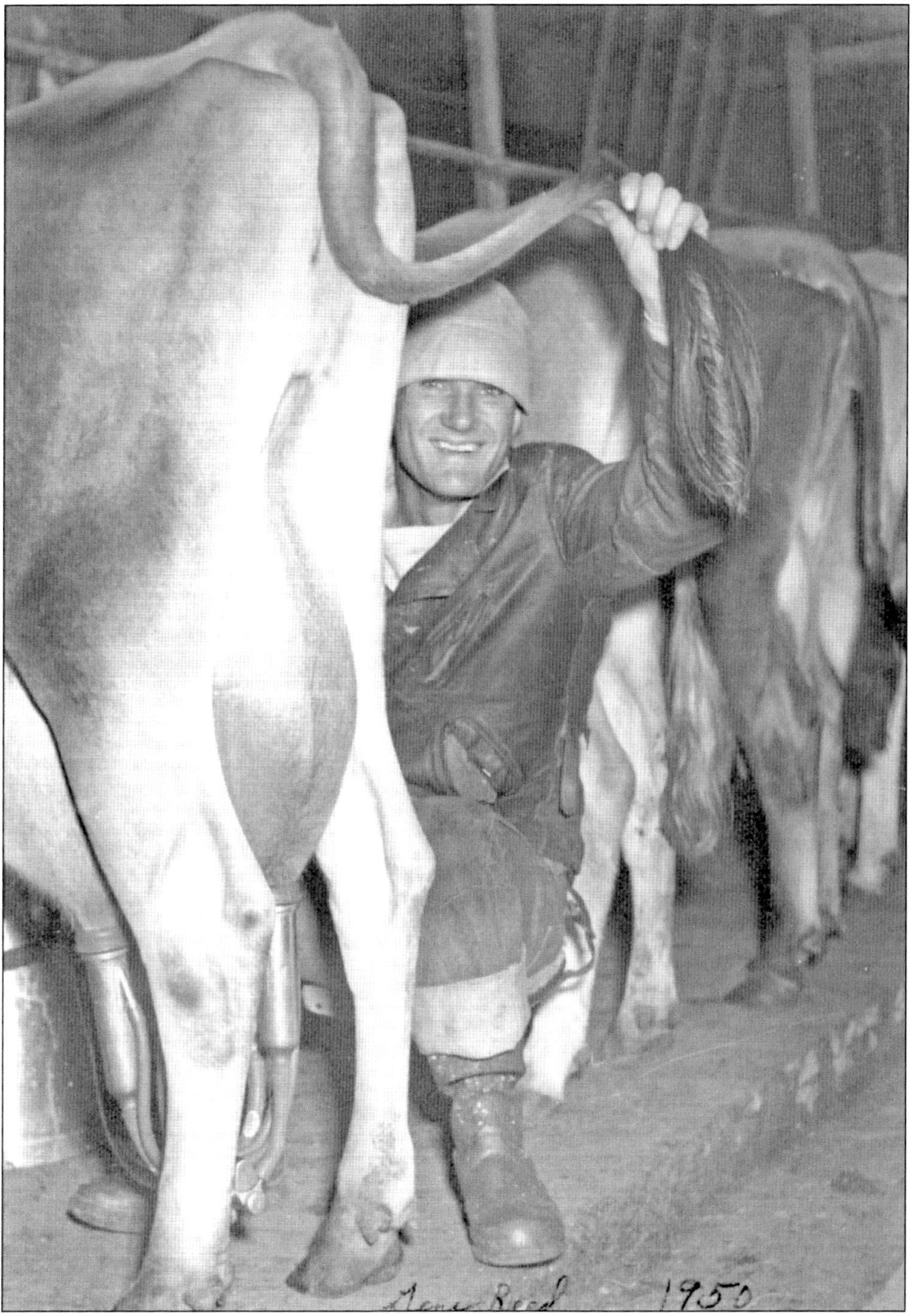

Milking one of his Jersey cows in 1950 is Eugene "Gene" Reed. He married Ruth Reed, daughter of Harlow and Emily Reed, in 1949. Gene was the third generation to farm on Reedsford Road. The Reeds likely shipped their milk to a variety of processors over the years. In 1902, Sugar Loaf Cheese Factory operated at the edge of Myrtle Point, while Sunrise Cheese Factory was located three miles up the South Fork. (AR.)

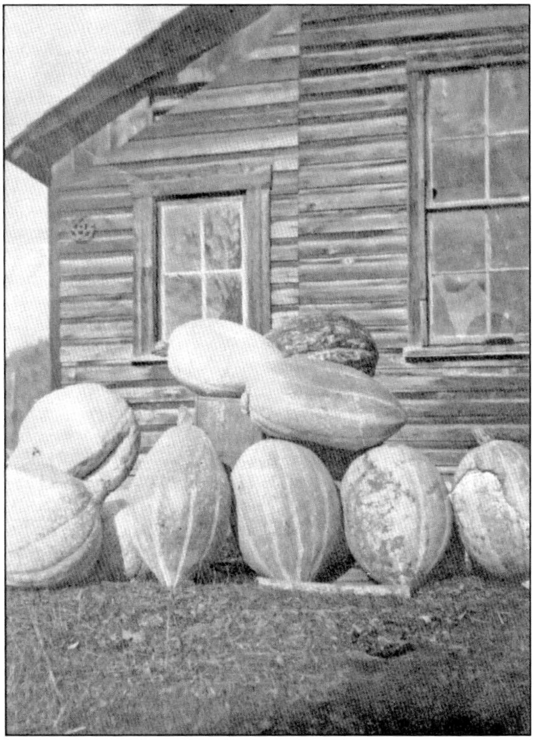

Carl and Vestie Bushnell grew these giant squash in their large garden on upper Catching Creek in the 1920s. Their farm was homesteaded by Hamilton Bushnell, a widower, in 1909. To reach the Bushnells' house, visitors crossed a short, low bridge over Koontz Creek, a tributary of Catching Creek. The couple was raising the first six of their nine children when they lived in this house. (RB.)

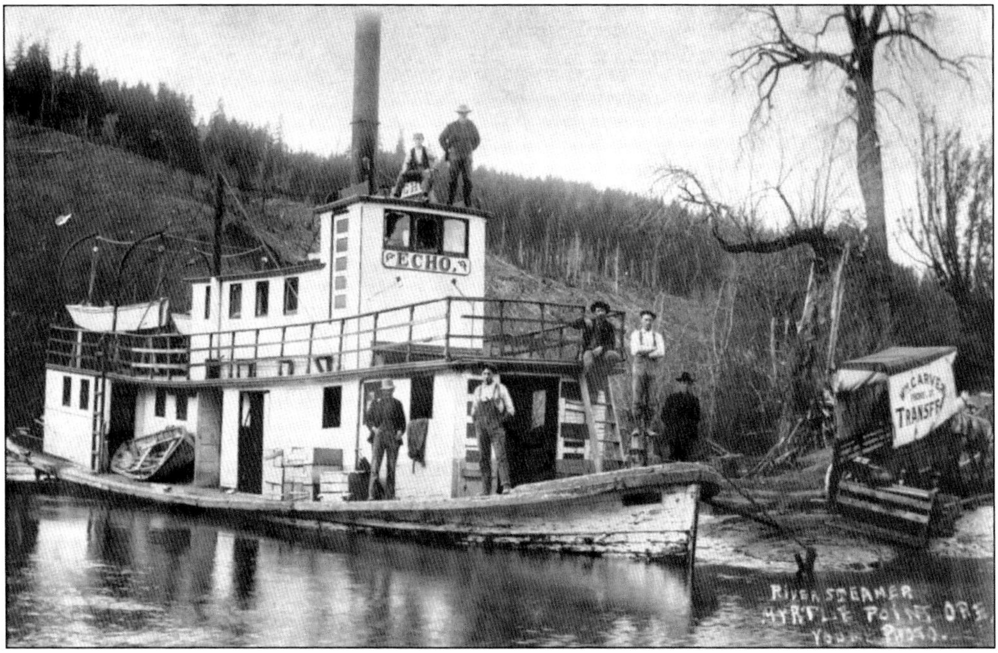

The *Echo*, a 66-foot stern-wheeler, meets a William M. Carver Transfer wagon at Myrtle Point around 1910. Russell Panter bought the *Echo* in 1908. His son, Thomas Walter Panter, is at far left on the lower deck. Charles Zevely stands with his arms crossed, and the man at far right is probably Wardro Crumley. Charles Henry James sits on the roof. In addition to running a freight business, Carver owned a Myrtle Point livery stable in 1904. (DCM N3676.)

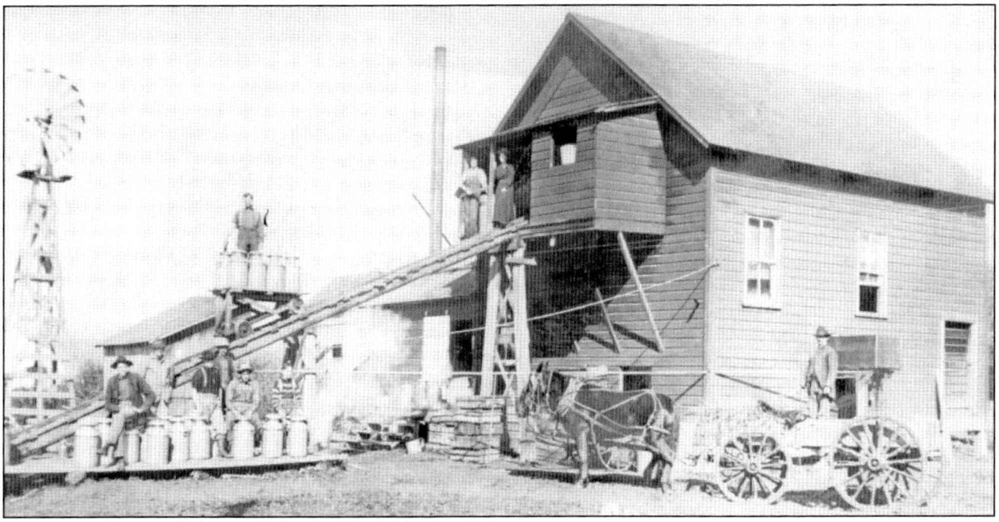

A trolley system hauls milk cans from riverboats to the second story of the Norway Creamery in the early 1900s. At the top of the ramp stand two women, the one at left wearing overalls. When a cheese factory was added to the creamery, its upstairs community room hosted basketball games, dances, plays, and home economics meetings. (CVM.)

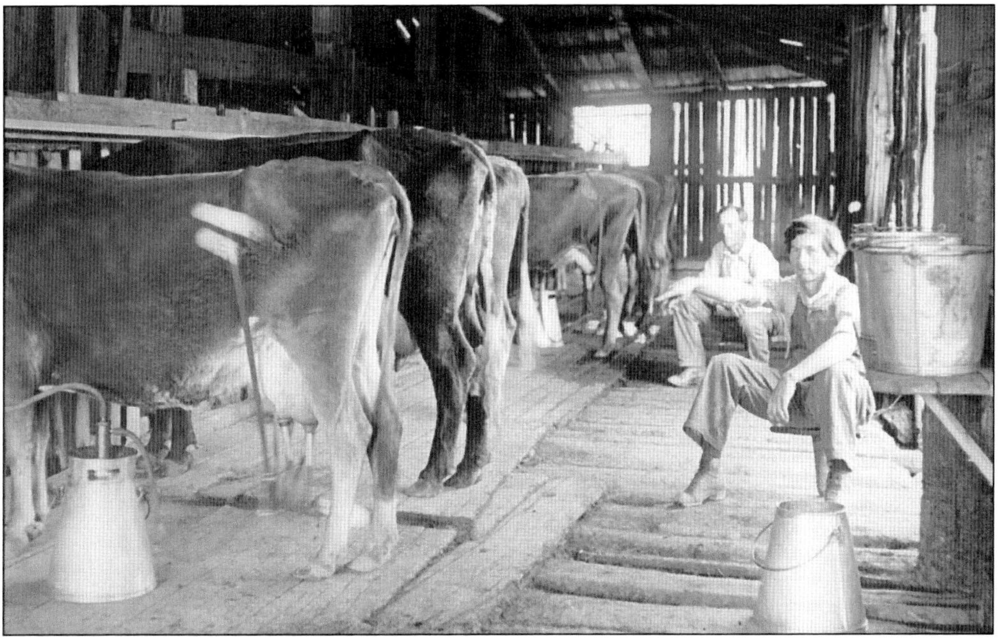

John "Jack" Fabry, in the background of this image, moved in 1904 to the Belieu place on Catching Creek, where he ran a dairy for over 40 years. Fabry's unidentified milker (foreground) points to a Hurman Milking Machine, possibly newly installed. Bickford Bartlett, who also lived on Catching Creek, was an agent for Hurman Milking Machines. Fabry was a bachelor who usually had a husband-and-wife team working for him on the farm and in the house. (WS.)

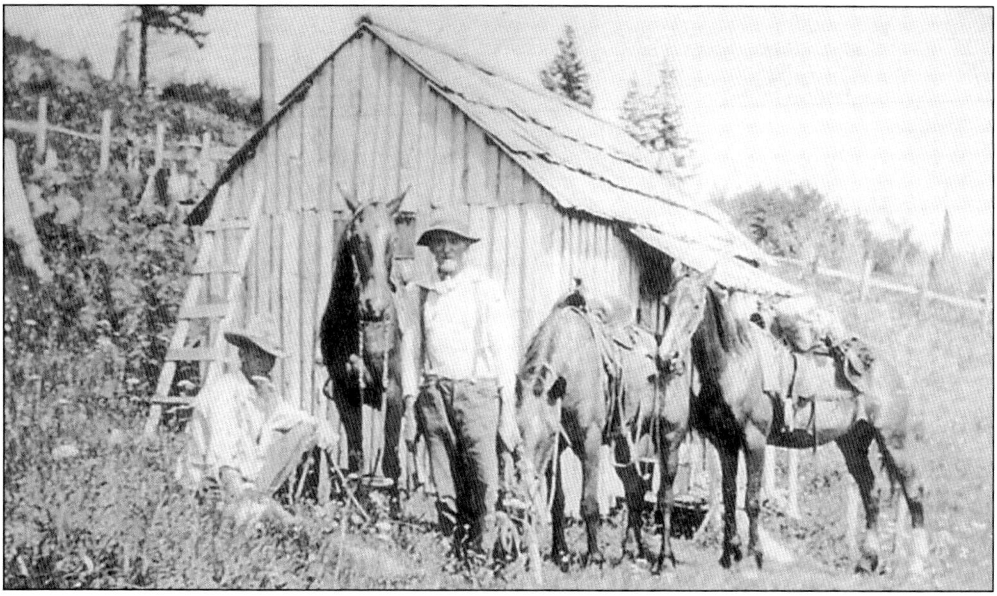

Beyond the head of Catching Creek, on the ocean side of Catching Creek Mountain, was Four Mile Cabin, also called King Cabin. George King (seated) bought the cabin from Jack Burk (standing). In 1925, they rode to the cabin, probably to check cattle and bring home some venison. The cabin burned in 1936 when humidity dropped to eight percent and fires blazed throughout Coos County. (CK.)

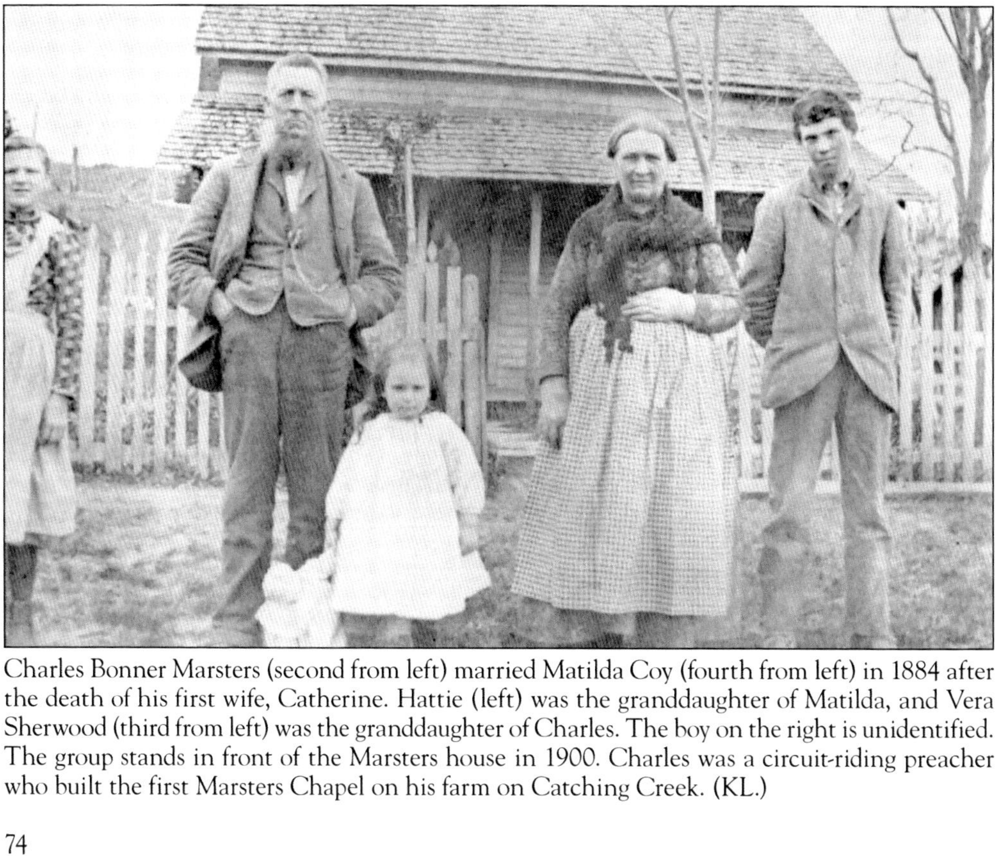

Charles Bonner Marsters (second from left) married Matilda Coy (fourth from left) in 1884 after the death of his first wife, Catherine. Hattie (left) was the granddaughter of Matilda, and Vera Sherwood (third from left) was the granddaughter of Charles. The boy on the right is unidentified. The group stands in front of the Marsters house in 1900. Charles was a circuit-riding preacher who built the first Marsters Chapel on his farm on Catching Creek. (KL.)

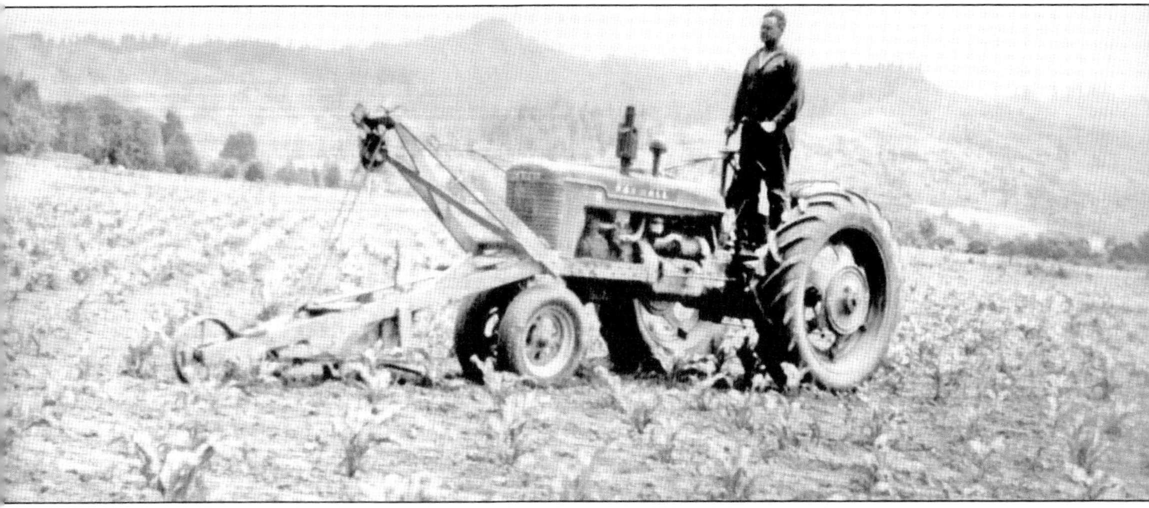

George Hall, who hummed tunes while driving his Farmall H tractor, tills the corn he planted in cross rows in the 1940s. Hall farmed on Old Broadbent Road on the place where Lewis and Catherine (Wimer) Strong had run a dairy farm in the 1800s. He also taught school. George was born on the Hall homestead near the Vern Lundy place on lower Catching Creek. (EHK.)

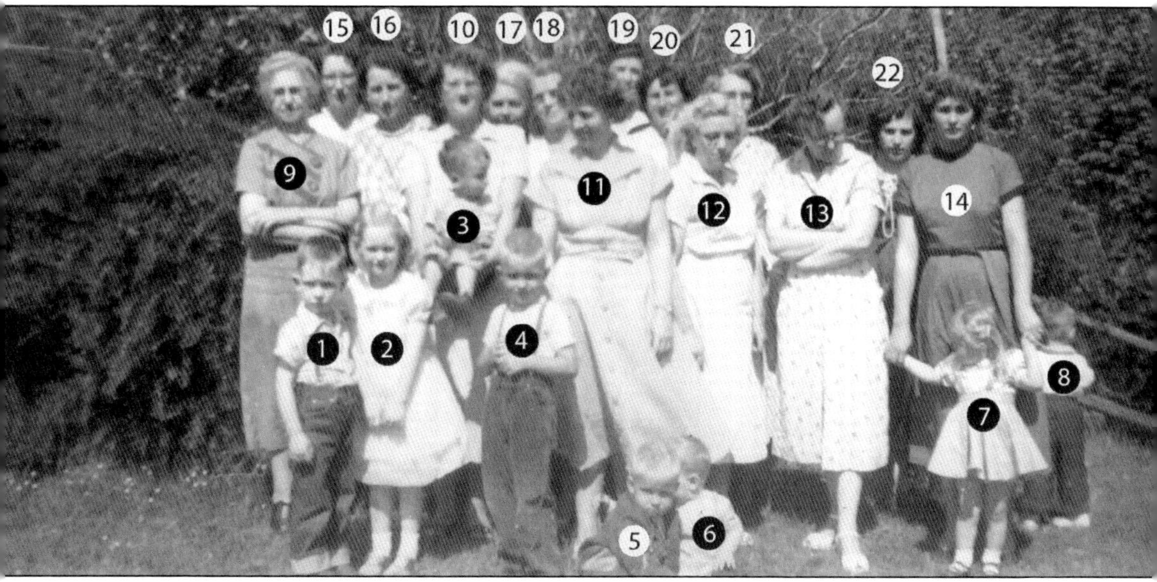

Catching Creek Friendly Neighbors began in 1937 as Ladies Aide, meeting at the Marsters Church. Later, members changed the name of the group and met in homes, often working on crafts. In attendance at this early-1950s meeting are, from left to right, (first row) Calvin Higgins (1), Connie Higgins (2), Richard "Dick Bushnell (4), Terry Bushnell (5), unidentified (6), Bobbi June Bushnell (7), and Larry Bushnell (8); (second row) Amy (Goble) Davenport (9), Bonnie Higgins (15), Mary (Smalley) Bartlett (16), Pearl Rema (10; holding Warren Rema Jr., No. 3), Lucy Wood (17), Eda Breuer (18), Gladys (Bushnell) Smith (11), Millie (Bushnell) Lakey (19), Vestie Bushnell (20), Thelma Bushnell (12), Mildred King (21), Elsie King (13), Daisy Bushnell (22), and Dorothy Bushnell (14). (CCFN.)

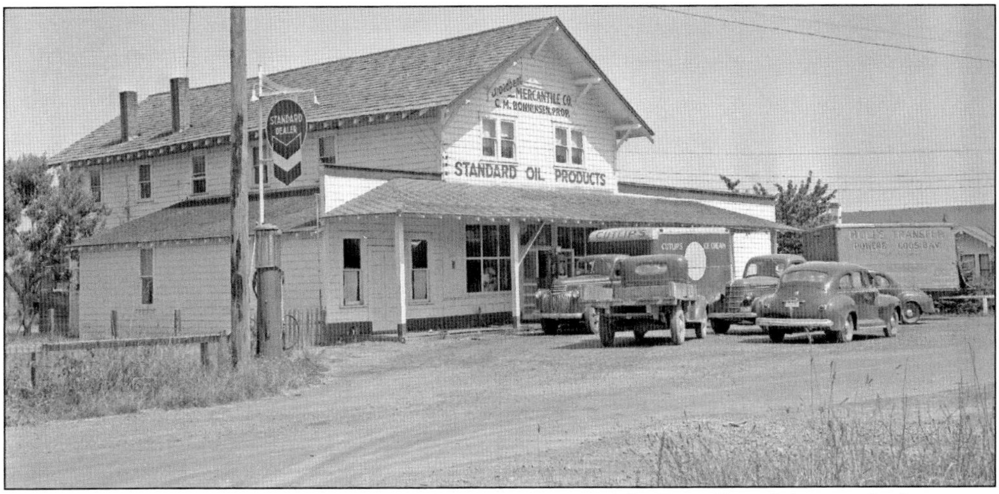

This 1940s signage proclaims C.M. Bonniksen proprietor of the Broadbent Mercantile Company. Inside the store was a post office, a tavern, and grocery items including Cutlips Ice Cream, made in North Bend. Other owners of the store include George and Catherine Nelson and Fred True. Broadbent, named for Charles Broadbent, gained a railroad station about 1915 and a post office in 1916. (CHMM 27 986-N897.)

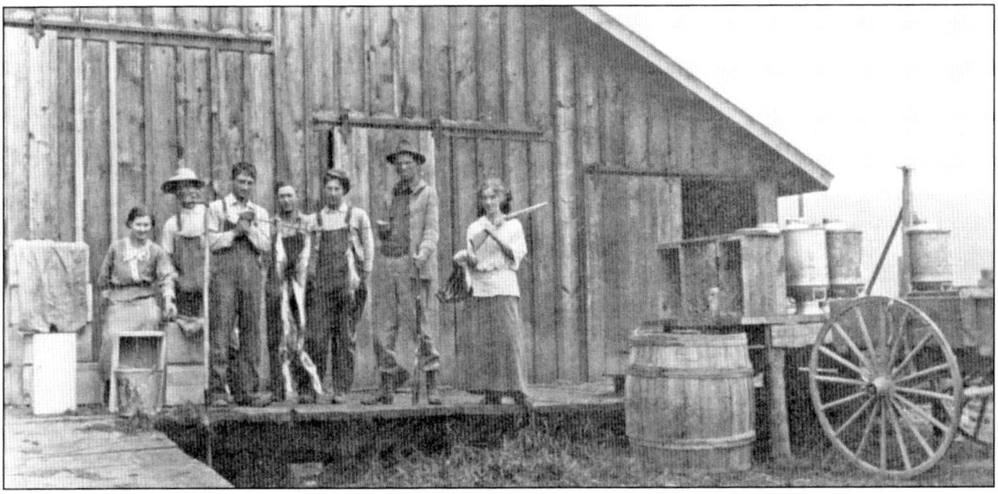

Back from a successful deer hunt in the early 1900s are members of two Arago families, the Stauffs and the Roots. In front of the barn are, from left to right, Nettie Stauff, Hessie Stauff, two unidentified young men, Sam Root, Jim Stauff, and Naomi Root. Naomi, born in 1888, married Caleb Robison, a neighbor, in 1917. She taught in several schools, beginning as early as 1912, including West Norway School in 1922. (WS.)

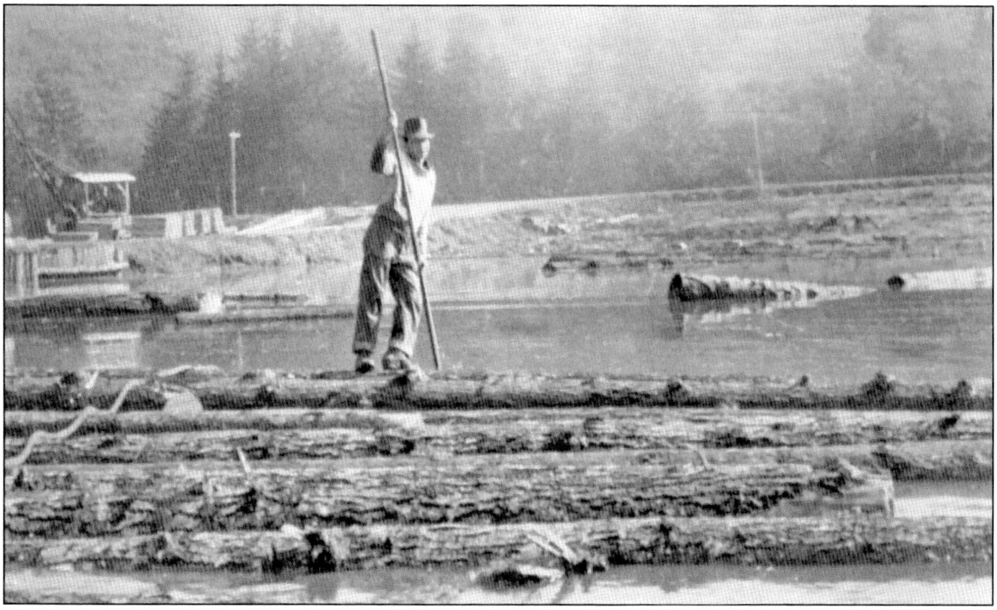

Caulk boots help Mike Labart stay upright on a slippery fir log in the Cheney Studs millpond in the late 1940s. Beyond the millpond, next to a yarder, are stacks of the eight-foot-long two-by-fours sawed at the mill, each stamped with the image of a stud horse. Ben Cheney built this sawmill near Broadbent, about a mile from the Powers Junction. (WL.)

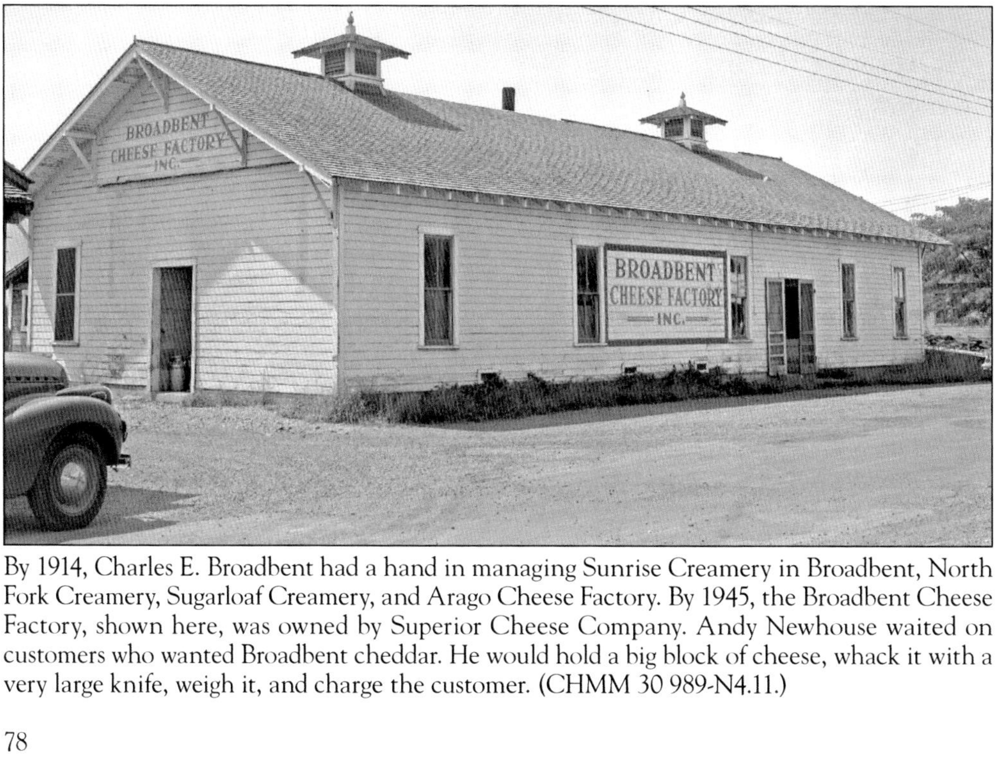

By 1914, Charles E. Broadbent had a hand in managing Sunrise Creamery in Broadbent, North Fork Creamery, Sugarloaf Creamery, and Arago Cheese Factory. By 1945, the Broadbent Cheese Factory, shown here, was owned by Superior Cheese Company. Andy Newhouse waited on customers who wanted Broadbent cheddar. He would hold a big block of cheese, whack it with a very large knife, weigh it, and charge the customer. (CHMM 30 989-N4.11.)

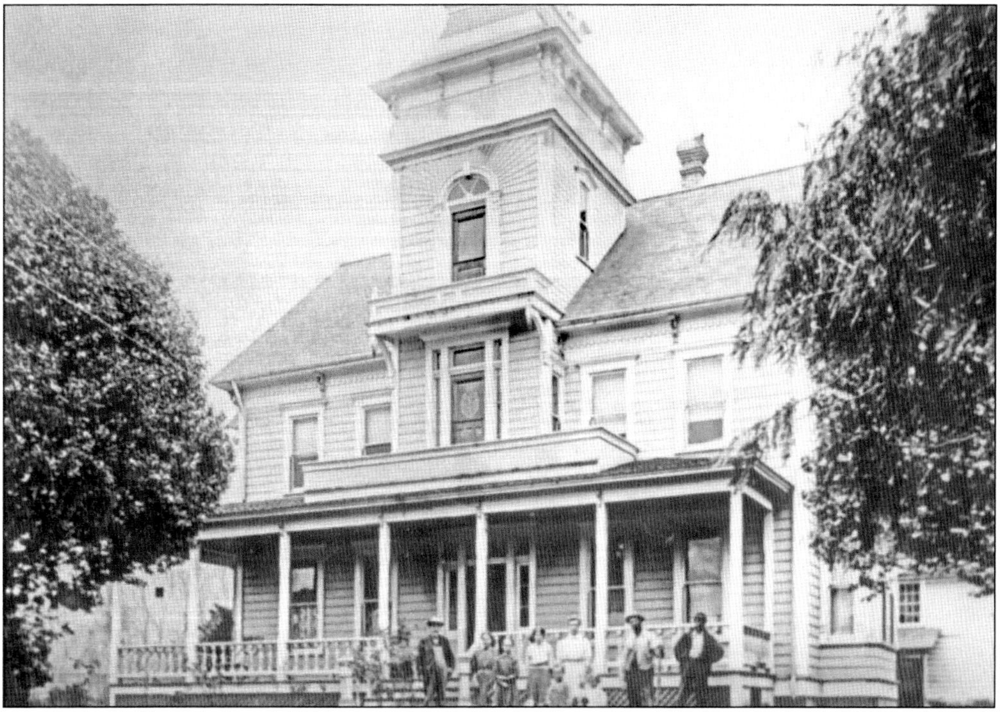

Theobald Mannel Hermann stands outside his house with the family of his son George in about 1915. Before it burned, this house stood near the Hermann Cemetery in Broadbent. Pictured are, from left to right, (first row) Roderick Hermann and Naomi Hermann; (second row) Theobald Hermann, Virna Hermann, Rowena Hermann, possibly C. Conger, George Hermann, and possibly Earl Conger. (PD.)

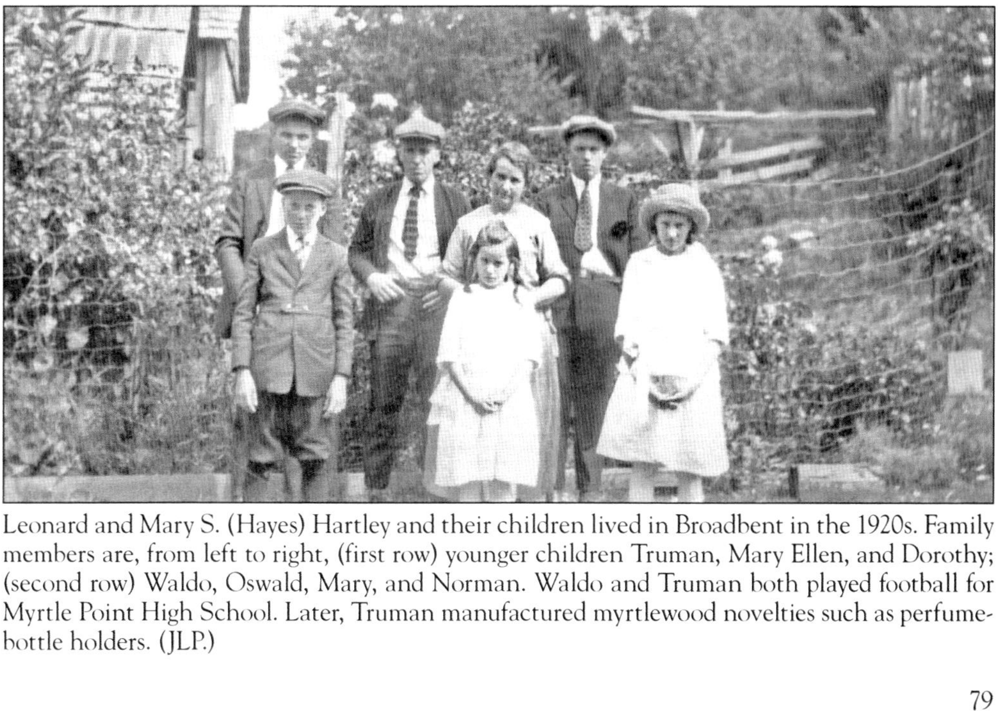

Leonard and Mary S. (Hayes) Hartley and their children lived in Broadbent in the 1920s. Family members are, from left to right, (first row) younger children Truman, Mary Ellen, and Dorothy; (second row) Waldo, Oswald, Mary, and Norman. Waldo and Truman both played football for Myrtle Point High School. Later, Truman manufactured myrtlewood novelties such as perfume-bottle holders. (JLP.)

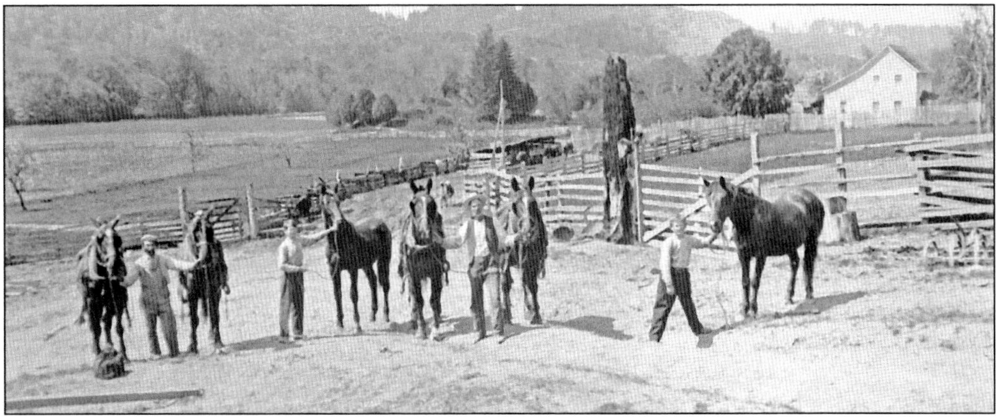

Selden Warner (third from left) leads a team of horses toward a wagon tongue in about 1915. A ranch hand (left) holds the bridles of a second pair of workhorses. Warner's sons Ellis (second from left) and Roland (far right) hold the rope halters of saddle horses. Selden Warner raised crops and milked cows near Broadbent. At one time, there were 22 dairies in a three-mile stretch between Powers Junction and Dement Creek. (CHMM 74 992-8-1986a.)

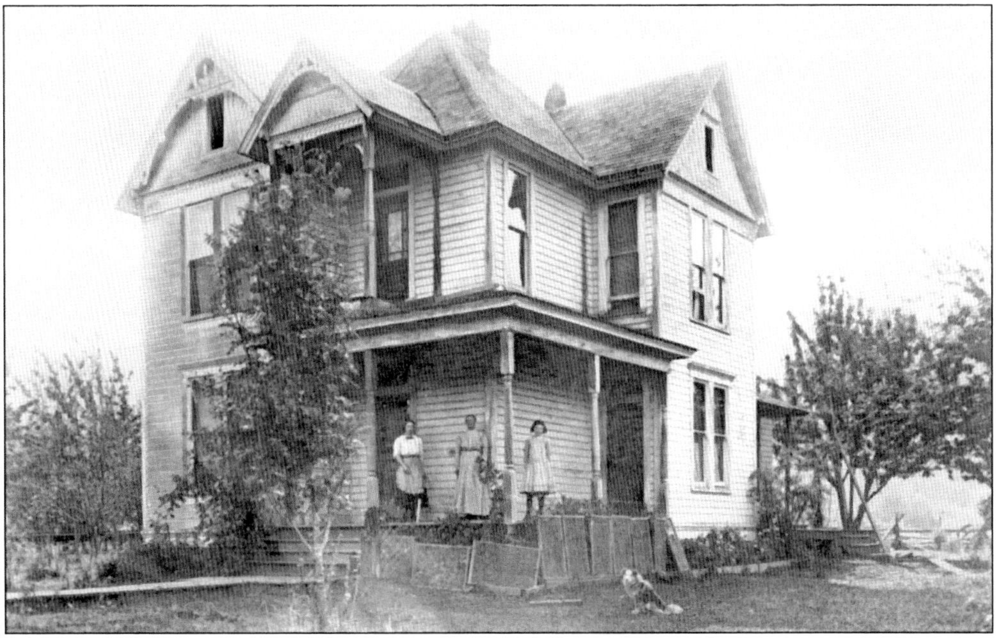

In their home in Gravelford, John D. Bennett and his wife, Mary Bell (Bunch) Bennett, provided room and board for students at Gravelford Academy. John D. was a sawmill operator, farmer, and bridge builder. When he was away building bridges, Mary Bell ran their farm. They donated part of their farm, a grove of myrtle and maple trees beside the river, to Coos County for a park, now named Bennett Park. (KD.)

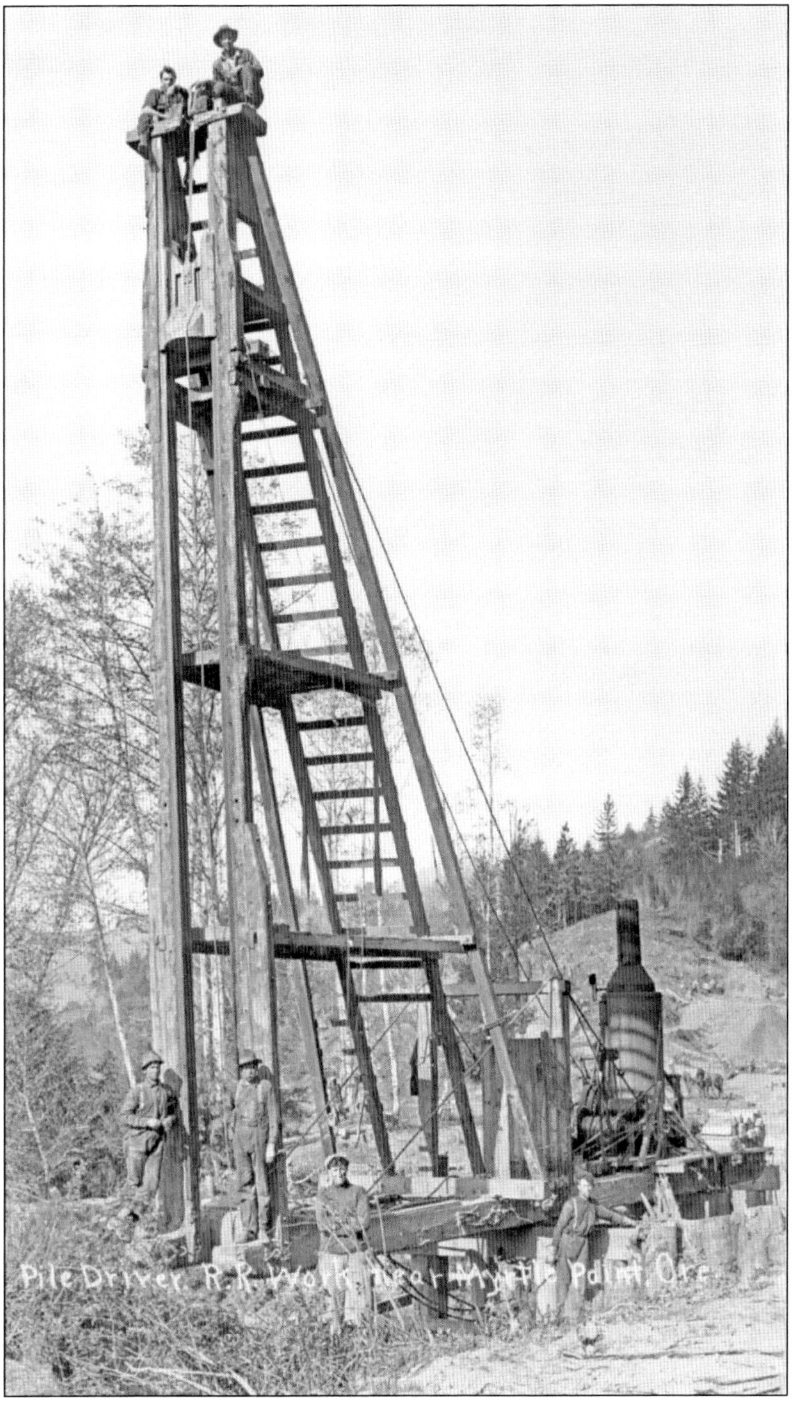

This pile driver near Myrtle Point around 1912 was powered by a steam boiler, seen at right. When Smith-Powers Logging Company built the railroad between Myrtle Point and Powers, log pilings supported eight main railroad bridges and miles of elevated train tracks. Port Orford Cedar logs were dragged or floated to the site, lifted into position in the frame, and then driven into the ground. (WL.)

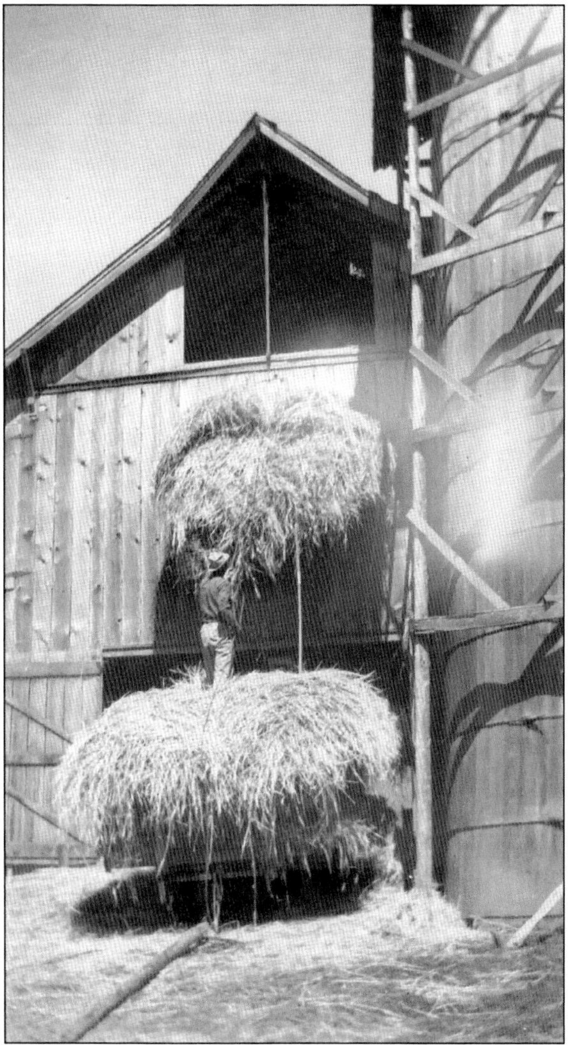

A derrick system lifts loose hay from the wagon into the haymow at a Hoffman barn, possibly in the 1940s. This barn had a double-harpoon hay fork that held the hay when it was lifted. Inside the barn was a pulley system connected to a track. To make silage, cut grass or corn was put in the silo (right). (DH.)

In 1915, the road to Powers curved through Carman Acres in Gaylord. Gaylord was also known as Etelka and Roland Prairie. The road was straightened and paved between 1941 and 1942. Julia (Grant) Carman, wife of James W. Carman, was Etelka's postmistress from 1891 to 1909, and the post office was in the couple's house. Three of the Carmans' six children—Robert, Clinton, and Asa—continued farming in Gaylord. (CK.)

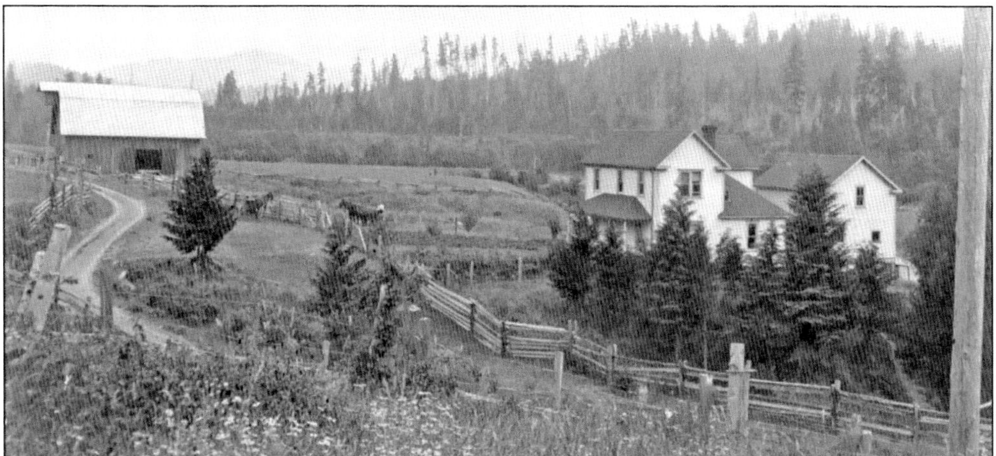

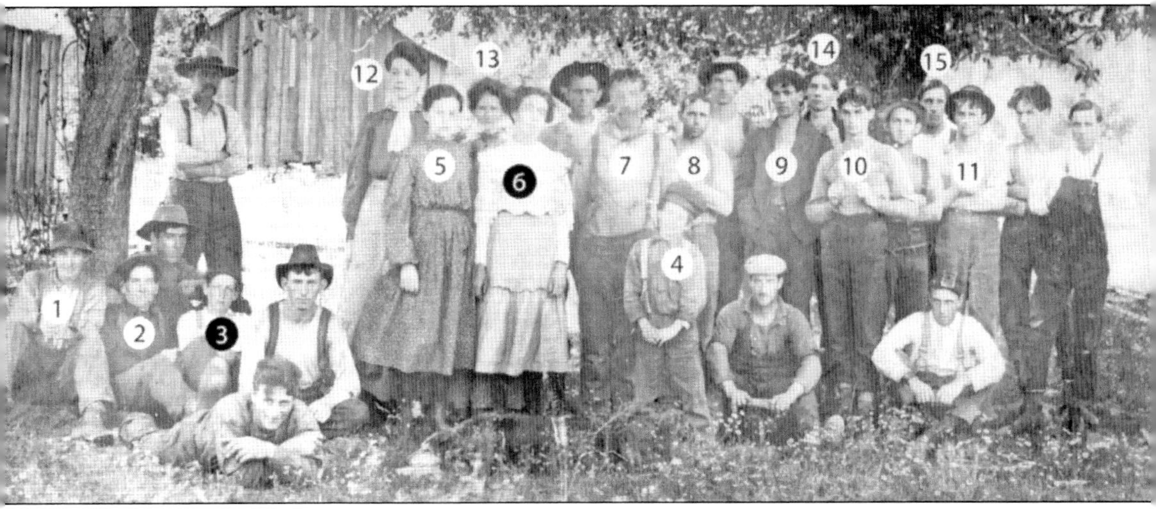

It was an all-cousin crew that Alex Adams, camp push (logging camp foreman), and his wife, Mary Isabelle "Izzie" (Ward) Adams, hired on at Cecil C. Carter's logging camp in Gaylord. Identified under the tree at left in this 1906 photograph are Clarence Adams (1), Allen "Dude" King (2), and George King (3). The young boy standing at center is Earl Adams (4), and standing behind him are, from left to right, Effie King (12), Lottie W. Carey (5), Gladys "Osa" Adams (13), camp cook Izzie (6), unidentified, camp push Alex (7), William "Willie" Warner (8), unidentified, George Adams (9), Leslie "Bud" King (14), William "Bill" Cribbins (10), unidentified, Fred Spires (15), Manley Cribbins (11), and two unidentified men. Also pictured (but not identified) are Dutch Prey, Bill Miller, Jim Green, Emory Robbins, Roy Neal, and Johnie Warner. (CK.)

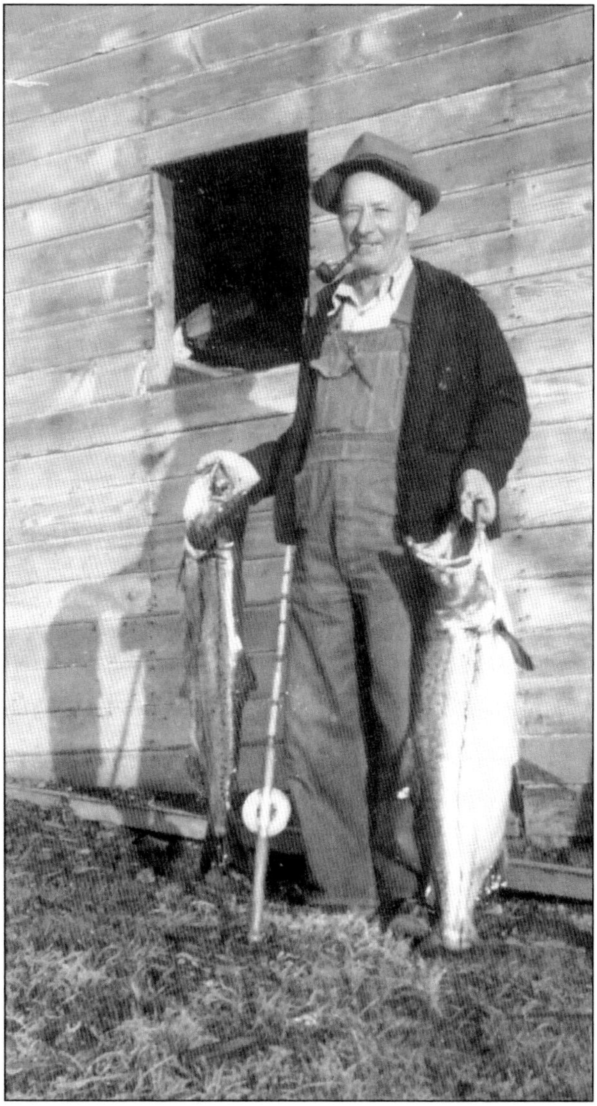

Luther Daniels pulled these salmon from the South Fork on November 22, 1947. Daniels was fishing the South Fork near this barn owned by Leland Barklow. Another place Daniels liked to fish was "Powerline Pole" in Norway. (CK.)

The day's task for Charles Hoffman and his dog Rover is to plow a field that will grow corn for silage. Rover rode on the tractor between the driver's knees. This Oliver Row Crop Model 60, shown in 1944, replaced horses on Hoffman's farm. Hoffman's grandparents Abraham and Jemima (Flett) Hoffman filed a donation land claim three miles south of Myrtle Point in 1854. (DH.)

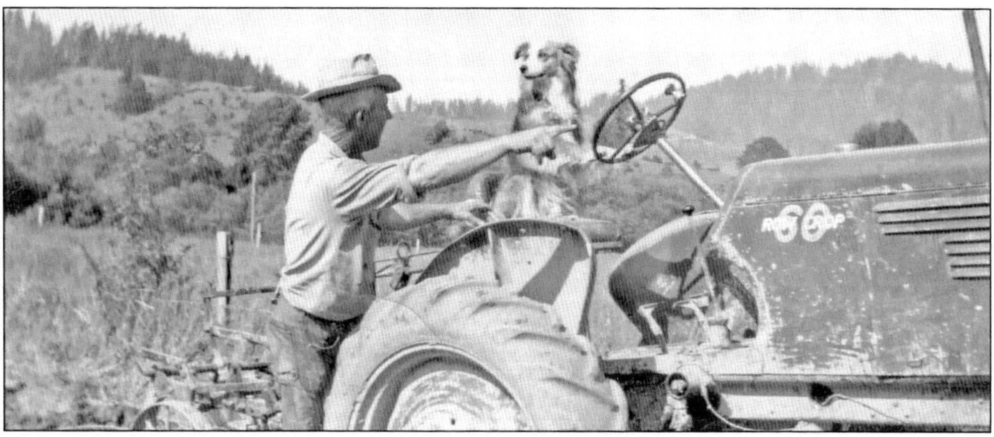

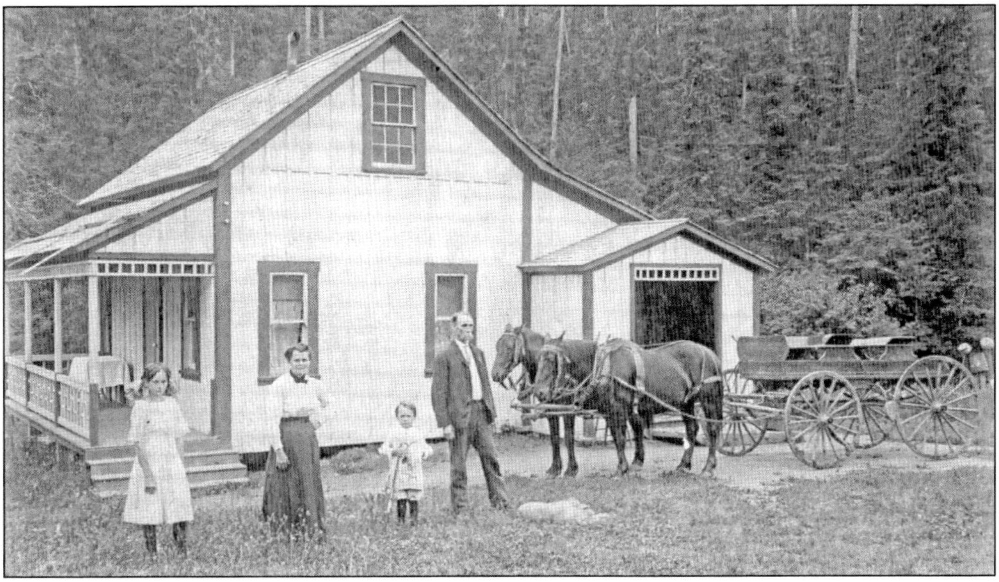

Some of the earliest rural post offices in the Coquille River drainage were established at Enchanted Prairie, Hermannville, Bancroft, and Eckley. Living at Enchanted Prairie in about 1913, in this house about one mile east of Bridge, were Richard Alonzo Cribbins (right), Frances "Fannie" (Ward) Cribbins (second from left), their daughter, Flossie (left) and their son, Alma (third from left). Harnessed to the family's buckboard are Chub and Dan. (KLD.)

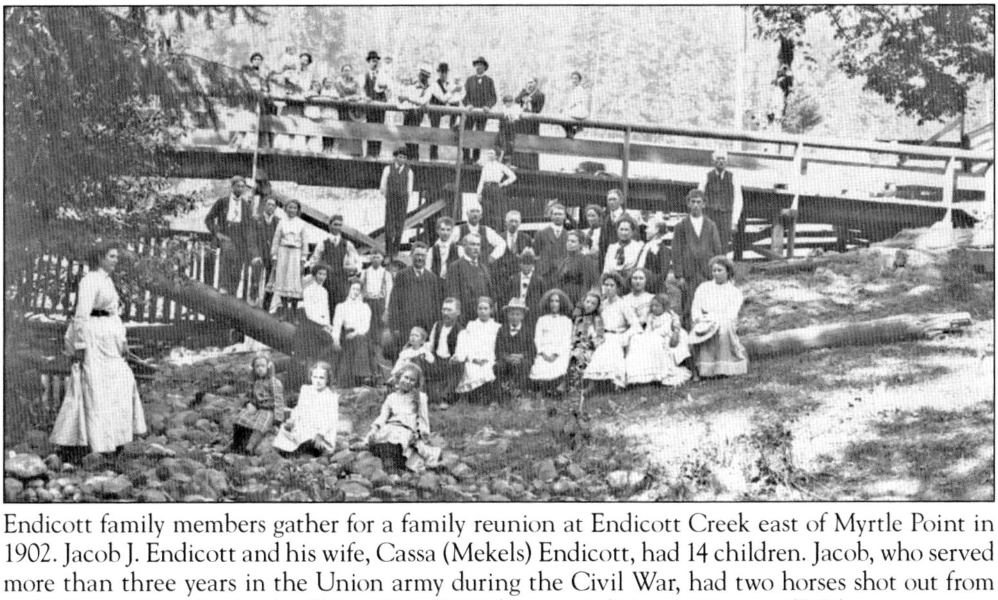

Endicott family members gather for a family reunion at Endicott Creek east of Myrtle Point in 1902. Jacob J. Endicott and his wife, Cassa (Mekels) Endicott, had 14 children. Jacob, who served more than three years in the Union army during the Civil War, had two horses shot out from under him. After the death of his wife in 1905, he married Fannie Warner. (RG.)

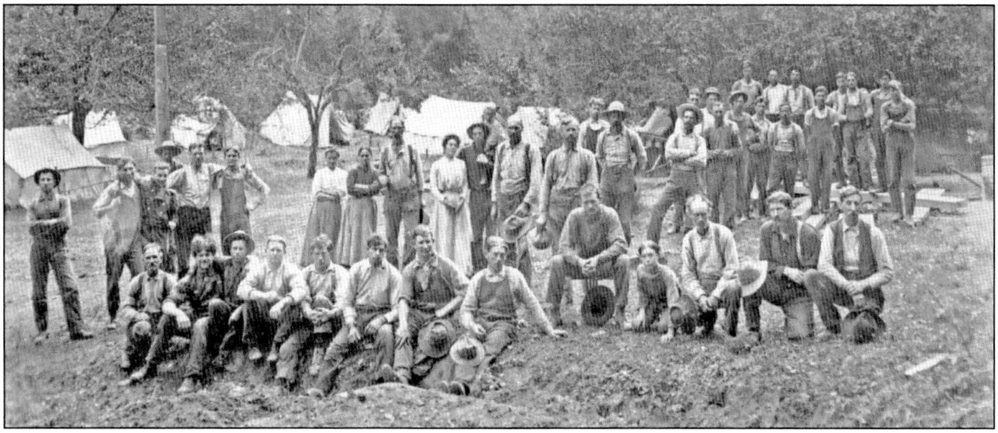

This road crew set up a camp near the Middle Fork of the Coquille River in the early 1900s, probably between Sugarloaf Mountain and Bridge. Frazier Hoffman worked on this crew improving Highway 42. (DH)

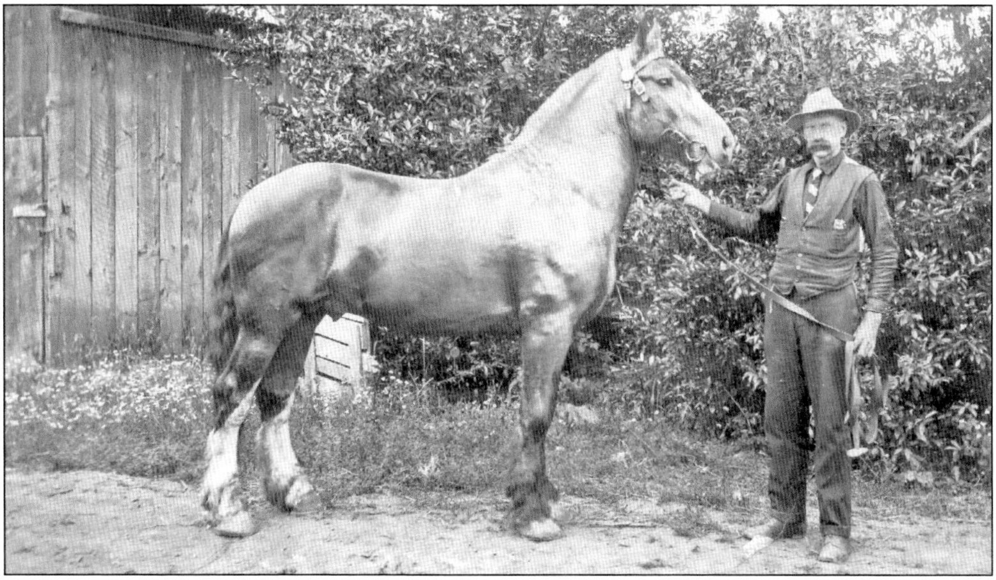

In this 1915 image, the registered Clydesdale stallion named Robert Burns shows the conformation that won a blue ribbon at that year's Coos County Fair. At right is the stud's owner, George W. Martin, who ranched on Sugarloaf Mountain. The photograph was intended for use in advertising. (CP.)

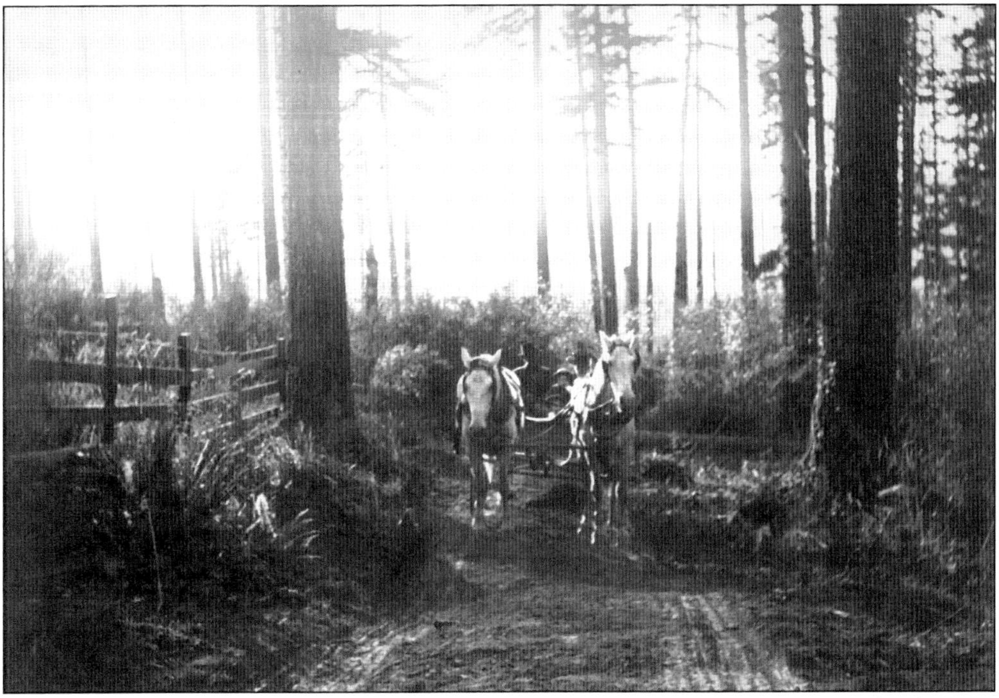

Taking the old road from their ranch at Echo Valley to Myrtle Point in 1898 are Lloyd and Emma Spires and their two sons. The elder son is Roy; the younger, Elton. This road on Bald Hill stayed to high ground, avoiding the bottoms that flooded in the winter. (KL.)

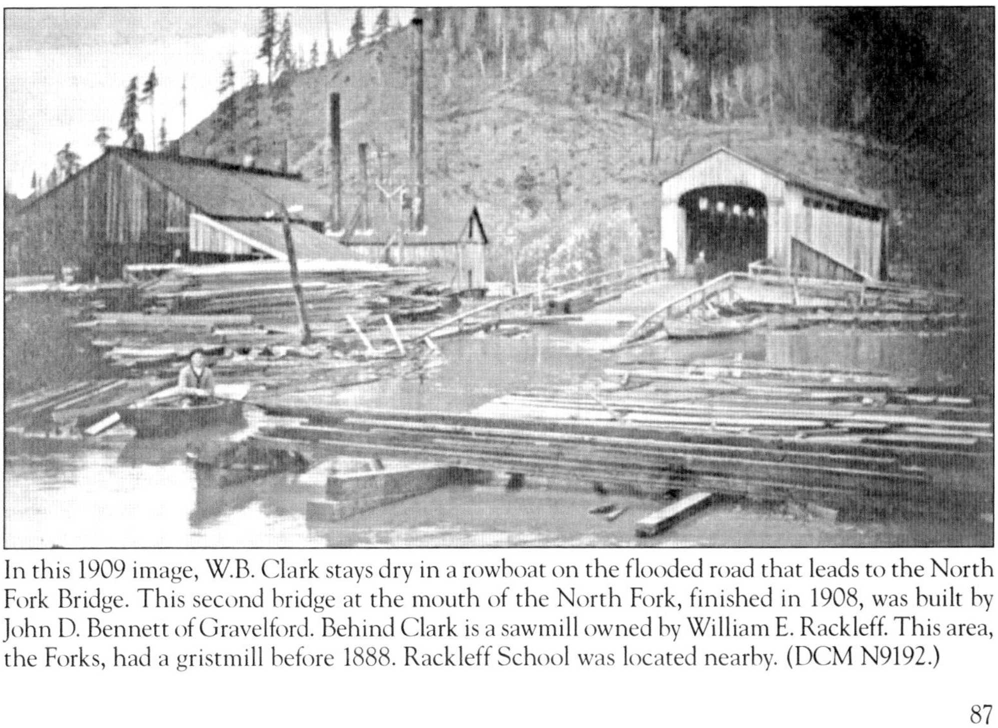

In this 1909 image, W.B. Clark stays dry in a rowboat on the flooded road that leads to the North Fork Bridge. This second bridge at the mouth of the North Fork, finished in 1908, was built by John D. Bennett of Gravelford. Behind Clark is a sawmill owned by William E. Rackleff. This area, the Forks, had a gristmill before 1888. Rackleff School was located nearby. (DCM N9192.)

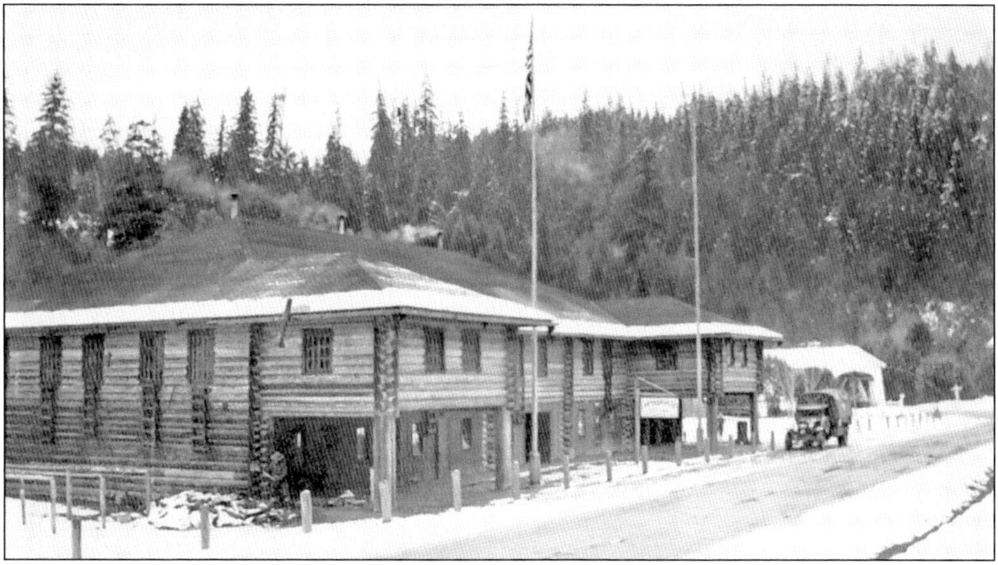

Built in the late 1920s to serve as a dude ranch, this log lodge had a ballroom upstairs. In 1932, the Civilian Conservation Corps housed enrollees in the ballroom while they built Camp Bradford on land across the Middle Fork. Hugh Sherwood dismantled the 1,500-log structure, moved the logs to Yachats, reassembled the building, and opened it as Sherwood Lodge in 1951. Visible at right is a covered bridge over Upper Rock Creek. (LK.)

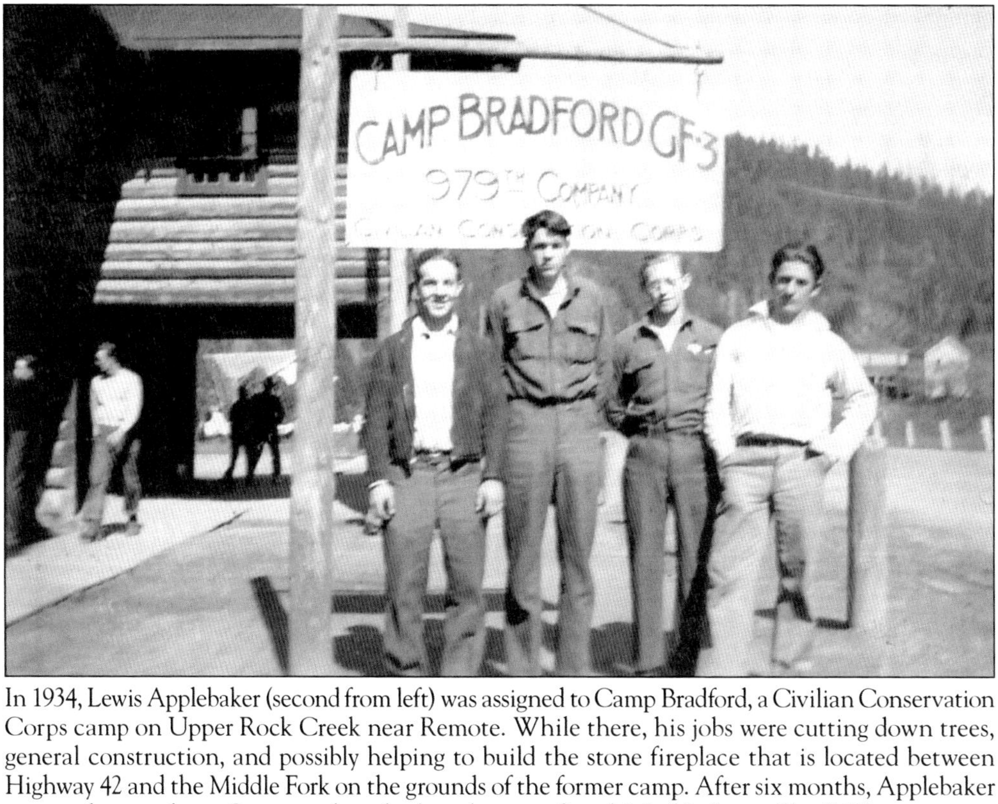

In 1934, Lewis Applebaker (second from left) was assigned to Camp Bradford, a Civilian Conservation Corps camp on Upper Rock Creek near Remote. While there, his jobs were cutting down trees, general construction, and possibly helping to build the stone fireplace that is located between Highway 42 and the Middle Fork on the grounds of the former camp. After six months, Applebaker returned to southern Oregon, where he later became fire chief of Jacksonville. (LK.)

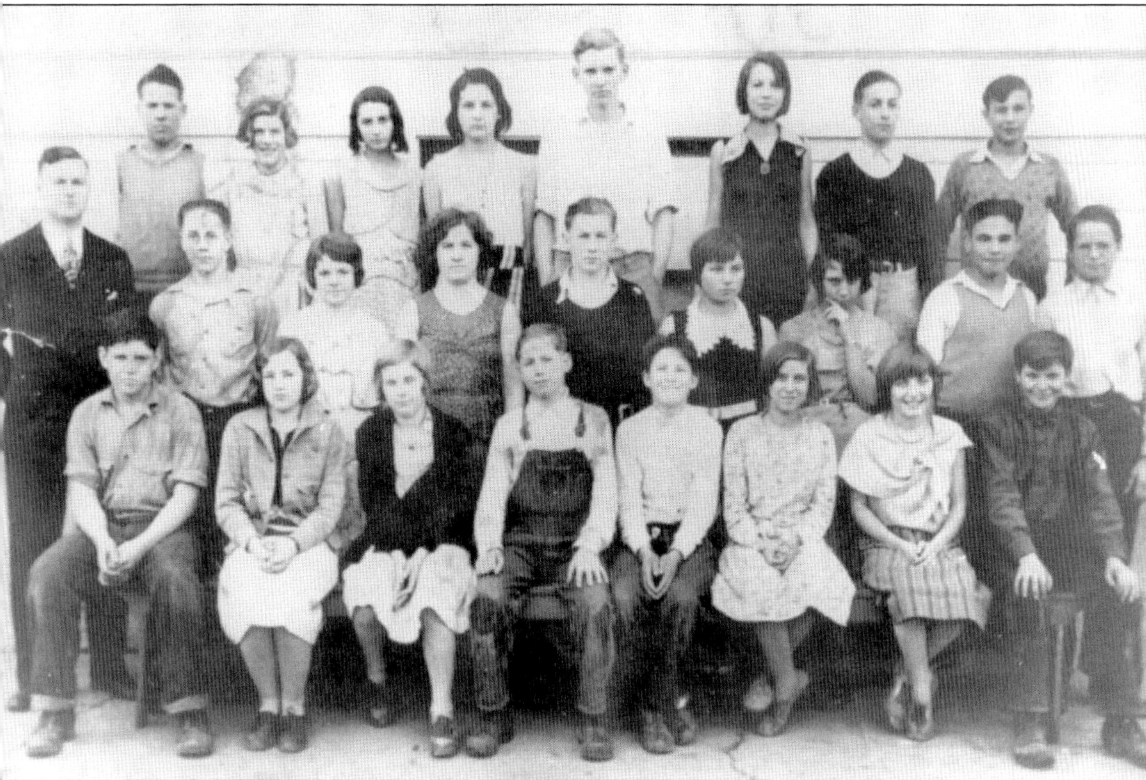

Harry Lasswell's seventh- and eighth-grade students at Bridge around 1933 are, from left to right, (first row) Kenneth LaBranch, Florence McMullen, Marion Bryant, Don Zinn, Melvin Clayton, Lita Shields, Myrtle Beckett, and Raymond Kirkendoll; (second row) Clyde Bartlett, Rayvenol Ramsey, Dorothy Sutphin, Merle Bryant, Connie Knight, Addie Farmer, unidentified, and John Koch; (third row) Ezra Zinn, Nell Koch, Annie Culver, Olive Buzzard, Vernon Shields, Maxine Scarborough, Glenn Cribbins, and Ernie Bryant. Lasswell stands to the far left. (CK.)

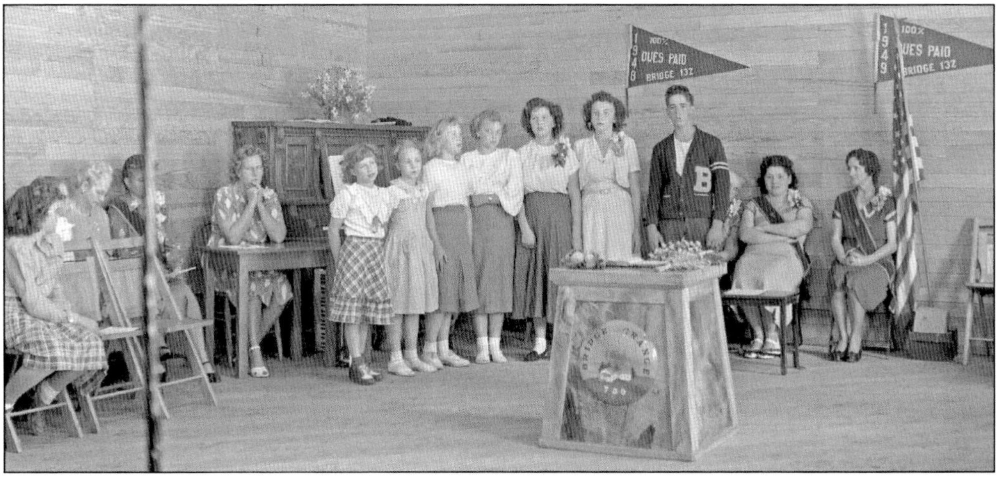

Juvenile Grange members were installed in 1949 at the Bridge Grange Hall. Participating in the ceremony are, from left to right, three unidentified people, Blanche Davis, Anna Waterman, Paula Lancaster, Audrey Waterman, Martha Lancaster, Alice Magill, Lila Hardman, Elma Jean Magill, Jack Dolph, unidentified (behind Jack Dolph), LaVada Hardman, and Elsie Mack. Dolph wears a letter sweater for Bridge High School. (CHMM 165 995-1.6706.1.)

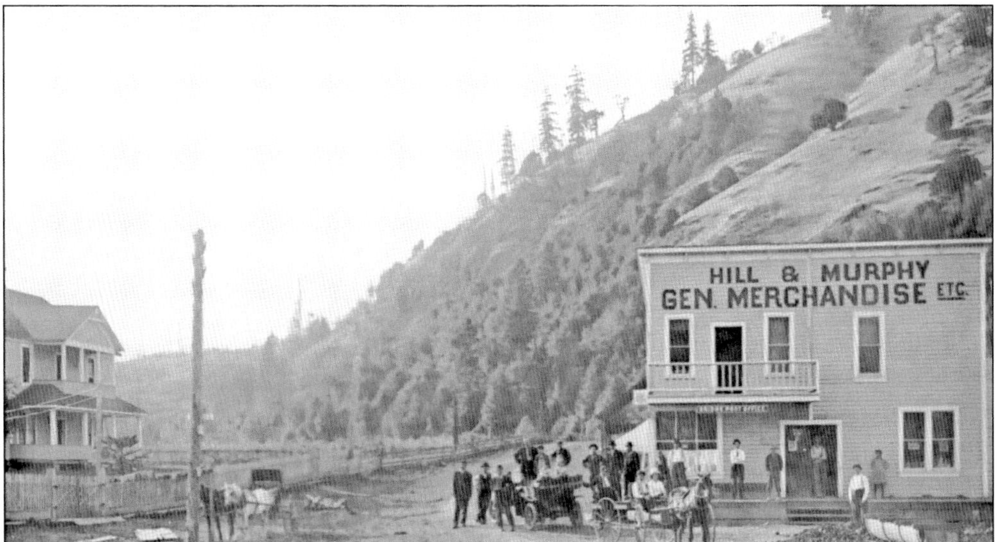

Anderson Mountain rises above the Hill & Murphy store. Inside the store was the Bridge Post Office, which opened on July 6, 1894. A covered bridge crossed Big Creek near this site before 1912. The first story of the house at left still stands today. (CHMM 168 959-317a.)

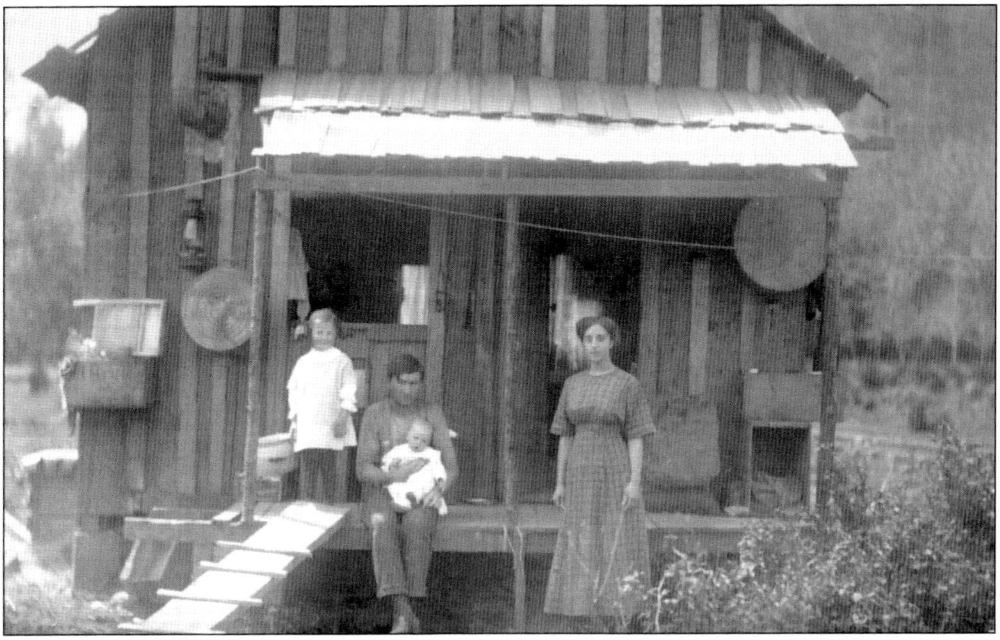

Dora (Hoover) Carlson (right) was born in 1896. A washtub hangs to the left of the open window of her house, near a scrub board. The larger tub to the right would have been handy for Saturday-night baths. Dora and her husband, Wayne (pictured), are shown with the first two of their five children, Helen and Jack (held by his father). Their other three children were Max, Artha, and Donna Jean. Dora's parents were Willis Aaron Hoover and Artha Catherine (Royer) Hoover. (JLP.)

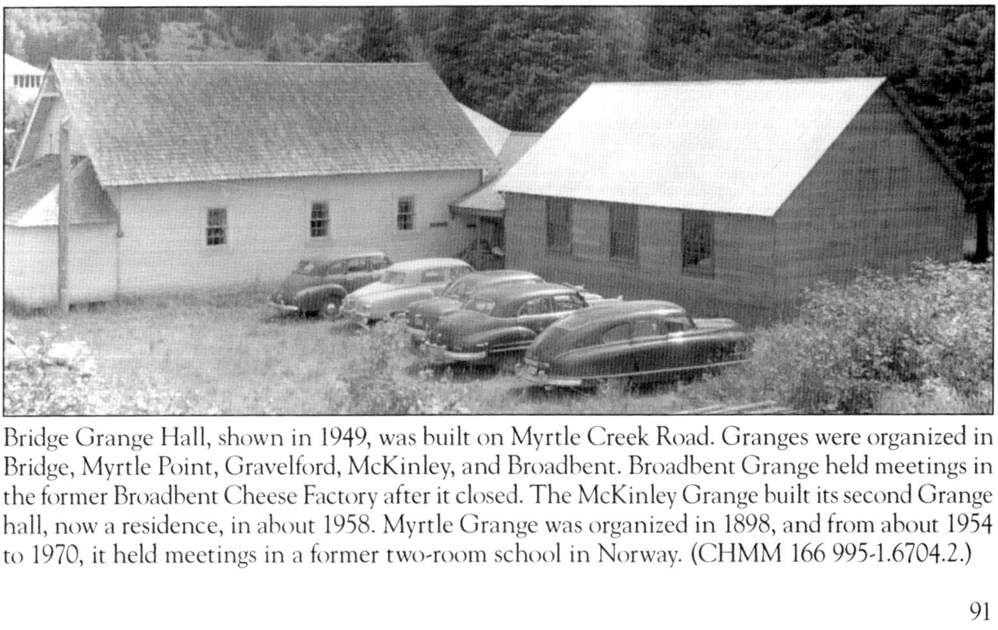

Bridge Grange Hall, shown in 1949, was built on Myrtle Creek Road. Granges were organized in Bridge, Myrtle Point, Gravelford, McKinley, and Broadbent. Broadbent Grange held meetings in the former Broadbent Cheese Factory after it closed. The McKinley Grange built its second Grange hall, now a residence, in about 1958. Myrtle Grange was organized in 1898, and from about 1954 to 1970, it held meetings in a former two-room school in Norway. (CHMM 166 995-1.6704.2.)

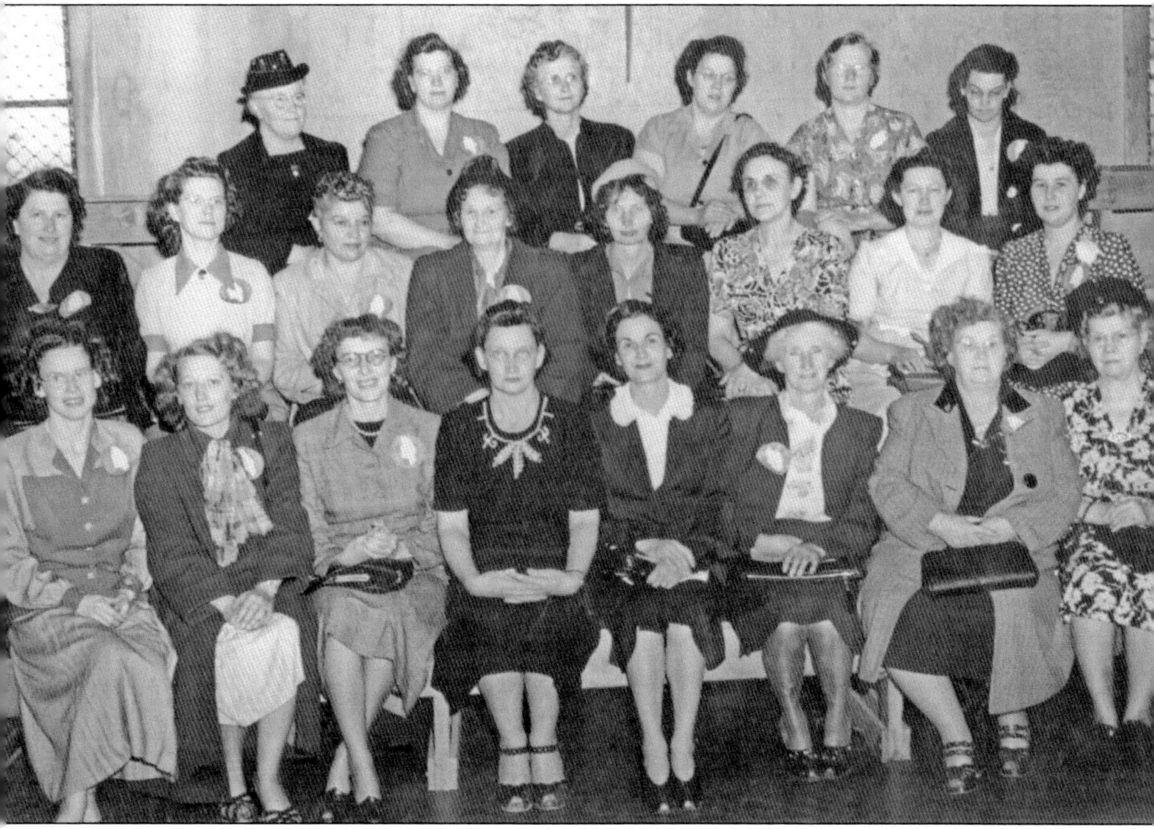

Members of the Bridge-Remote Extension group, meeting in the Bridge Grange Hall in 1946 or 1947, are, from left to right, (first row) Nell Koch, Edna McKinley, Sylvia Goodman, Amanda Waterman, Lou Richmond, Eva Jennings, Bessie Ocheltree, and Dora Van Alstein; (second row) Catharine Hardman, Carol Kennedy, Blanche Davis, Vivienne Fish, Mildred Hudson, Maude England, Grace Jewett, and Dorothy Nelson; (third row) Eula Schmann, Marion Brown, Irene Young, Eldis Sell, Anna Waterman, and Nana Winningham. (JLP.)

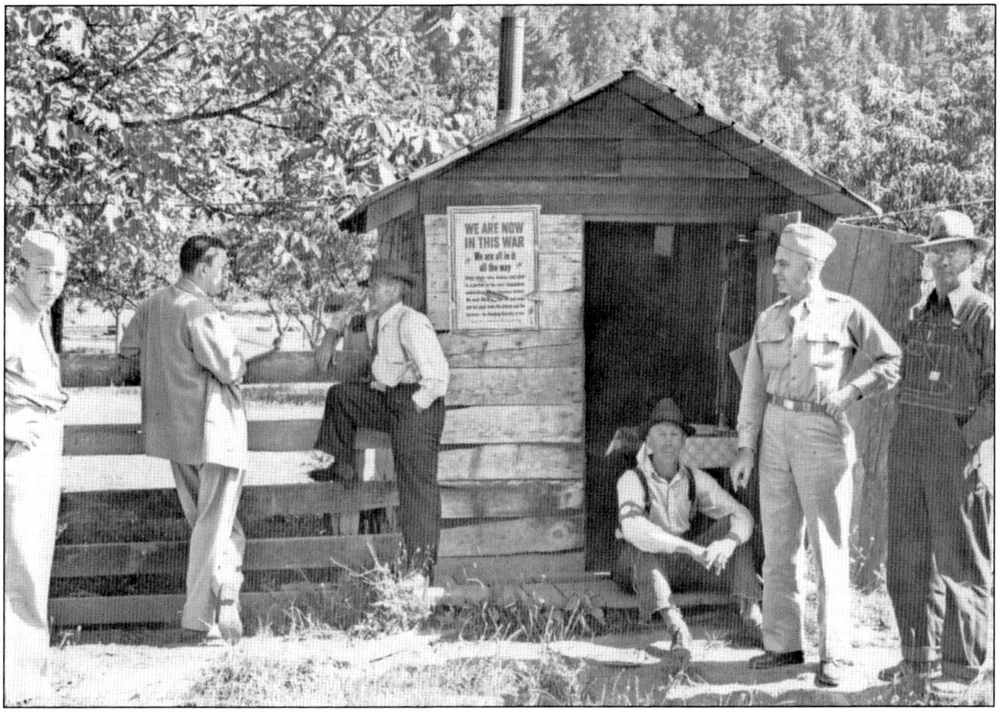

Volunteer plane spotters looking for American and Japanese airplanes took shifts in shacks like this one, likely in Remote. Laurence B. Jennings (third from left) talks with an unidentified man, while Jack Wyrick sits in the doorway. In Bridge, students were daytime spotters. The shack at Cherry Creek was manned by Dora and McKinley adults and youth. In Myrtle Point, Mayor Jack Dunn took the first plane-spotting shift. (JLP.)

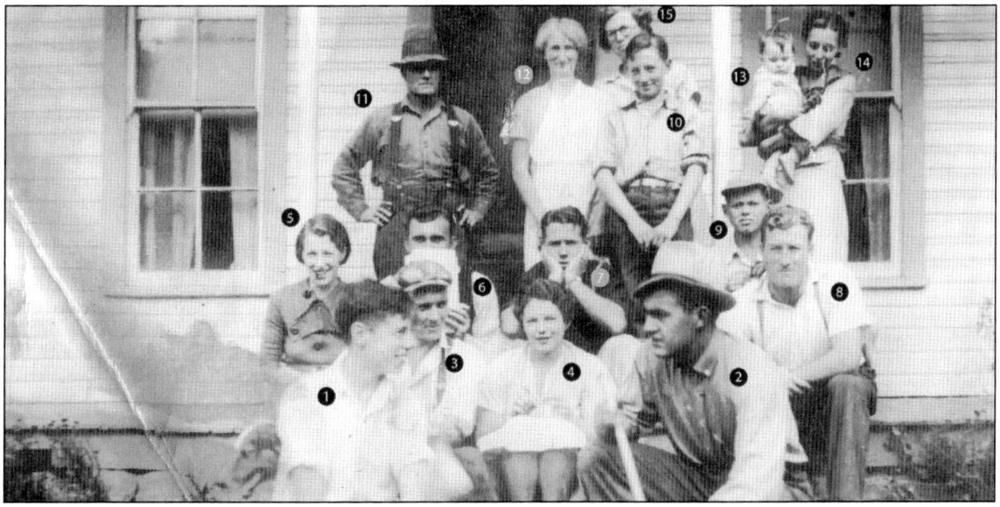

Outside a building that possibly is a former school near Remote are, from left to right, (first row) Wayne Jennings (1), Dow Beckham (2); (second row) Ivan "Ike"" Cribbins (3), Maude Jennings (4), and Powell Lancaster (8); (third row) Erma Jennings (5), Curt Beckham (6), and two unidentified young men (7 and 9); (third row) Laurence B. Jennings (11), Eva Dolly Jennings (12), unidentified (15), Gene E. Jennings (10), and an unidentified woman and child (13 and 14). Both Beckham brothers taught school, worked in the woods, and wrote local histories. (JLP.)

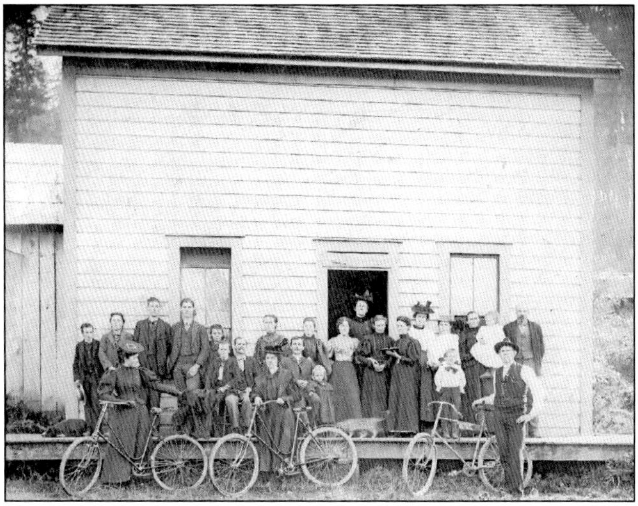

This building may have housed students at Gravelford Academy, a Seventh-day Adventist institution open from about 1897 to 1920. At Gravelford Academy in 1917, the monthly tuition for resident students ranged from $2 for first graders to $4 for twelfth graders. The 1917 catalog states, "The managers require all unmarried students whose parents or guardians do not reside near the Academy to board at the Home, and to room in the buildings owned or controlled by the school." (KD.)

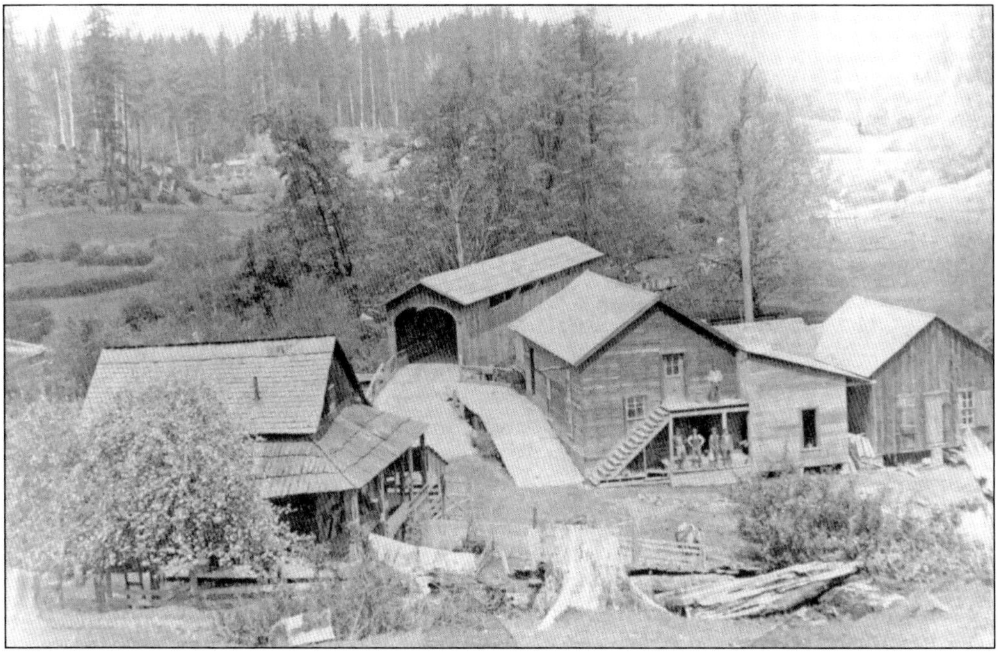

Gravelford had a covered bridge, a cheese factory, a post office, and a store located about a half mile up Brady Road. Here, men stand in front of the cheese factory that Fred Moser started around 1896. Like May Bunch, who opened a store in 1898, Moser had a store in Gravelford. He served as Gravelford postmaster from 1900 to 1918. He and his wife, Ida (Segessman) Moser, both born in Switzerland, had four children. (PD.)

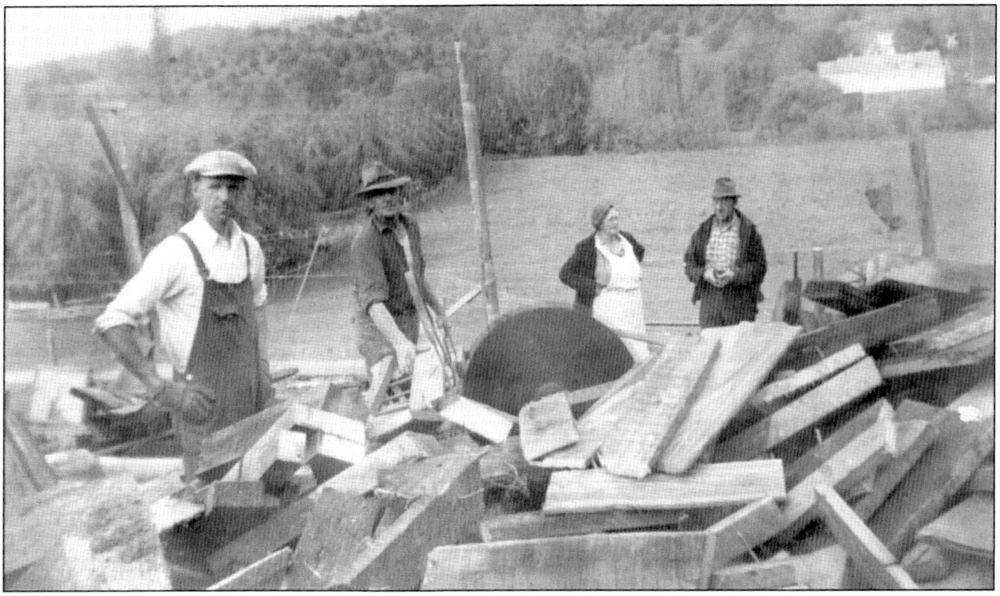

Running fir slabs through a buzz saw for firewood in the early 1940s are Paul Davis Sr. (left) and Harvey Barklow. Frank and Dovie (Lewellen) Southmayd, parents of Davis's wife, Opal, are also pictured visiting this Brady Road farm. In the background is Gravelford Cheese Factory, built on the northern bank of the North Fork. Behind Davis is his orchard of apple, pear, and prune trees. (PD.)

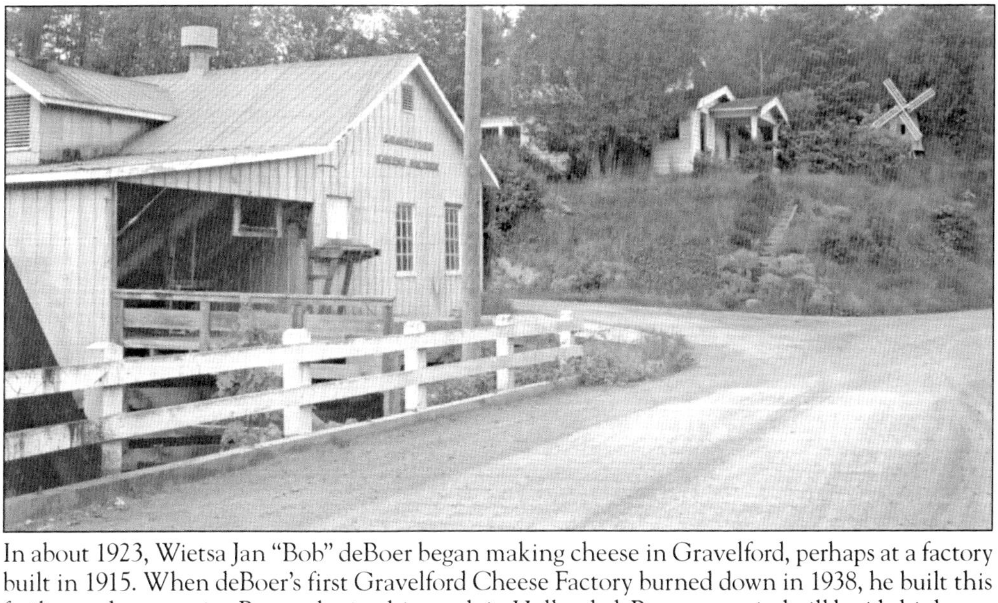

In about 1923, Wietsa Jan "Bob" deBoer began making cheese in Gravelford, perhaps at a factory built in 1915. When deBoer's first Gravelford Cheese Factory burned down in 1938, he built this facility at the same site. Remembering his youth in Holland, deBoer put a windmill beside his house above Gravelford Road, where he lived with his wife, Gertrude (Heffley) deBoer, and their two daughters, Betty and Helen. The cheese factory closed in about 1944. (CHMM 96 969-N3.2 h.)

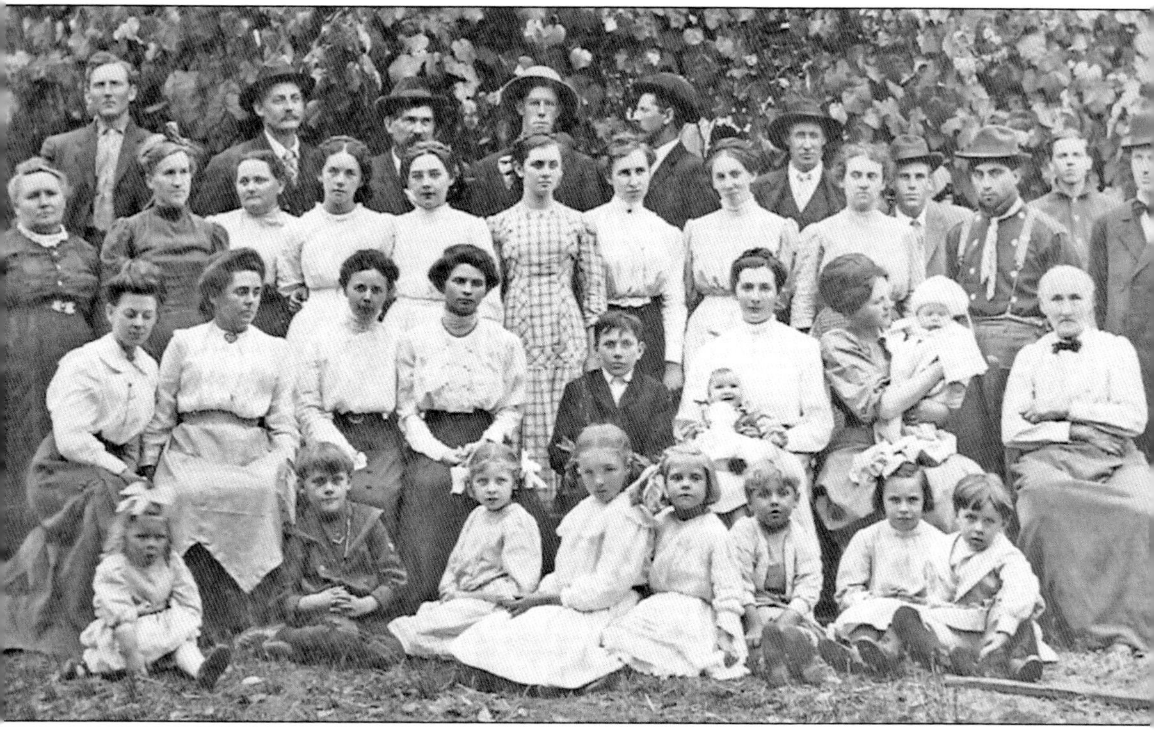

At a reunion near Gravelford in about 1910 are, from left to right, (first row) all unidentified; (second row) Clara B?, Alice (Stemmler) Luttrel, unidentified, Selata Howe, unidentified, Dora Gearhart holding Hazel Gearhart, probably Aletha (Krantz) Slagel holding Margaret Slagle, and Rachel C. Walker (sister of Charles Fletcher Leatherman); (third row) Lottie Young, Georgia Bunch, unidentified, Gladys Krantz, ? Young, Grace Krantz, unidentified, Opal Dugger, unidentified, ? Laird, and Harvey Seggle; (fourth row) Oscar Bunch, ? Luttrel, unidentified, Lloyd Leatherman, unidentified, Charles Fletcher Leatherman, Neal Gearhart, and unidentified. (HL.)

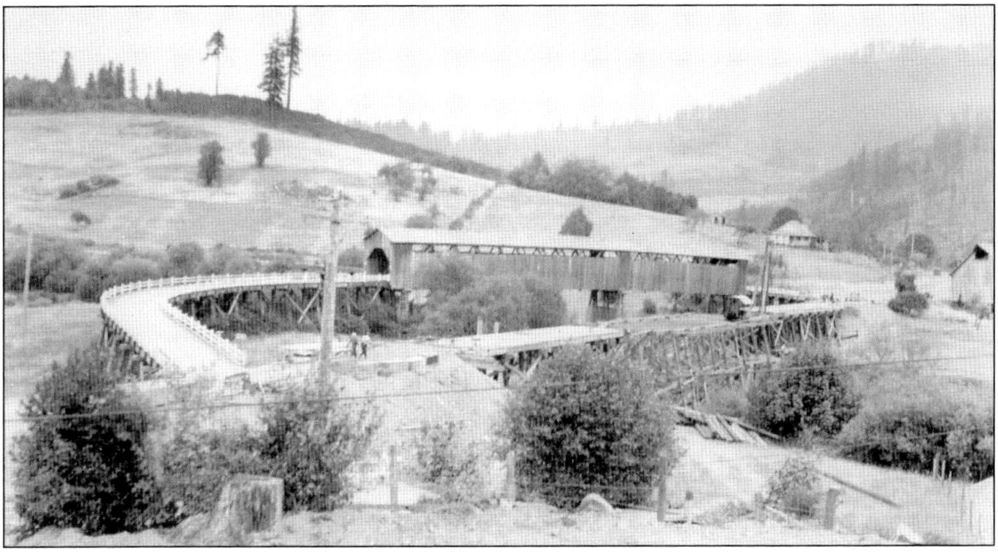

Cooper Bridge over the North Fork, four miles northeast of Myrtle Point, is named after William O. Cooper, who owned a ranch at the end of the covered bridge when it was built by George Reidinger around 1900. A replacement bridge is under construction. In the background is a house once owned by Sylvia Culbertson. (PD.)

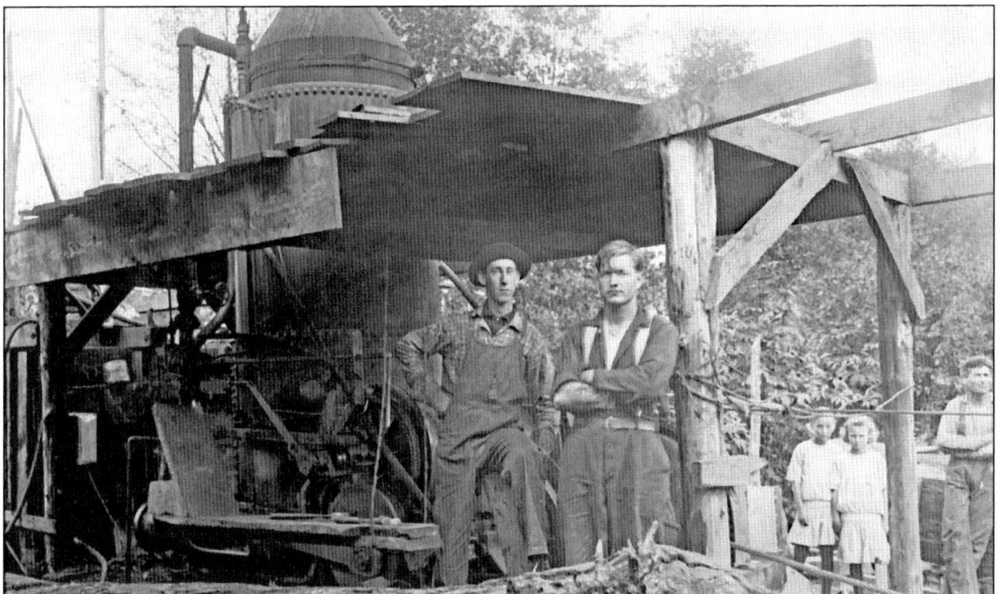

Bill Olson and his wife, Edna (Gill) Olson, logged their land on Elk Creek in the hills south of the East Fork. Standing near the steam donkey around 1923 are, from left to right, Ed Crumley, Bill, Helma Olson, Helen Gill, and Dick Gill. Bill arrived in Coquille on his 21st birthday, April 1, 1910, and worked for a year or two on Rink Creek for the Aasen brothers, Ed and John. (GO.)

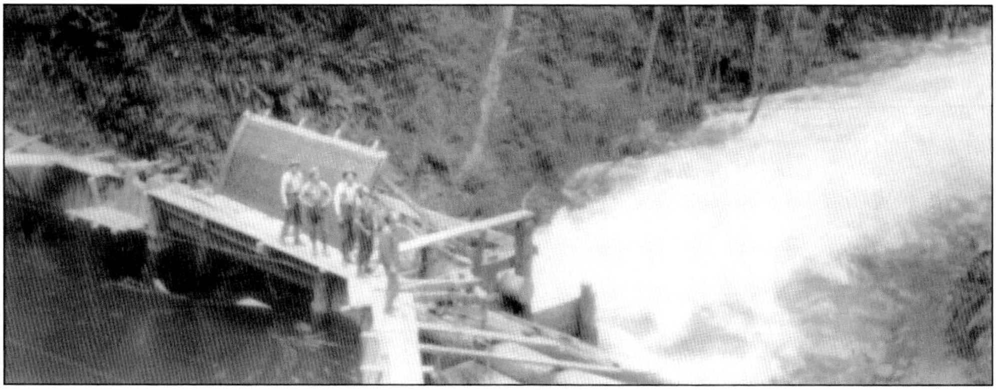

At splash dams like this one on Elk Creek, there was a lot of excitement when the men released the ponded water and the logs. Men ran along the banks with their peavies in hand. When a log got hung up, they pushed it off. The logs especially got stuck on gravel bars. (GO.)

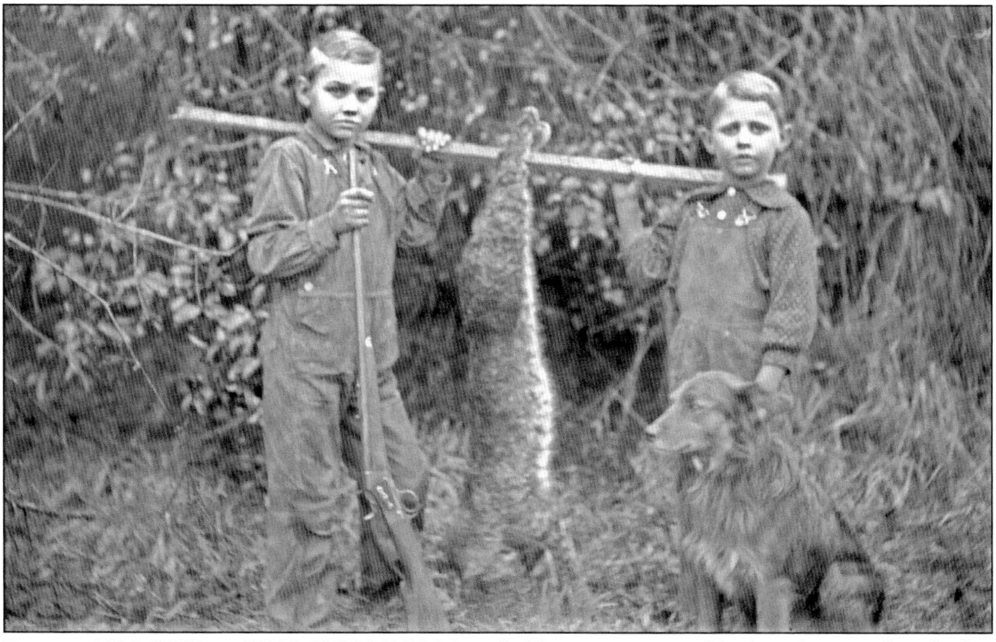

Born in 1900, William Webb "Wild Bill" Mast (left) was not very old when he posed with this bobcat. His brother, Lloyd "Winker" Mast, was even younger. The Mast brothers lived in Lee Valley with their parents, Hardee and Maude Dora (Brown) Mast. (CHMM 190 006-56.20.)

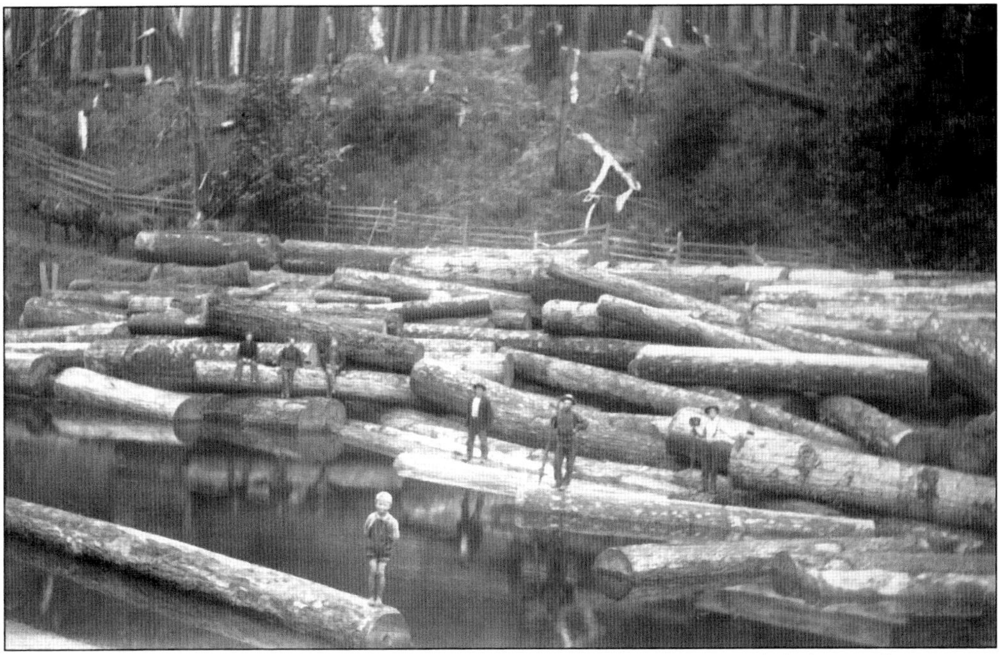

This young Mast boy might have waded in the cold water of the North Fork before walking out to the end of this log. A few miles away in Dora, John Gearhart had the 1937 contract for running all the logs out of the East Fork of the Coquille River. Gearhart's nephew Calvin Bigelow slipped and fell into the river while breaking up a log jam; unable to get out, he drowned. (CHMM 182 006-56.4.)

Barn builders erect the Mast barn in Lee Valley. William Mast and his wife, Charlotte, started farming in Lee Valley in 1873. Mast served one term as Coos County commissioner and was the postmaster when the Lee Post Office was established in 1888. It closed by 1929. (CHMM 192 006-56.26.)

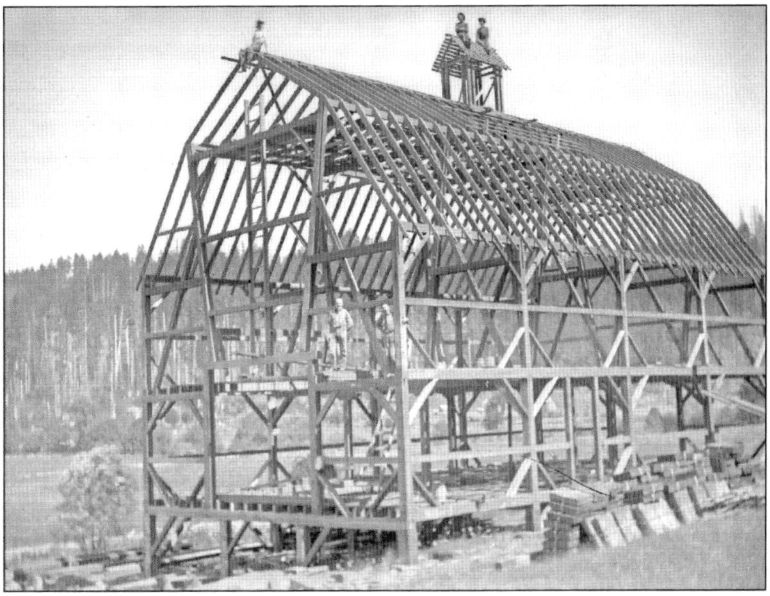

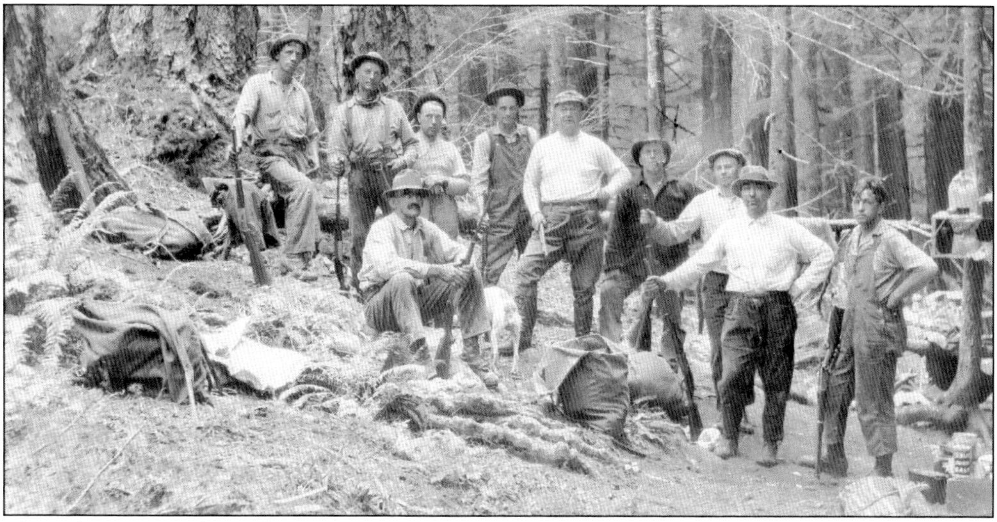

These hunters at their elk camp include Ernest "Ernie" Krewson (far right) and Walter Laird (second row, sixth from left, smoking a cigar). Both men lived in Sitkum, one of the settings for Krewson's book *Tioga's Pigs*, which was published in 1955. Krewson, born in 1891, married Zilpha Benham, another Sitkum resident. (CL.)

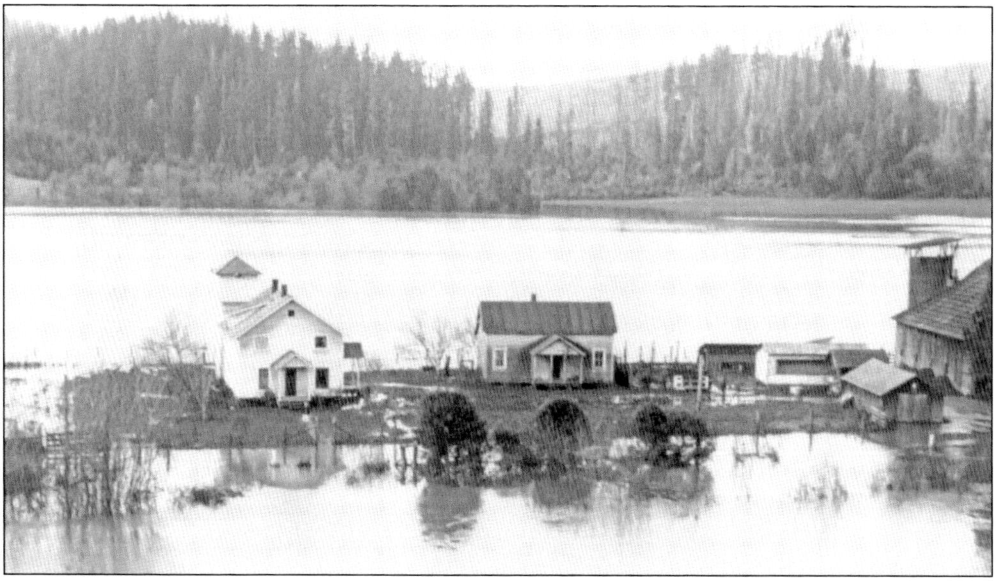

When the North Fork flooded on January 5, 1936, water covered much of Lloyd and Selata (Howe) Leatherman's dairy farm in Lee Valley near Fox Bridge. Their house (left) was built on high ground. The middle building, a former creamery that Lloyd Leatherman moved to the farm, was the home of his parents, Charles and Della (Layman) Leatherman, and his grandmother Matilda Layman. (HL.)

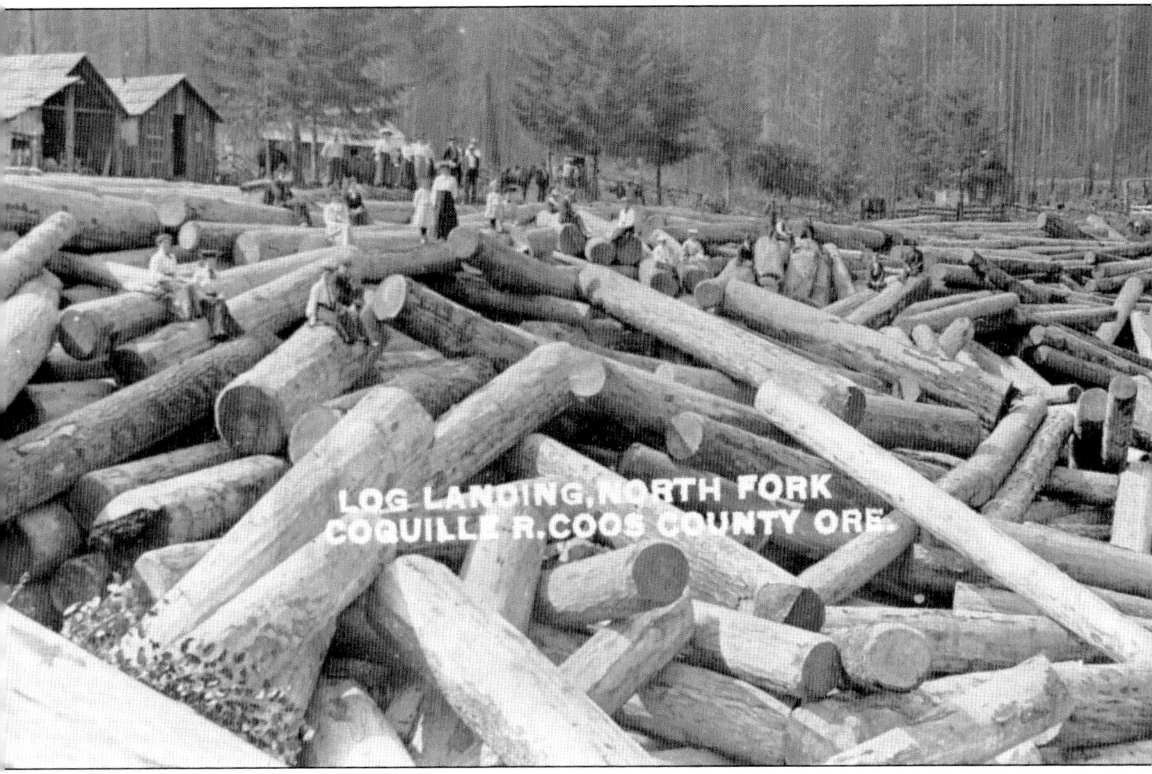

Stranded in McKinley or Fairview, these logs will float downstream when winter rains raise the North Fork of the Coquille River. Rivermen used peavies and sometimes dynamite to break up logjams. Log drives on the North Fork started in 1898, and loggers built a series of splash dams on the upper North Fork. (DCM N3175.)

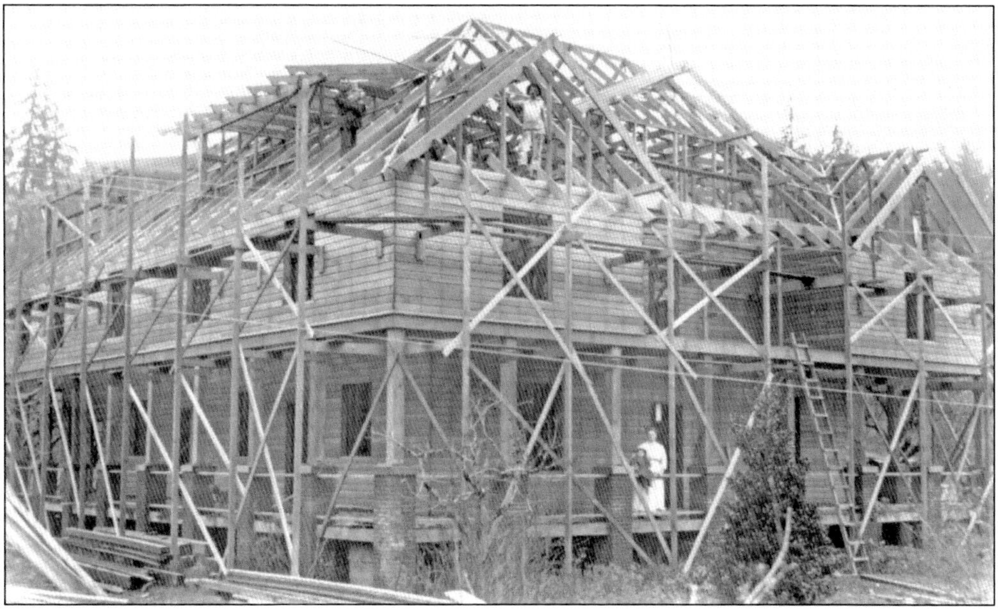

Edwin Abernethy used his engineering skills to design this house in Dora near Steel Creek around 1905. Standing in the third story are three men, one holding a young child. Abernethy sawed the lumber with his portable mill and fired the bricks in his kiln. A photographer and musician, he married Ethel Laird in 1922. His grandfather George Abernethy was Oregon's first provisional governor. (DL.)

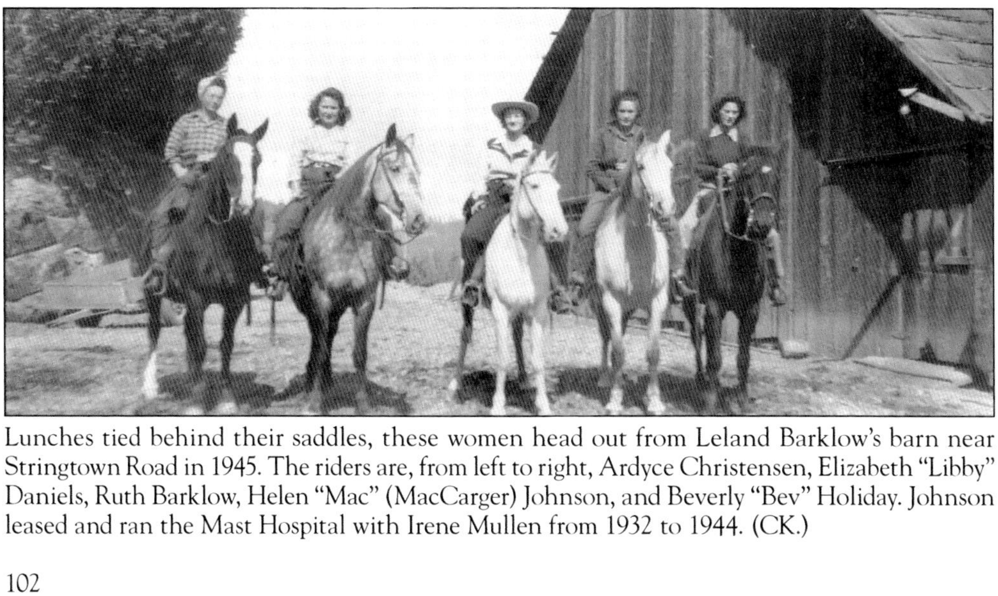

Lunches tied behind their saddles, these women head out from Leland Barklow's barn near Stringtown Road in 1945. The riders are, from left to right, Ardyce Christensen, Elizabeth "Libby" Daniels, Ruth Barklow, Helen "Mac" (MacCarger) Johnson, and Beverly "Bev" Holiday. Johnson leased and ran the Mast Hospital with Irene Mullen from 1932 to 1944. (CK.)

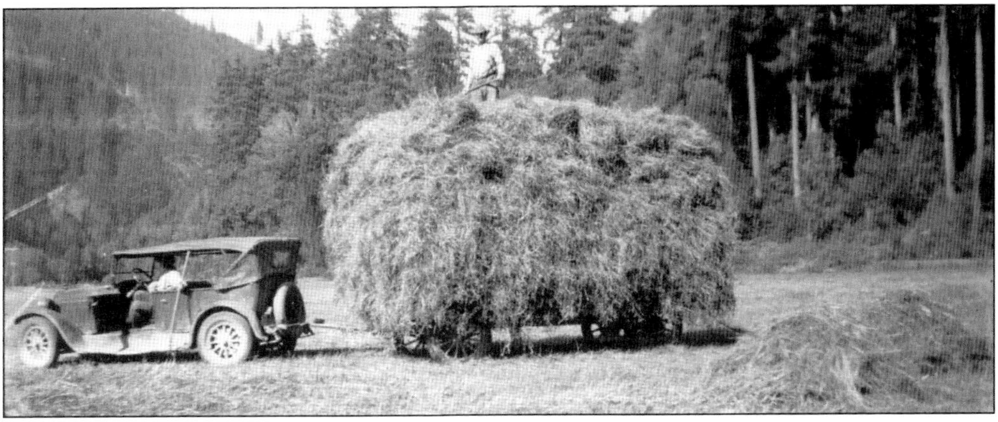

With one hand on a hay fork, another hand on the steering wheel, and the car door wide open, a woman is ready to spring into action. Harvested from a field in Sitkum, this load of loose hay has been stacked tall and square. The automobile probably dates from 1910 or later. (DL.)

Civilian Conservation Corps enrollees started building Camp McKinley in about 1933. The camp was located about 3.5 miles up Middle Creek Road on land leased from the Lawhorn family. Community members were invited to watch movies in the camp's mess hall. During World War II, the camp housed conscientious objectors who worked on roads, fought fires, and tended a tree nursery. (CVM.)

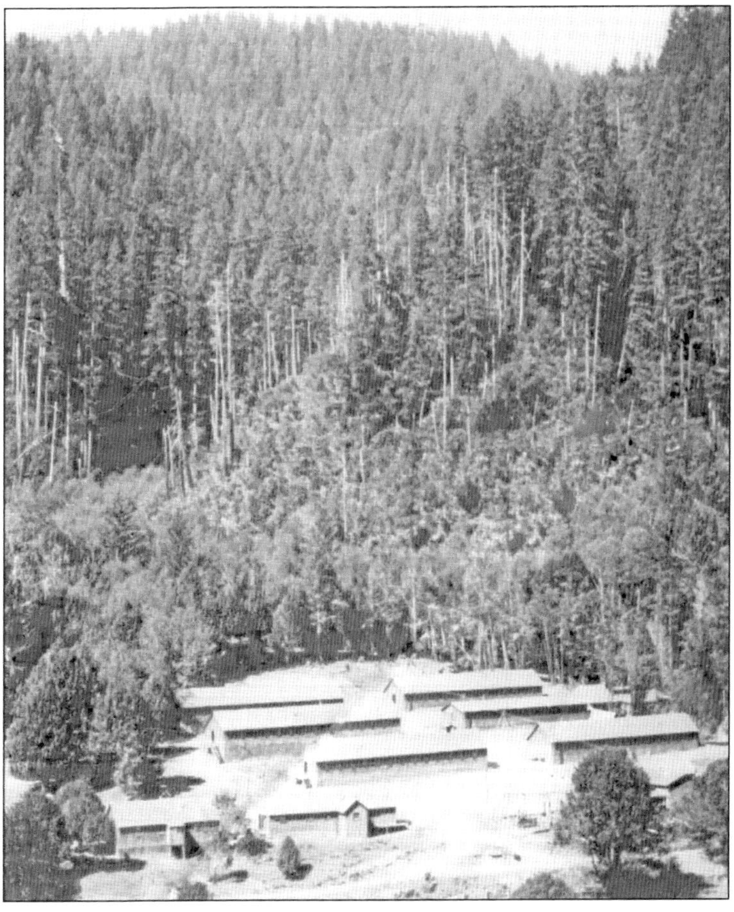

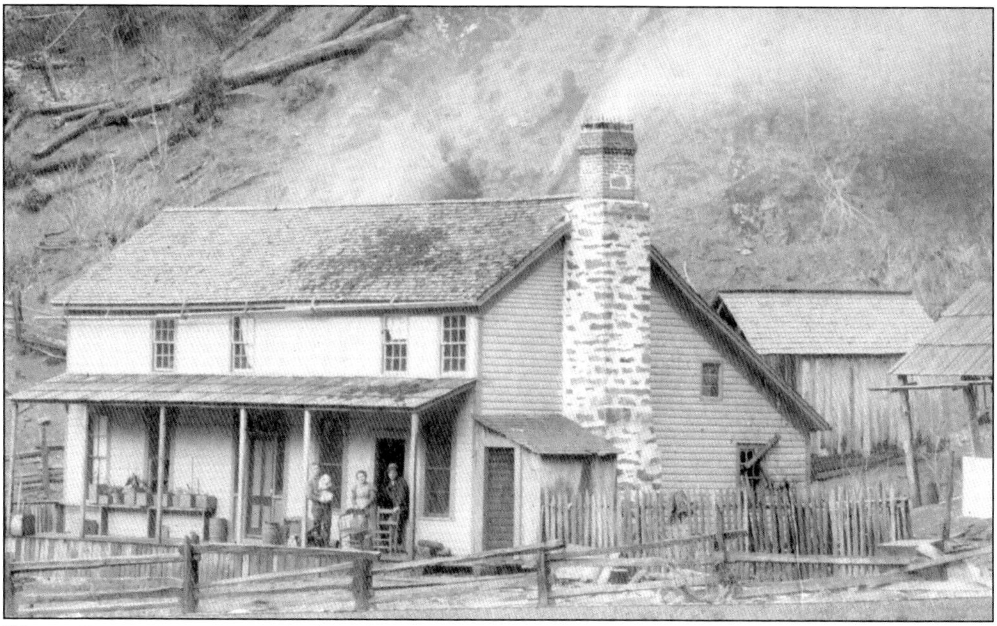

"Burnt June 10, 1904," is the handwritten note on this photograph of the Halfway House in Sitkum. This is one of three or four Halfway Houses where members of the Harry and Laird families offered sleeping space and meals to Coos Bay Wagon Road travelers. Walter Laird and his wife, Mayre (Hall) Laird, who cooked meals for paying guests from 1900 to 1934, were the last Lairds to operate the Halfway House. Room and board for one night at the Halfway House cost $1 in 1915. (DCM N4322.)

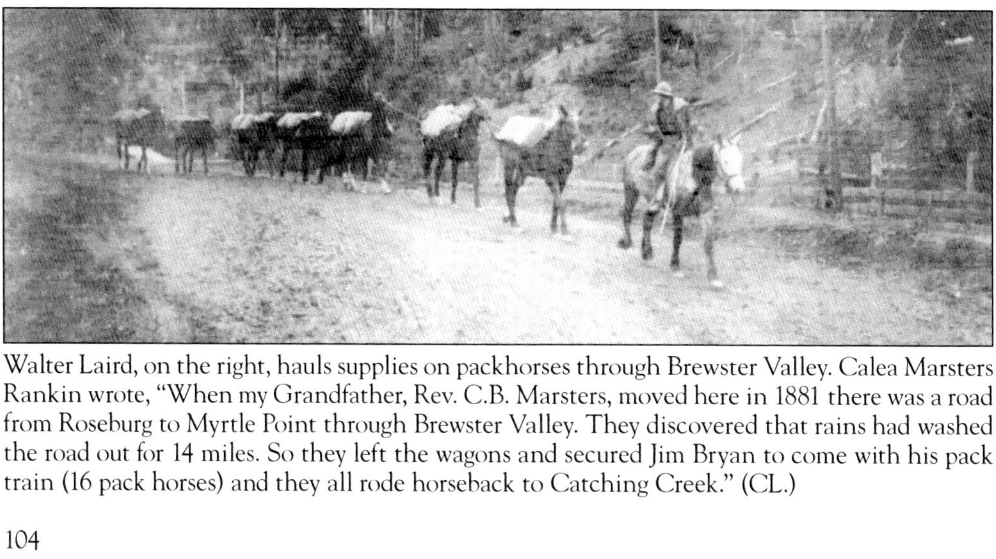

Walter Laird, on the right, hauls supplies on packhorses through Brewster Valley. Calea Marsters Rankin wrote, "When my Grandfather, Rev. C.B. Marsters, moved here in 1881 there was a road from Roseburg to Myrtle Point through Brewster Valley. They discovered that rains had washed the road out for 14 miles. So they left the wagons and secured Jim Bryan to come with his pack train (16 pack horses) and they all rode horseback to Catching Creek." (CL.)

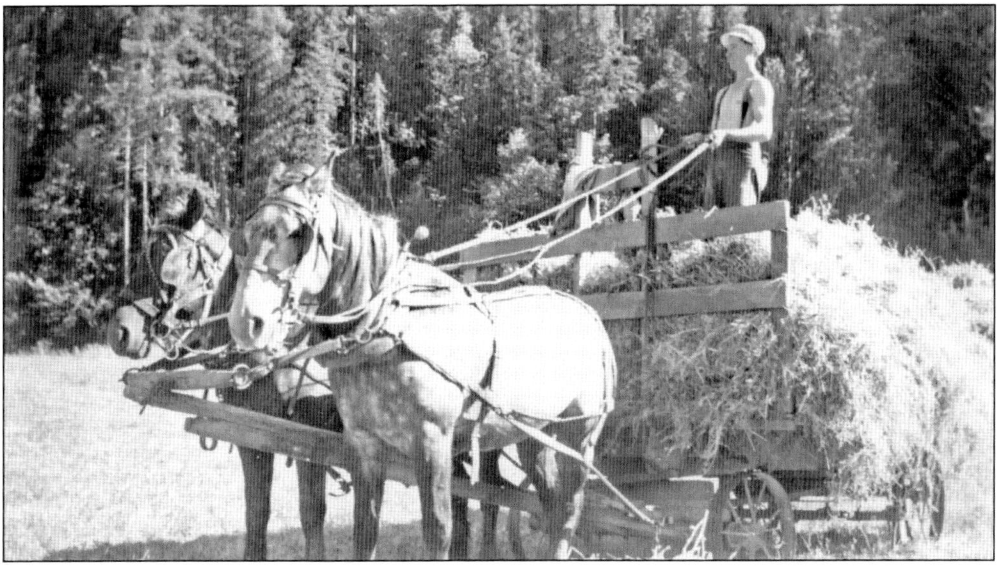

Gene Jennings guides Star, a dark gelding, and Babe, a light-colored mare. Jennings, who lived in Remote, was working for Grover and Alvin McQuigg near Gravelford. Hay was put into shocks with pitchforks, and the shocks of hay were then pitched onto a wagon. The load was judged to be full when the person on the ground could not lift the hay any higher. Jennings would be killed in a car accident in 1943 at age 19. (JLP.)

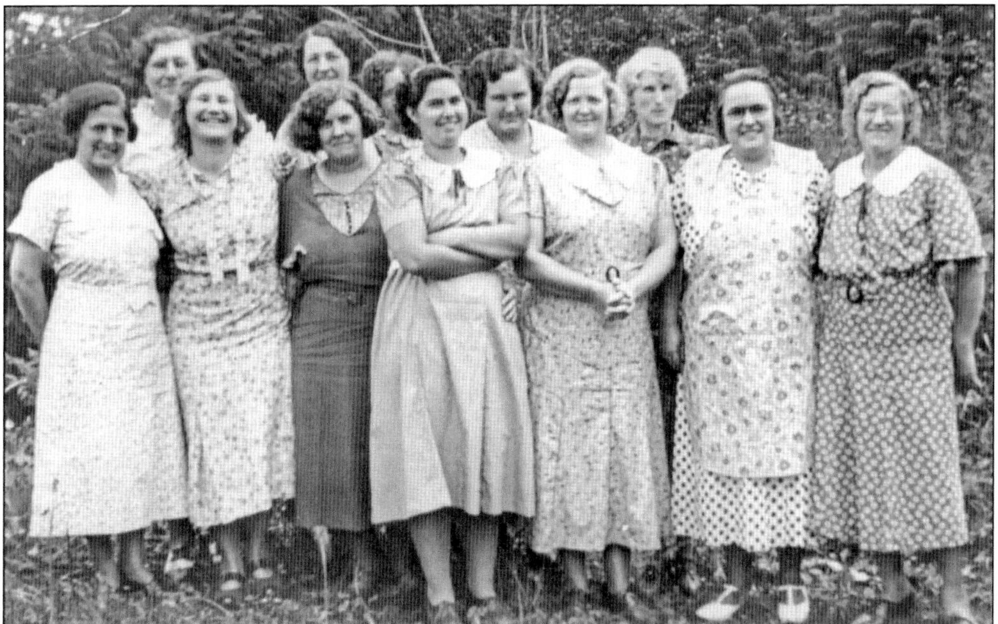

Carding wool was the task chosen by Wilma Shepherd when the Dora Friendly Club held its first meeting at her house on January 20, 1932. Club members that year are, from left to right, (first row) Ethel (Laird) Abernethy, Laura Minard, Cecil Walker, Mary Bunch, Elena Minard, Grace Durnam, and Georgia (Hollenbeak) Bunch; (second row) Jesse Swan, Zilpha (Benham) Krewson (a nonmember visiting from Sitkum), Josie Bennett, Wilma (Bunch) Shepherd, and a Mrs. Buell. (MJC.)

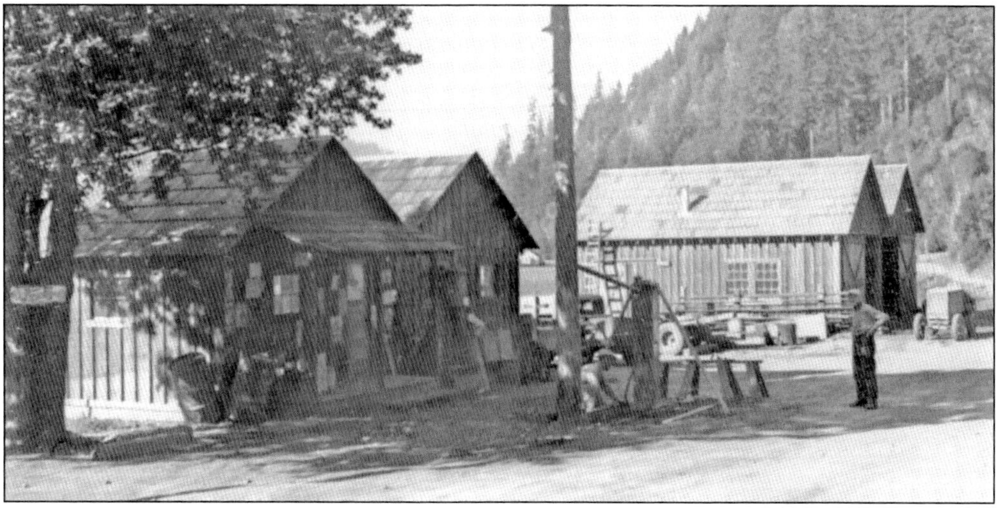

In front of the LB&L (Laird, Benham & Laird) office in about 1940 stands a gas pump; beyond it is the truck shop. Partners in the firm, which had a white cedar–logging camp in Sitkum, were Ivan Laird, Julius Benham, and Kenneth Laird. In 1936, Lennie (Benham) Krewson handed off cooking duties at the camp to Mildred (Laird) Benham. Truck drivers in 1938 were Kenneth Laird, Elmer Wilson, Tom Howe, Milton Mast, and Lendon Jenkins. (DL.)

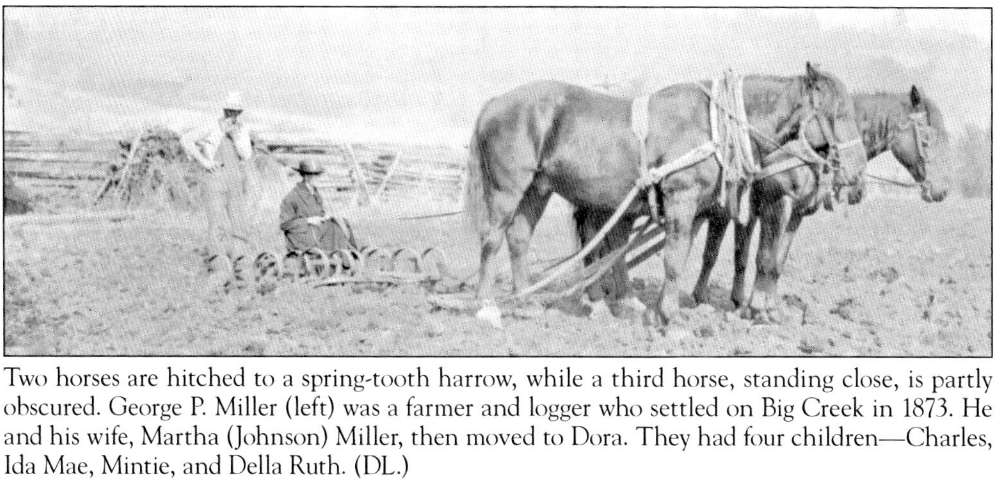

Two horses are hitched to a spring-tooth harrow, while a third horse, standing close, is partly obscured. George P. Miller (left) was a farmer and logger who settled on Big Creek in 1873. He and his wife, Martha (Johnson) Miller, then moved to Dora. They had four children—Charles, Ida Mae, Mintie, and Della Ruth. (DL.)

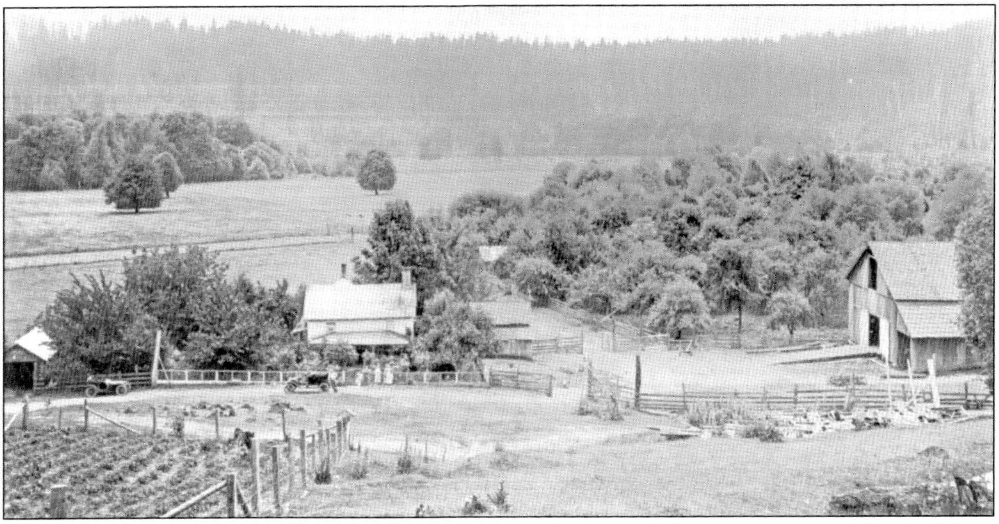

Charlotte "Lottie" Mast, widow of William Mast, was living with her youngest son, Hardee Mast, and his family in this Lee Valley house in 1911. Hardee and his wife, Maude (Brown) Mast, had four children. The house, built about 1882 and located near Hervey Bridge, stood until about 1960. In 1939, hundreds of people attended a family reunion at Shrine Grove, a site donated to the Masons by Hardee and his brother Webb. (BM.)

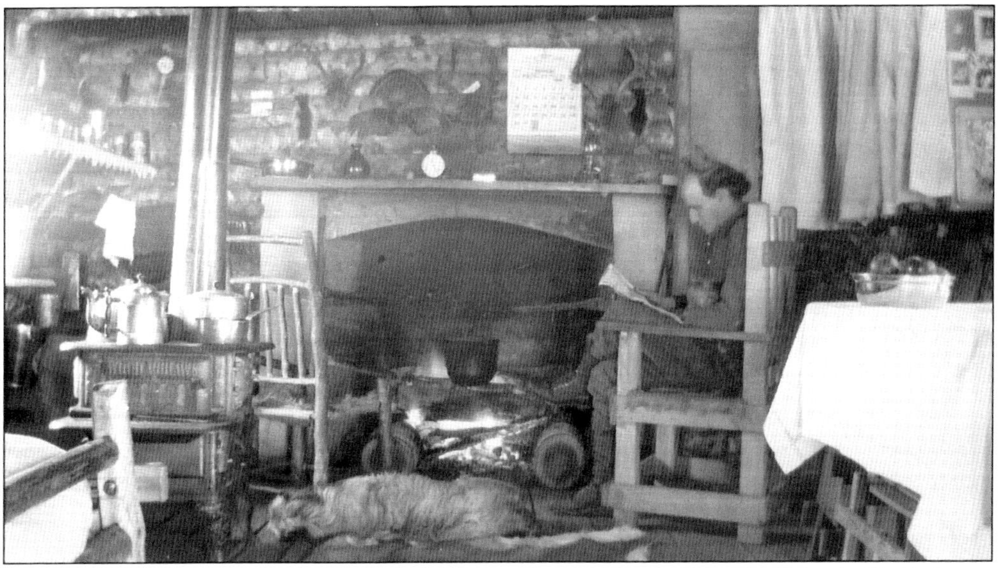

Pete Spani reads in his cabin on Easter morning in 1913. Pete and his wife, Maude (Fish) Spani, homesteaded near Catching Creek. They moved to California when their son, Paul, was about three years old. (LK.)

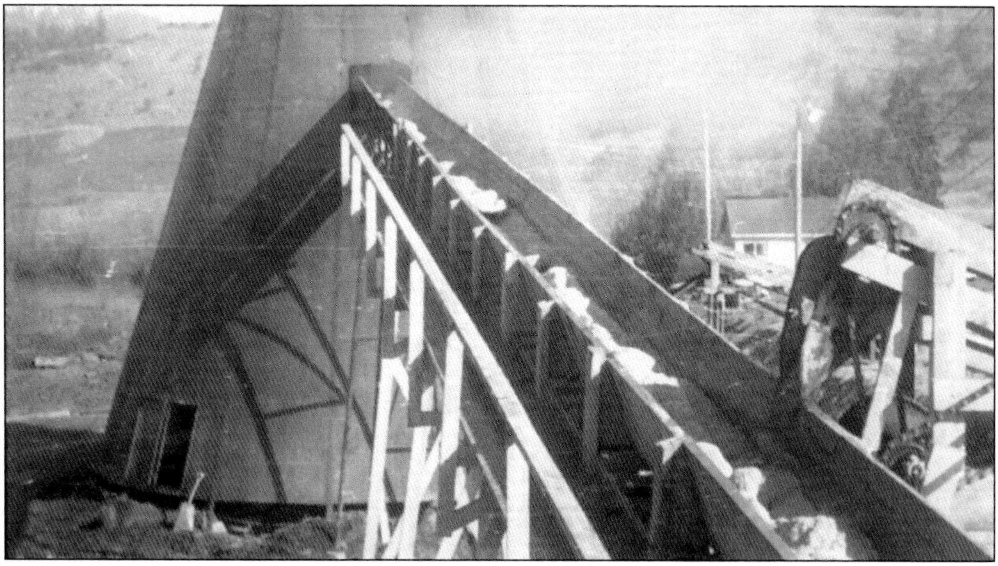

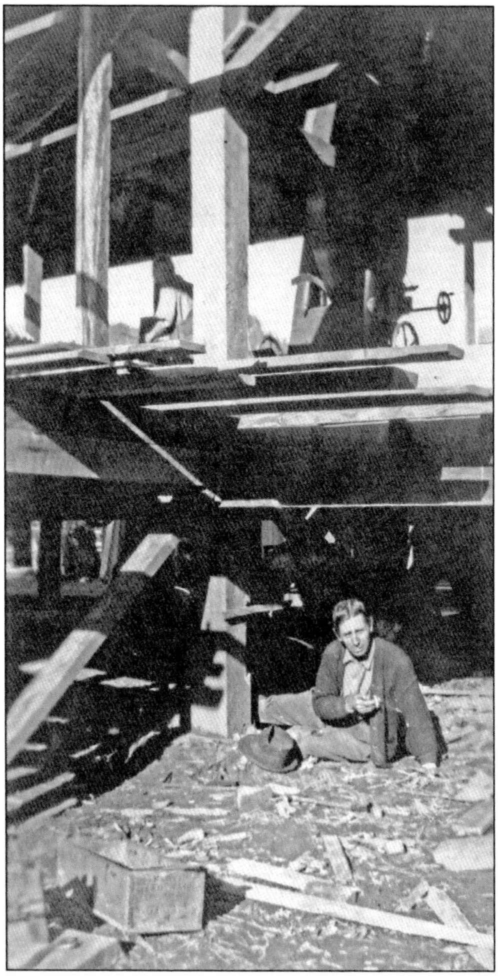

At the Cheney Studs sawmill in about 1948, sawdust rides the conveyor belt to the wigwam burner. From about 1946 to 1962, Cheney Studs sawed railroad ties and two-by-fours. It provided work for high school students, among others, helping them to go to college. Calvin Warner owned the land that Ben Cheney bought for the mill. (WL.)

Marshal Alford takes a smoke break beneath the planer at a Sitkum sawmill in about 1903. The mill was located near the bridge over the East Fork on Old Weaver Road. Perley Crowley converted the structure to a house in about 1939. After Crowley, the property was owned by Doc Clayton and later belonged to Elmer and Alice Strode. (DL.)

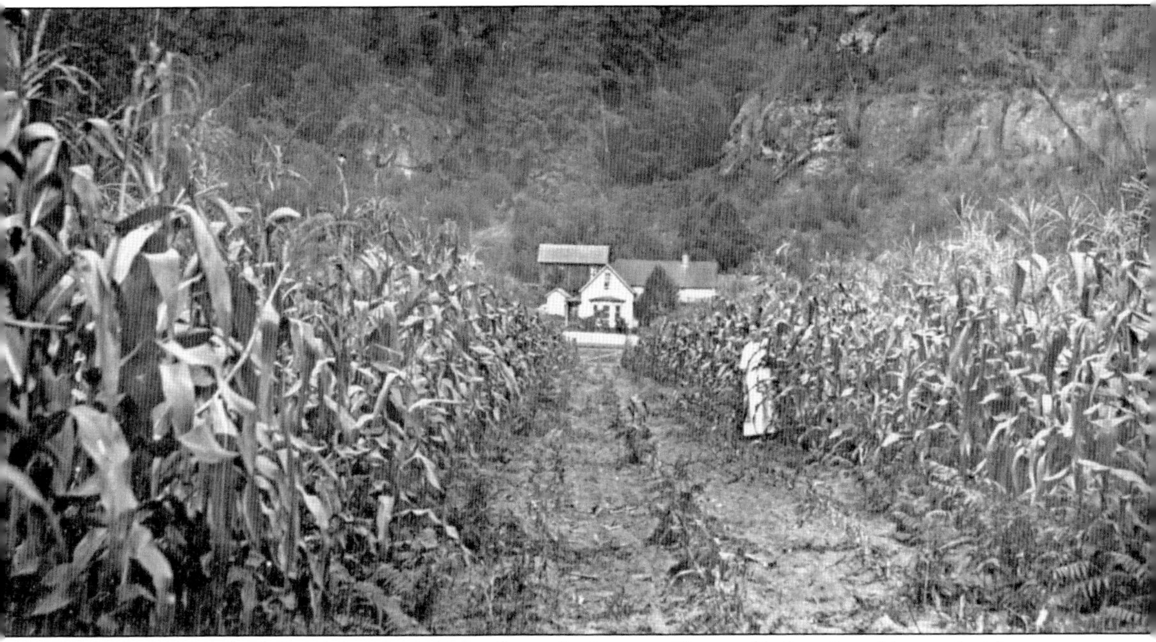

In Sitkum, a path through a cornfield leads to the home of James D. Laird and his wife, Nancy Belle (Harry) Laird. The post office was located in this house until 1964. Nancy Belle served as postmistress until 1917, when her daughter Ethel (Laird) Abernethy began her 35 years as postmistress. Nancy Belle operated a telegraph in this house from about 1875 to about 1917 and also raised nine children. (DL.)

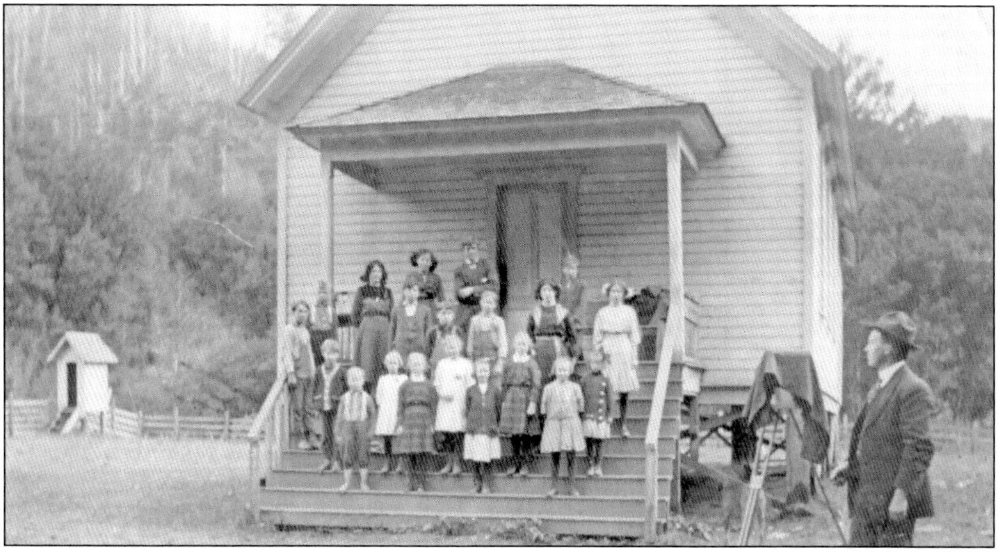

In 1911, Dora resident Ed Abernethy (right) brought his camera to Sitkum School. The twins in plaid dresses are Matilda (left) and Isabell Austin. In dark dresses on the upper steps at left are Zilpha (left) and Linnie Benham; their brother Julius Benham, wearing a jacket, stands in front of them. The boy in the back row is Bill Walton, and the girl at the far right is Lillian Austin, sister to the twins. (DL.)

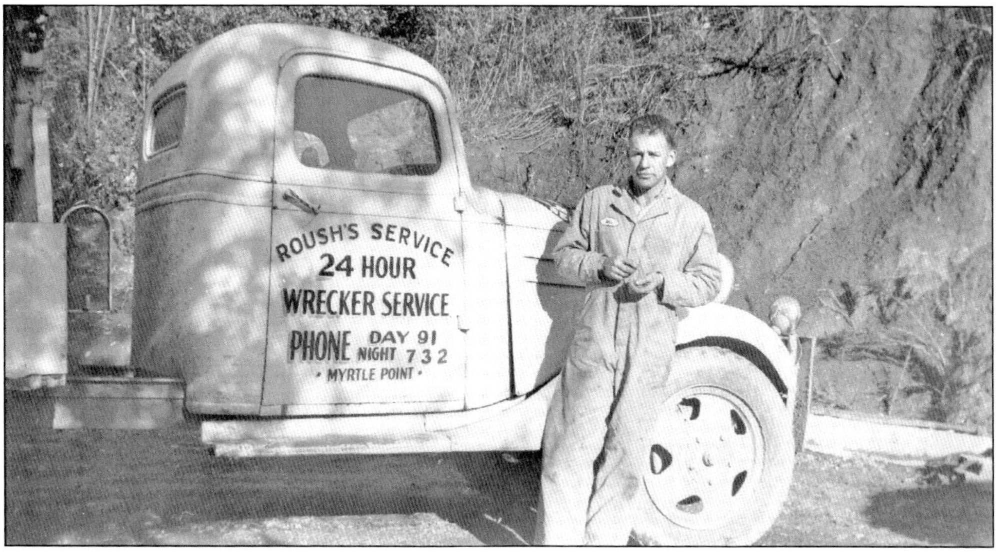

When Wesley Guy was not working at Thornton's Tire & Appliance, he answered wrecker calls. The wrecker, owned by Guy's brother-in-law Am Roush, was a Chevrolet truck made between 1938 and 1940. Guy and his wife, Laura Lee (Roush) Guy, moved to Myrtle Point in the mid-1940s. (BA.)

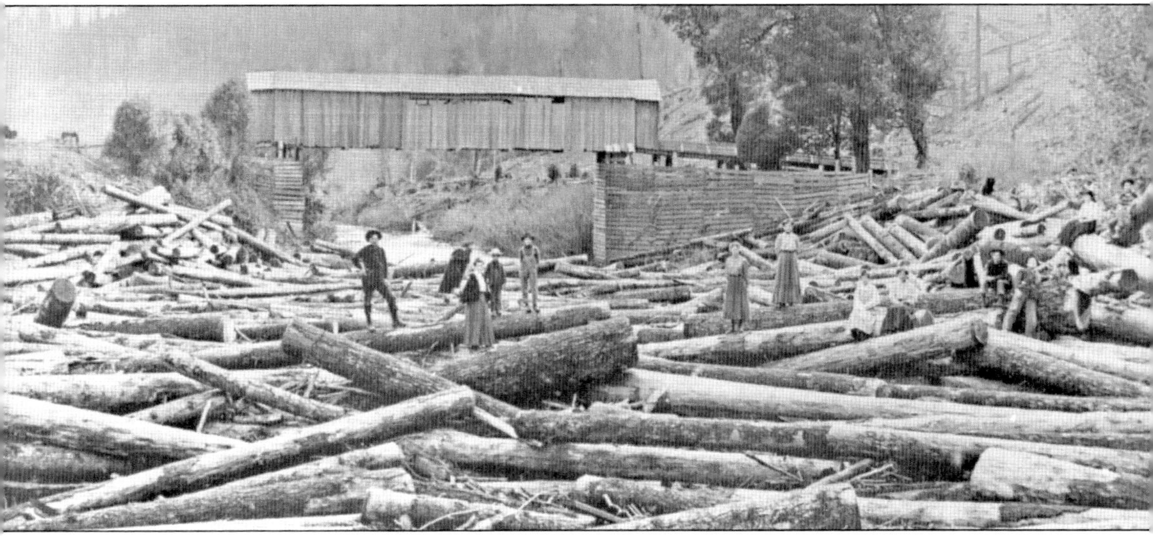

In 1886, master bridge builder John D. Fox of Lee Valley constructed this bridge over the East Fork where Minard Riffle powered Harvey Minard's gristmill. Minard bought the mill from Joseph Wright in 1882. Minard's wife, Roxana (Krantz) Minard, was the Dora postmistress. The post office was located in her home on the Elk Creek side of the river; the mail was sent across the river in a wire cage running on a cable. (DCM N3174.)

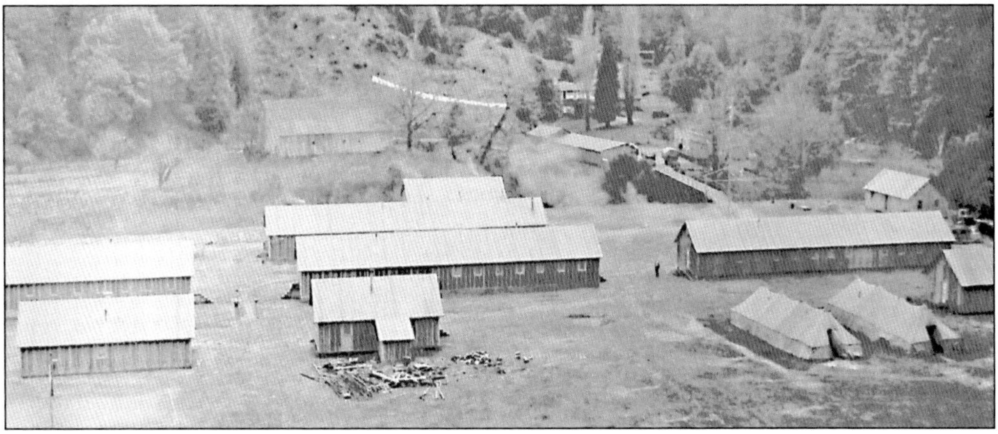

A bridge over the East Fork connects the barracks of Camp Sitkum to the Forest Service buildings and the adjacent county road in about 1934. The Civilian Conservation Corps camp was built on property leased from Richard Oren "Bob" Kirk and his wife, Nora Mae (Beaman) Kirk. In the background is a long line of wash on a clothesline attached to the Kirks' house, formerly the Halfway House. Army stake trucks took enrollees to Myrtle Point on Saturdays. (LK.)

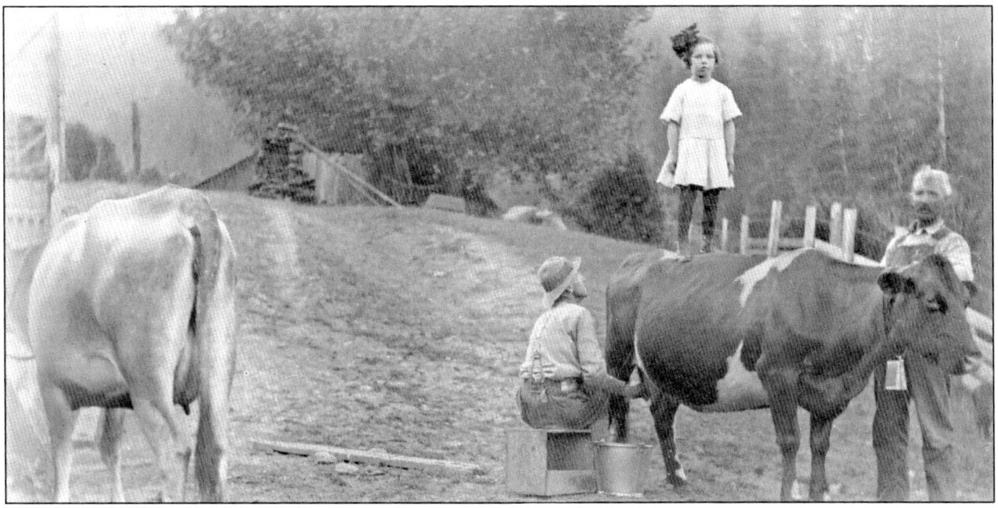

Hailey Laird milks while Gertrude Laird, his niece, balances on the cow's back. Gertrude, daughter of Binger and Anna (Weekly) Laird, was born in 1908. This photograph was probably taken in Sitkum when Hailey and Binger were visiting their parents, James D. and Nancy Belle (Harry) Laird. The man at right, who likely works for the Lairds, is unidentified. (DL.)

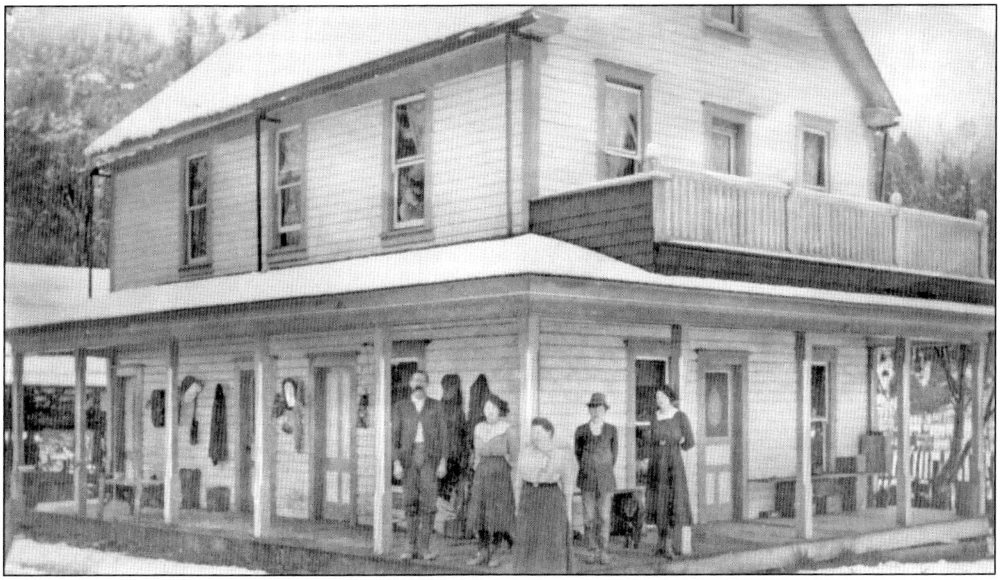

Standing in front of their house on a snowy day in about 1912 are, from left to right, James R. Benham, Linnie Benham, Callie (Mast) Benham, Julius Benham, and Zilpha Benham. This home was located on Brummit Creek Road where it intersects with the road to Brewster Rock Lookout. James, a bull puncher with three yoke of oxen, raised and trained oxen, mules, and horses. Meetings of the Brewster Valley Ladies Club were probably held here occasionally, because meetings were held in homes and Callie and, later, her daughters were club members. (DL.)

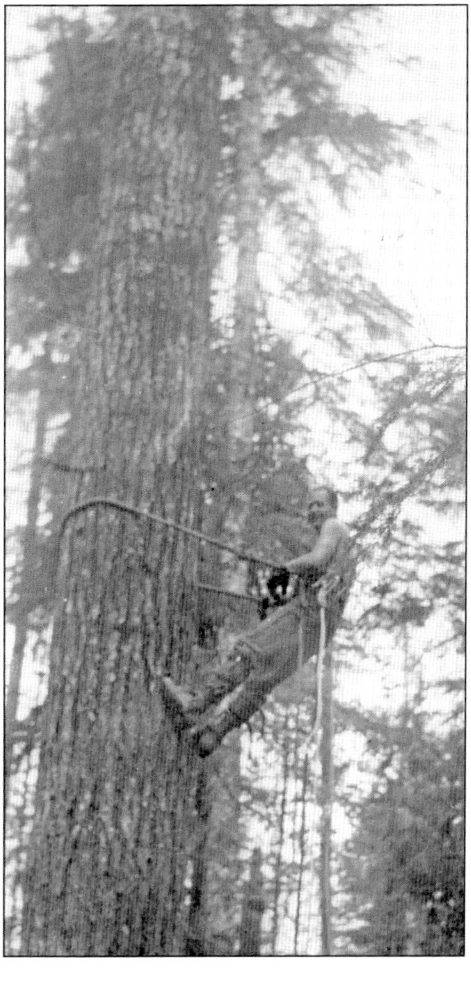

Roy Spires began working as a high-climber in the 1920s—topping trees and setting rigging for high-lead logging. On a rainy night in 1945, he rescued an Army flyer who was stranded in a fir tree. Spires climbed the tree in the dark; loaned his spurs and belt to the flyer, who then climbed down; pulled his gear back up the tree; and then climbed down himself. (KL.)

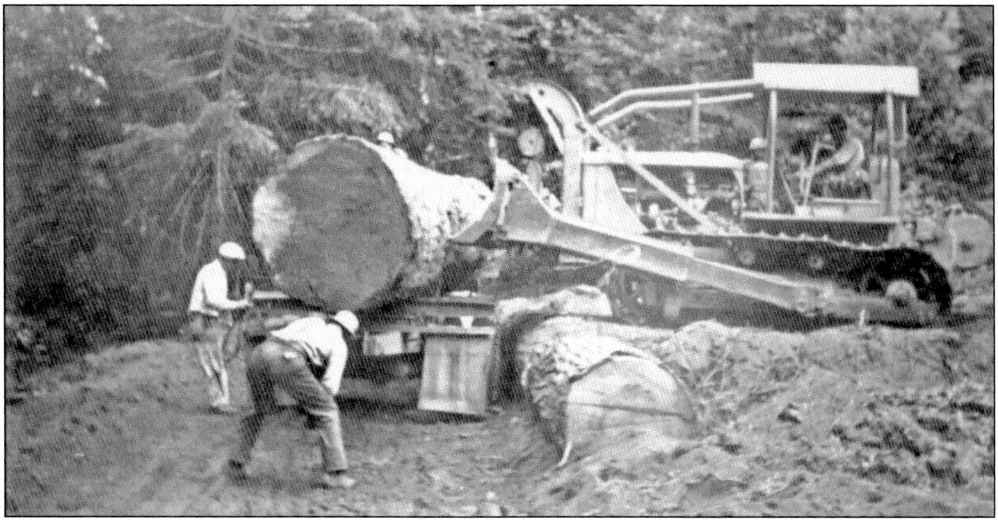

A truck gets a log centered up for the trip to the mill in 1950 or 1951. To load the log, the D-8 Caterpillar working for Train Logging, possibly with Swede Jennings at the controls, rolled it over the brow logs, where it dropped to the truck bed. The log looks to be more than seven feet in diameter. (MTBM.)

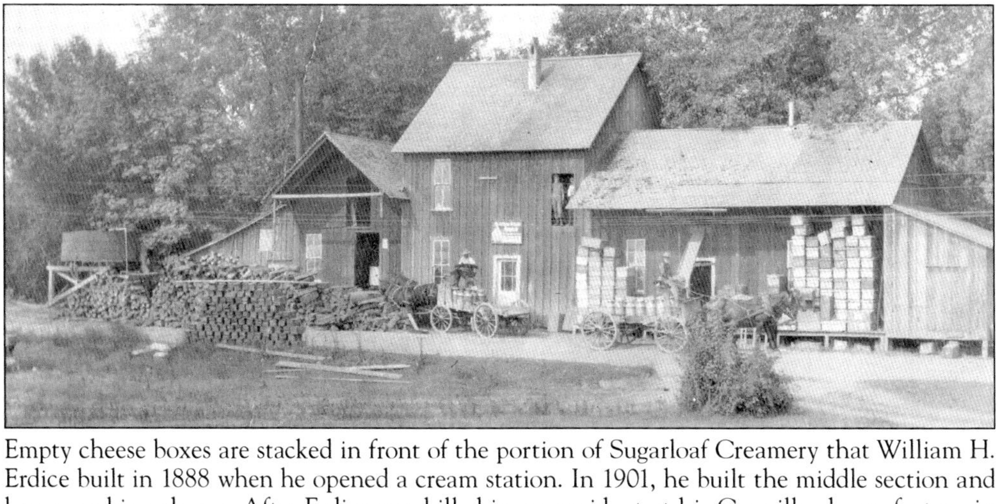

Empty cheese boxes are stacked in front of the portion of Sugarloaf Creamery that William H. Erdice built in 1888 when he opened a cream station. In 1901, he built the middle section and began making cheese. After Erdice was killed in an accident at his Coquille cheese factory in 1903, Charles E. Broadbent bought the Sugarloaf facility. It was located on Reedsford Road close to the site of the train depot. (PD.)

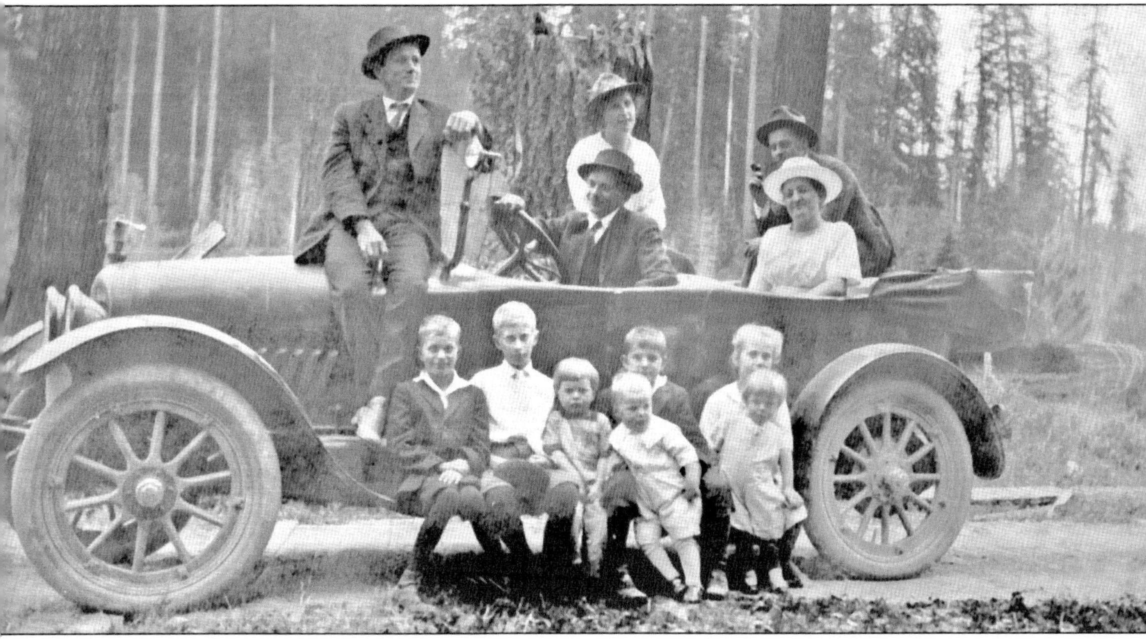

Ed Detlefsen sits on the hood of a touring car in 1918. In the front seat are Martin Schmidt and his wife, Marie (Reitz) (Dean) Schmidt. In the rear seat are Marguerite (Reitz) Detlefsen and her brother Adolph Reitz. The children are, from left to right, (first row) Fred Schmidt, Elton Schmidt, and Don Schmidt; (second row) Paul Detlefsen, Elbert Dean, Ray Detlefsen, and Helen Dean. Adolph died in a horse race in Norway, the community where both couples had dairy farms. Similarly, Marie's first husband, Robert Dean, was thrown from a racing horse and killed in about 1911. (FS.)

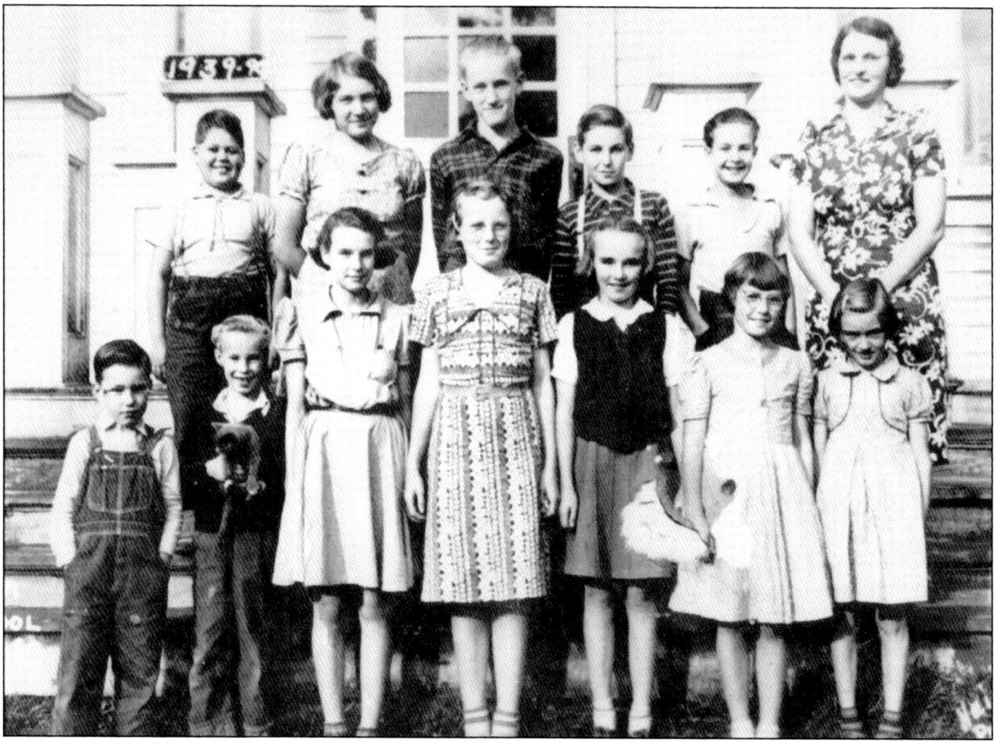

Wayne Gill holds the school cat near the front steps of Dora School. The school, now a residence, was located on Sitkum Lane near its intersection with Lone Pine. Students and their teacher during the 1939–1940 school year are, from left to right, (first row) unidentified, Wayne Gill, Faye Gill, Opal Faye "Dode" Groves, Colleen Shepherd, unidentified, and Myrna Oberman; (second row) LaWayne Howe, Hazel Oberman, Don Sylvester, Keith Thompson, Dick Gill, and Rosabel Brown. (DPL.)

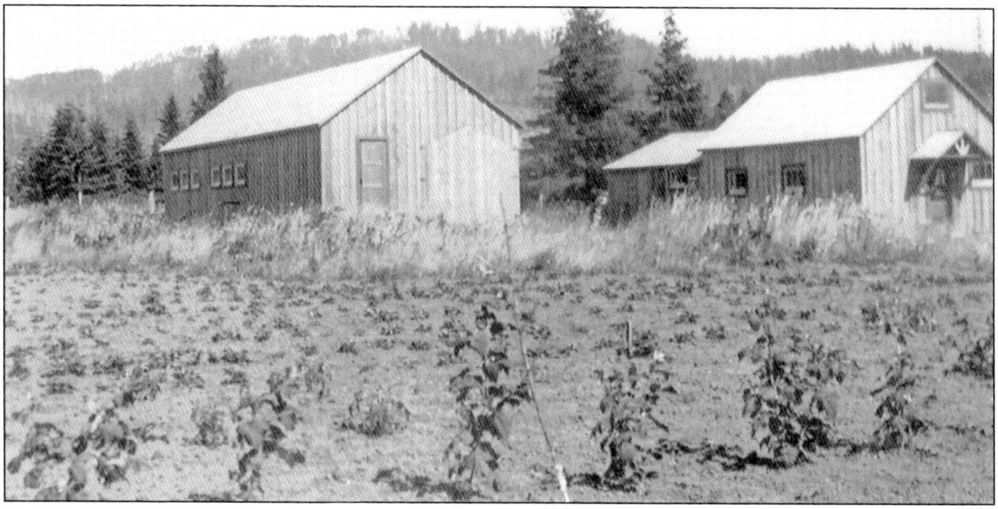

From 1944 to 1965, Jay Francisco, with help from his wife and two daughters, Ramona and Joanne, produced Francisco Potato Chips in this factory (left) on Cemetery Road just east of the Myrtle Point city limits. Francisco stirred the tub of frying chips with an oar. The family also raised and sold berries, but they did not grow potatoes. (JM.)

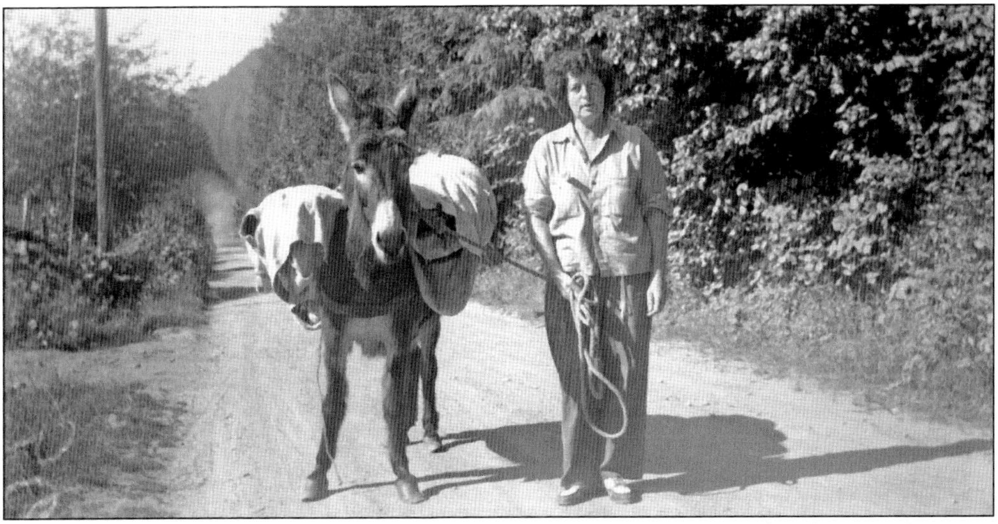

Her donkey loaded with ferns, Jesse (Courtwright) Watson stops near her home in Dora on Goldbrick Road in the late 1940s. Watson learned how to pick ferns from her daughter Winona "Sissy" (Watson) Osbon, who learned from Mattie Groves. Callison's, which shipped greenery by rail to eastern markets, paid 3¢ per bunch of 55 sword fern in 1933. Jesse and her husband, Ezra Watson, once owned the property in Dora that became the bulb farm. (BMM.)

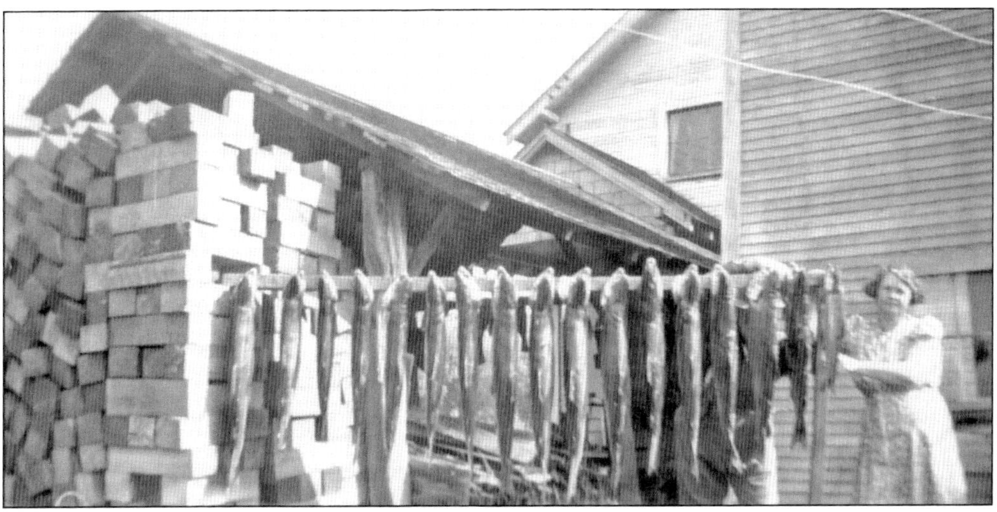

These 16 fish are ready for the smokehouse at Selata (Howe) Leatherman's home in Lee Valley. Leatherman's son Howard caught the salmon in the North Fork of the Coquille River in the 1930s. Fish were so plentiful in the early days that men sometimes got a wagonload and fed them to their hogs. After the splash dams were built, fewer salmon came up the rivers. (HL.)

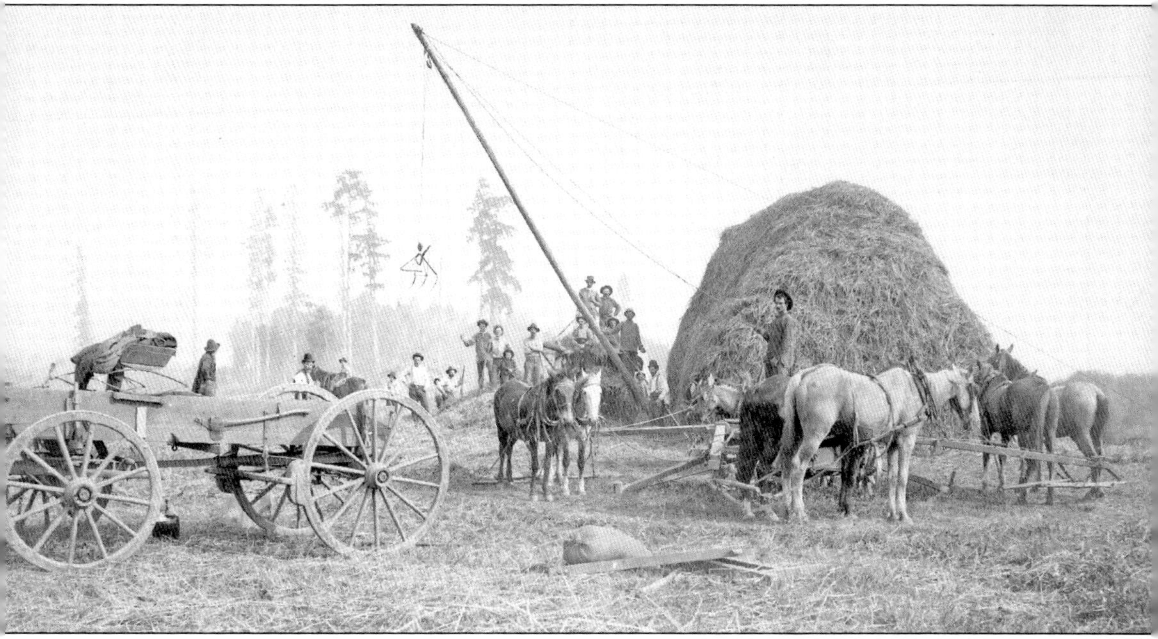

Brothers Charles and Louis Heller farmed on Cherry Creek near McKinley. Charles bought an Aultman-Taylor thresher in 1881. For 40 years, Charles hauled a thresher across Coos County; horses powered the thresher early on, before a switch was made to steam tractors. The Heller brothers married sisters who lived on a neighboring farm. Charles wed Amanda Culbertson; and Louis, Telitha Culbertson. (CHMM 41 988-P13.)

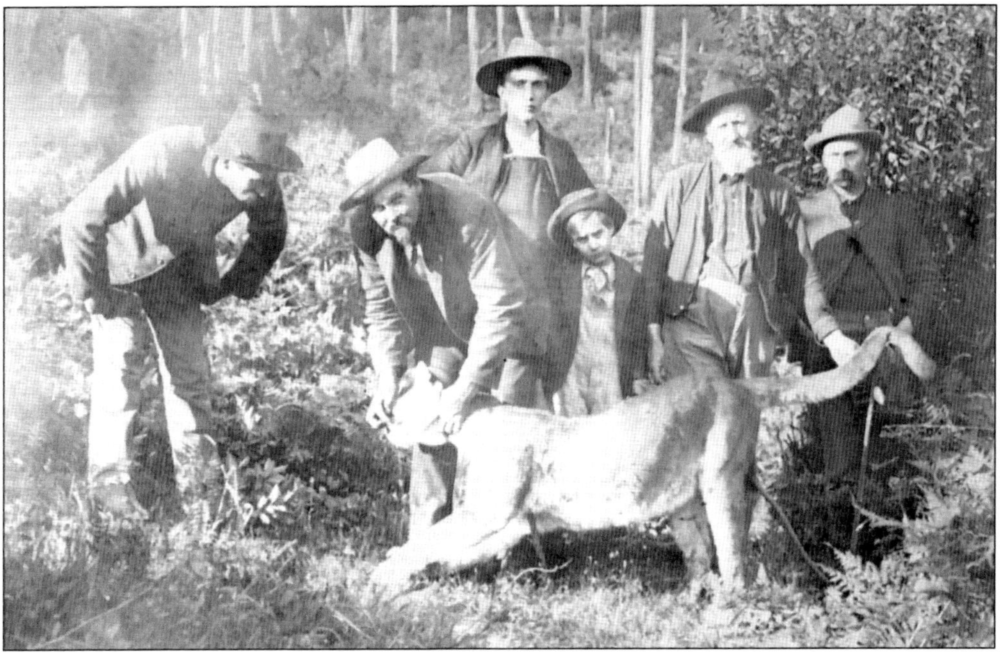

Mike Krantz shows the teeth of a cougar killed near Weekly Creek about 1911. The man taking a close look at left is unidentified. To the right of Krantz are, from left to right, Vance Weekly, Edwin Weekly, Isaac Taylor Weekly, and Bill Smith. This cougar might be eight feet long and weigh as much as 200 pounds. (AS.)

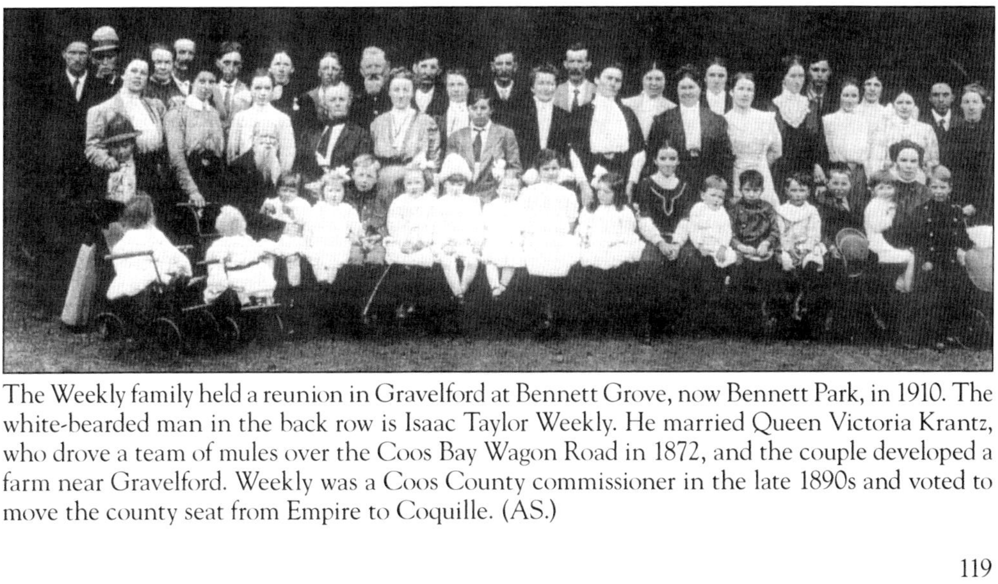

The Weekly family held a reunion in Gravelford at Bennett Grove, now Bennett Park, in 1910. The white-bearded man in the back row is Isaac Taylor Weekly. He married Queen Victoria Krantz, who drove a team of mules over the Coos Bay Wagon Road in 1872, and the couple developed a farm near Gravelford. Weekly was a Coos County commissioner in the late 1890s and voted to move the county seat from Empire to Coquille. (AS.)

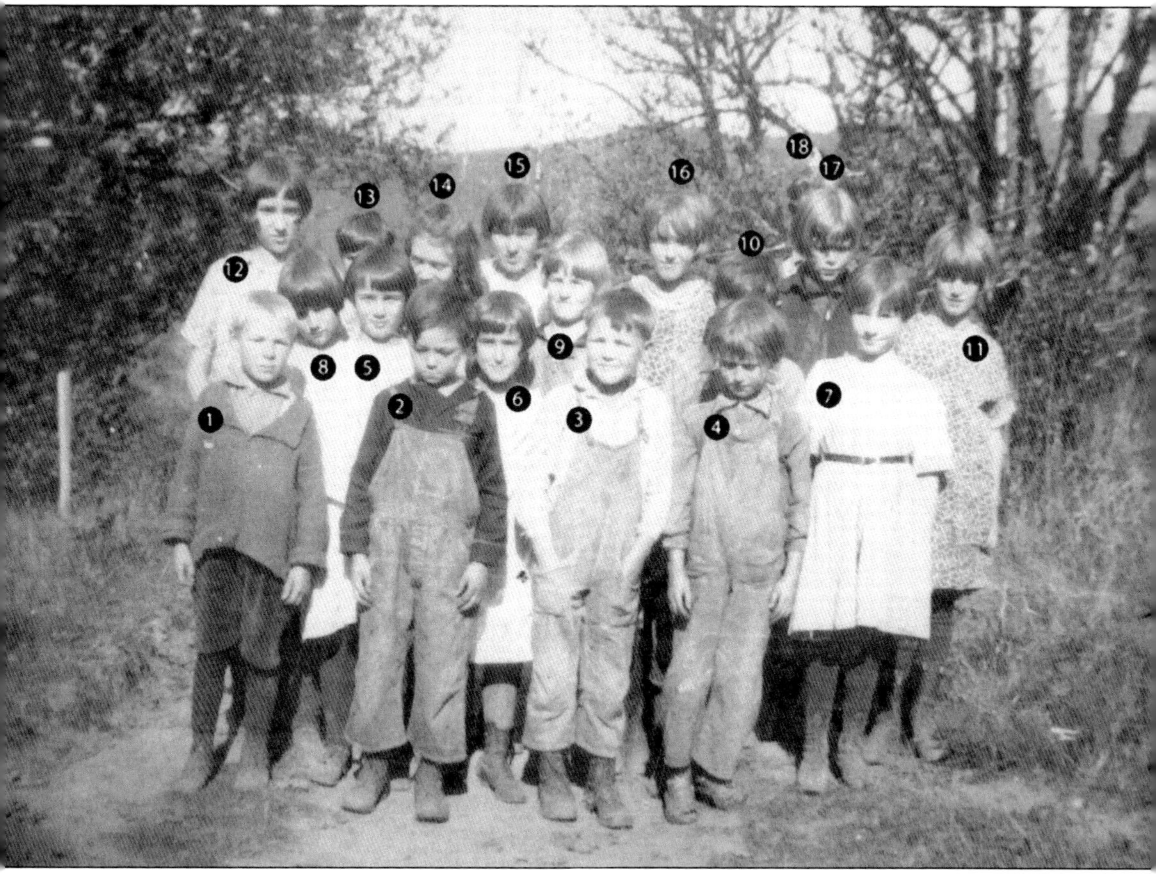

Shiloh School was located on the south side of the East Fork, a site reached today by crossing Crosby Bridge. Students at the school in 1925 include, from left to right, (first row) Jean Cotton (1), Donald West (2), Ellis Crosby (3), and Elvene Bennett (4); (second row) Freeda Strong (5), Lavina Albright (6), and Ada Belle Cotton (7); (third row) Myrl Weekly (8), Bernice Bennett (9), Walter West (10), and Doris Olson (11); (fourth row) Elsie Weekly(12), Harold Weekly (13), Mildred West (14), Iva Strong (15), Idaline Olson (16), Nellie West (17), and Louis West (18, mostly hidden behind Nellie). (AS.)

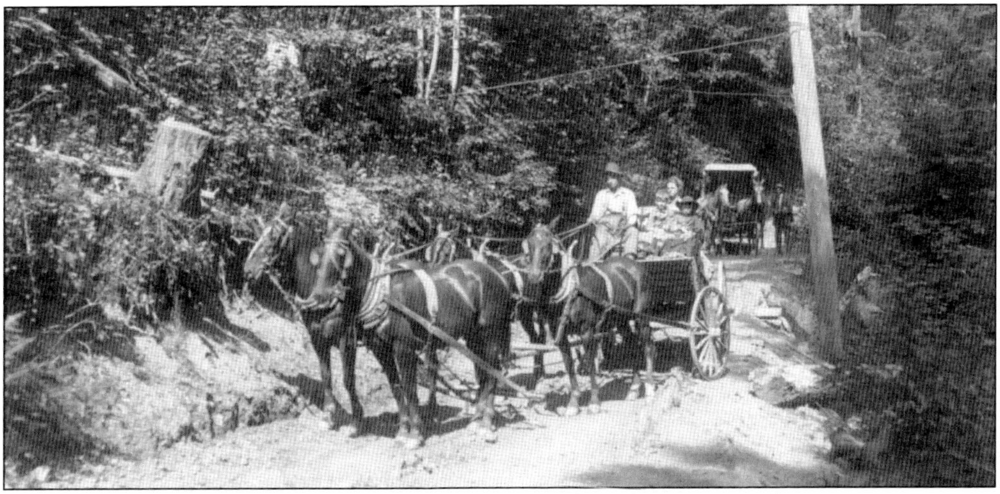

Four horses pull a stage on the Coos Bay Wagon Road in about 1909. When two wagons met, one team had to be unhitched. That team's wagon was then lowered over the side of the road to allow the other wagon to pull forward. (CL.)

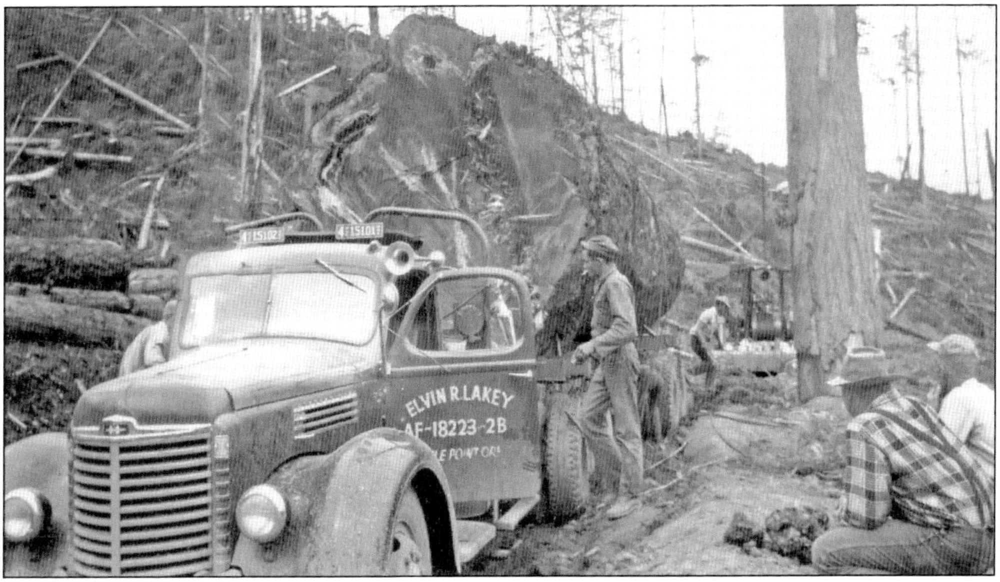

Brownie Coldiron Logging pulled this huge log out of the woods up Catching Creek and loaded it on Elvin R. Lakey's truck in the early 1950s. Norman Morris, Lakey's nephew, stands near the cab's open door. Because hauling the log on the highway to the Coos Bay Lumber Company mill in Coquille would have required a permit, Morris drove the truck to the reload facility at the depot, where the log was loaded on a railroad car. The reload was a place with equipment for transferring logs. (RB.)

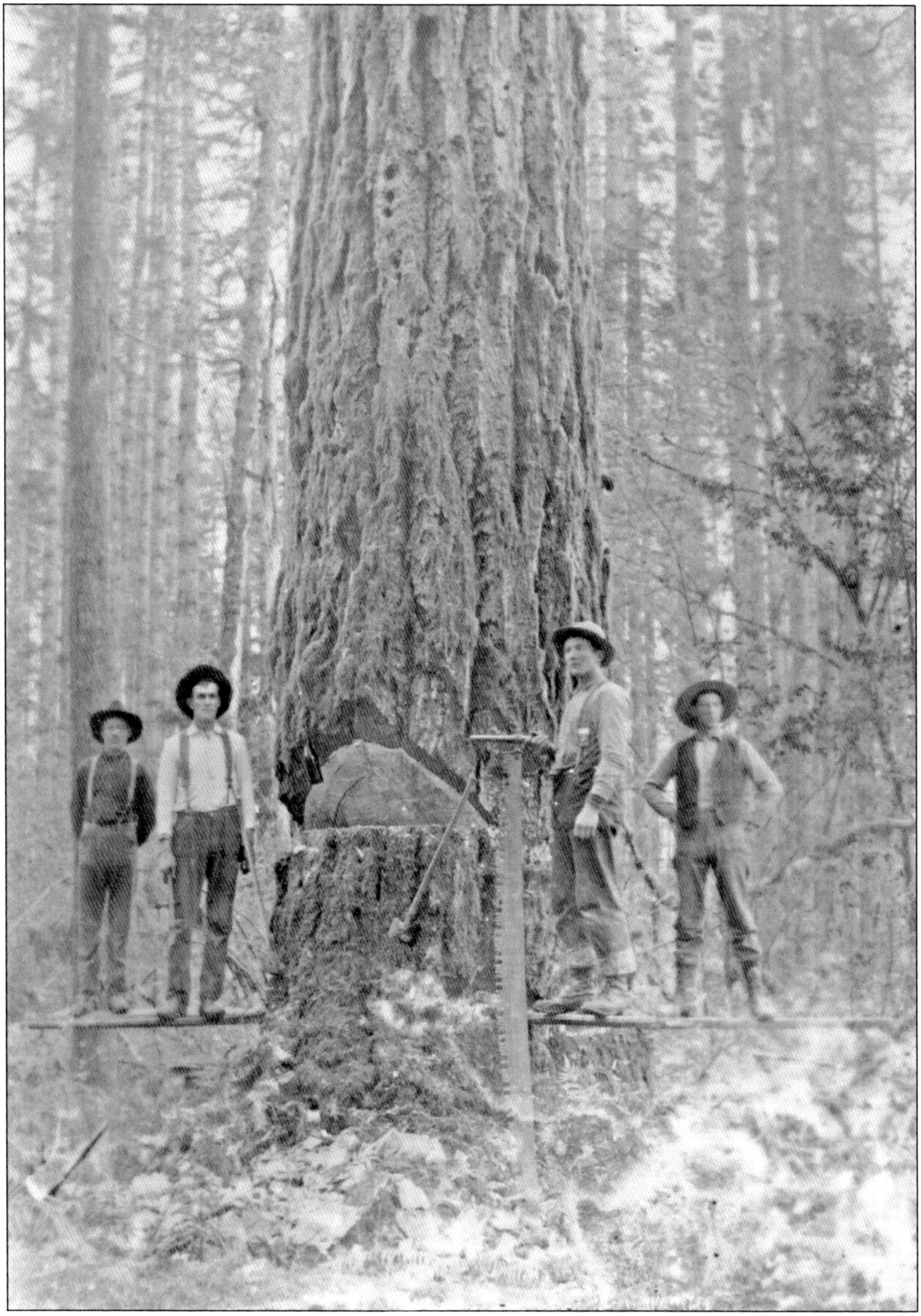

Standing on springboards and getting ready to fell this tree are four loggers. One (probably the man on the left springboard closest to the tree) is Marion Miller. Another (probably the man with his hand on the saw) is Oscar Bunch. Miller lived in Dora on Miller Road, while Bunch lived in Dora on the place later owned by the Stamen family. (DL.)

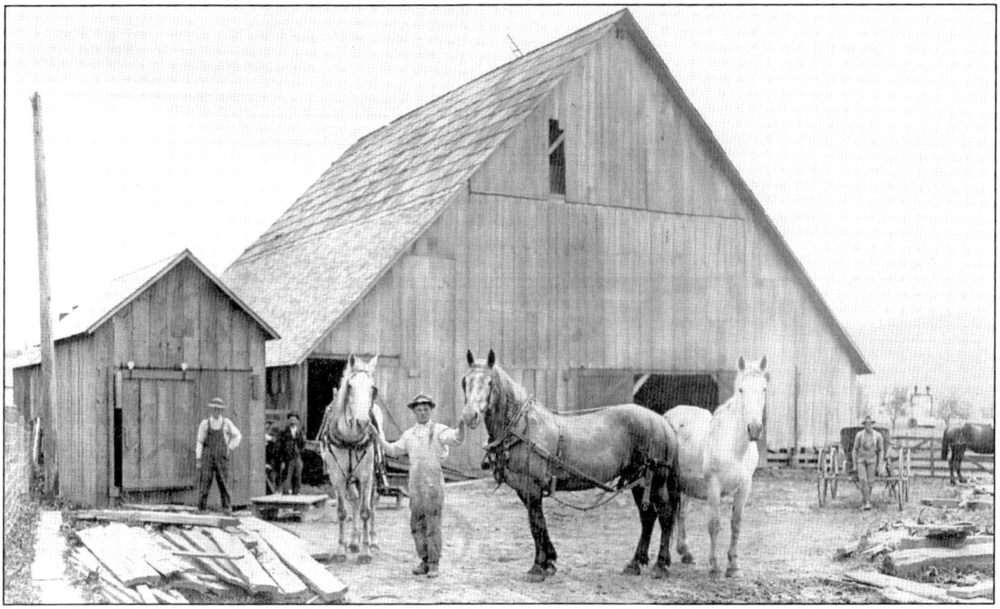

In this early-1900s image, Bill Bell holds the bridles of a team of horses at the Price and Laura (Hoover) Robison place in West Norway, across the river from the community of Norway. Roy Haney (left) stands near a sliding door, while Roy "Brownie" Robison (wearing a dark coat) stands near the alley between the two buildings. Leaning against a buggy to the right is Price Robison, Brownie's father. (HR.)

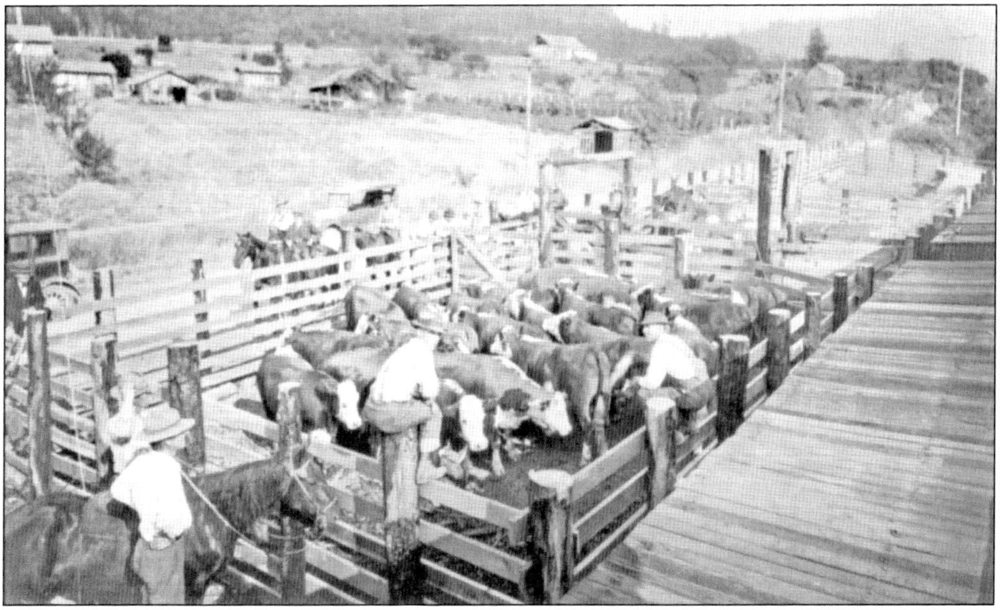

The cattle in this early-1900s photograph will soon be loaded into the boxcars visible at right at the Broadbent train station. Trains passing through Broadbent sometimes had over 100 cars loaded with logs from the Smith-Powers Logging Company operations near Powers. Trains stopped running through Broadbent around 1972. (SD.)

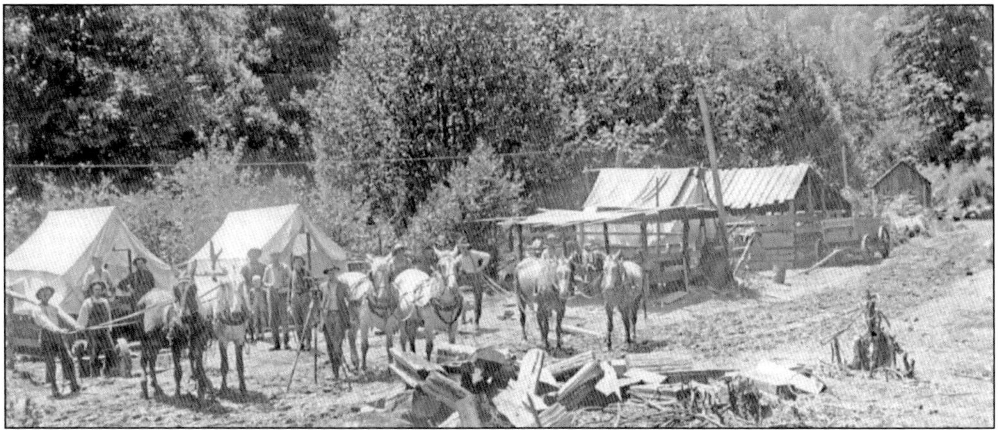

Jesse Laird's first paying job, in about 1921, was watering the horses and mules at this road camp. The crew was surveying and improving the Coos Bay Wagon Road. Laird lived with his parents, Walter and Mayre Laird, at the Halfway House in Sitkum. The Coos Bay Wagon Road climbed steeply from Reston, in Douglas County, and then dropped into Brewster Valley before winding its way to Dora, Fairview, and Sumner. (CL.)

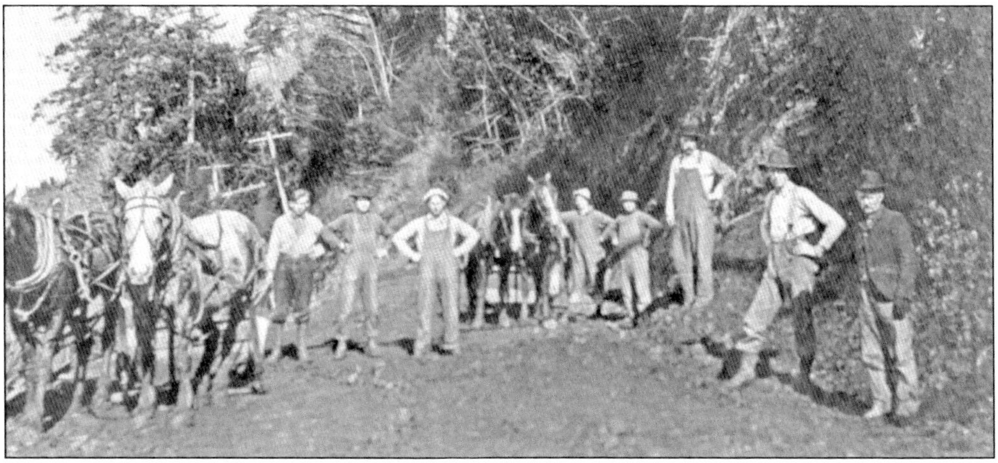

Road boss John W. Clinton (far right) has a crew using teams of horses and a fresno scraper to work on the road between Myrtle Point and Coquille in about 1898. The road crew includes, from left to right, Dude Harrison, Bill Neideigh, Walter Barklow, Ray Clinton, Gene Cole, Frank Nelson, and Jim Barkdoll. (CCS.)

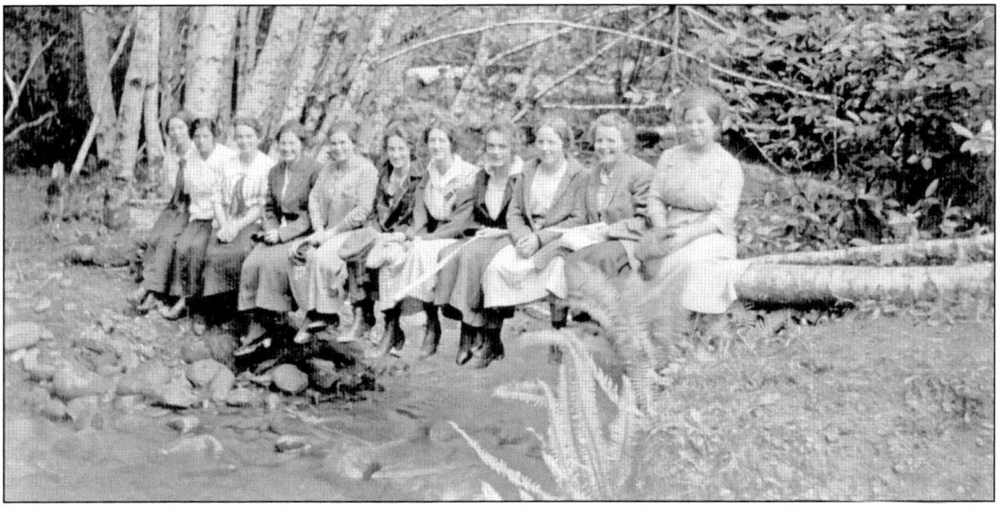

A fallen alder tree over a creek in Sitkum is a precarious bench for women on an outing in the early 1900s. For unknown reasons, one woman holds a yardstick, and another holds a wooden fork. The companions are, from left to right, unidentified, Ethel Laird, Wanda Harry, Linnie Benham, Myrtle Harry, Mildred Laird, Zilpha Benham, Lila Smith, Bonnie Laird, Mary (Hall) Laird, and Berta Laird. Mary sits between her twin daughters. (DL.)

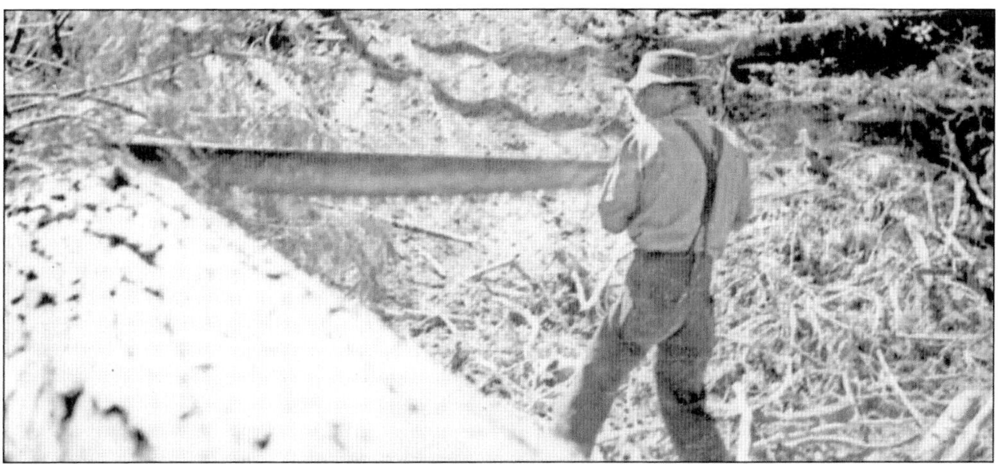

Using a seven-foot Atkins or Disston bucking saw, Lloyd Winningham bucks a tree in the late 1940s. Crosscut saws were also called hand briars, misery whips, and Swedish fiddles. (CB.)

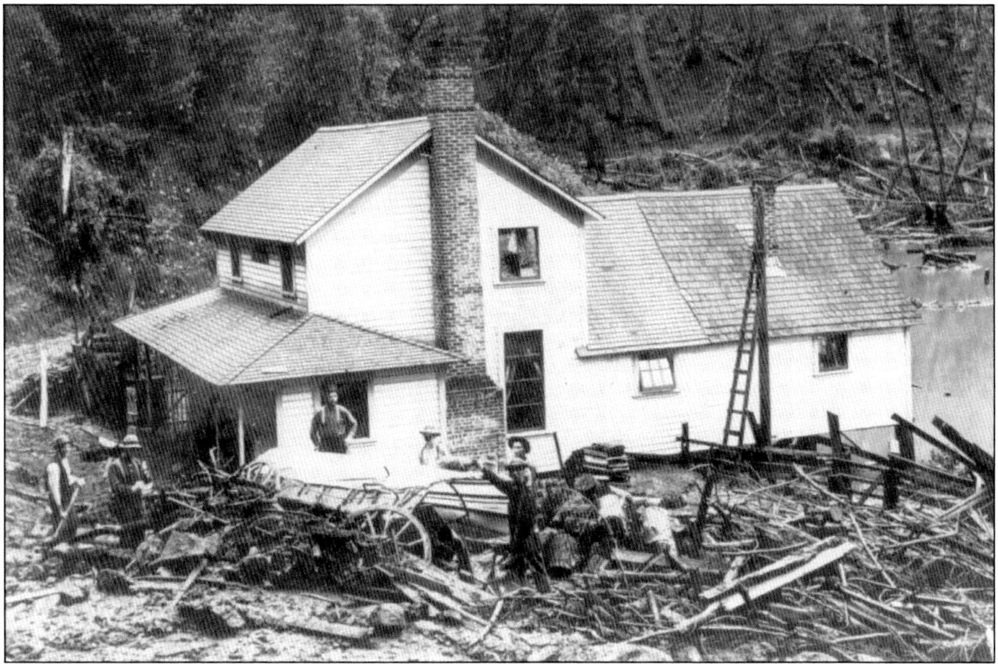

The Even Neva "Nevy" Harry house in Sitkum was in the path of a landslide that knocked over a wagon in the early 1900s. Floodwater covers the area behind the house. Nevy Harry, born in 1859, married Phoebe Turner, and they had four children. Later, this house was owned by Kenneth and Eleanor (Neideigh) Laird. (DL.)

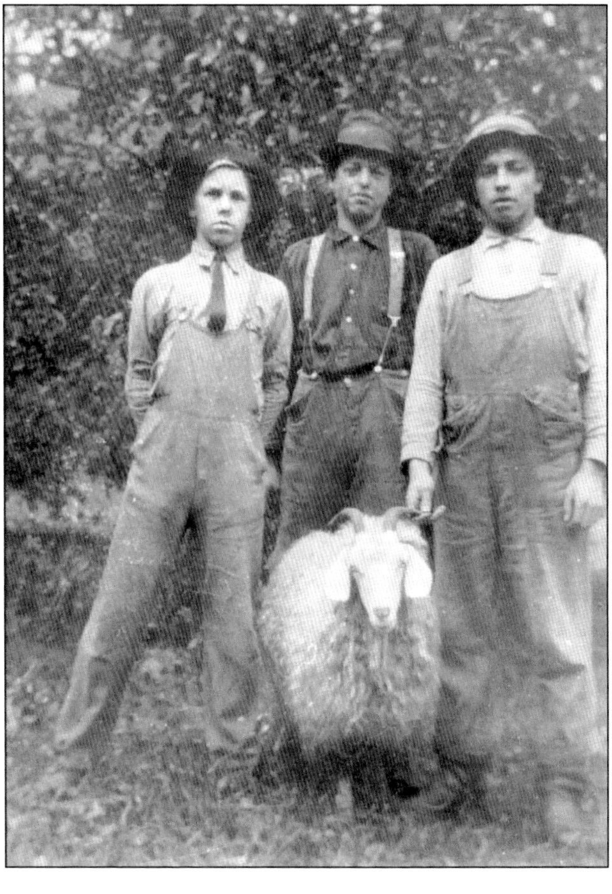

Clifford Laird (right) holds the horn of his goat while standing with two Sitkum friends, Charley Austin (left) and Julius Benham. In 1917, when Laird was 16, he and his brother Ivan were using a crosscut saw to fell an alder in Sitkum near the home of their parents, James and Nancy Belle (Harry) Laird. The tree split and fell on Clifford, who died minutes later. (DL.)

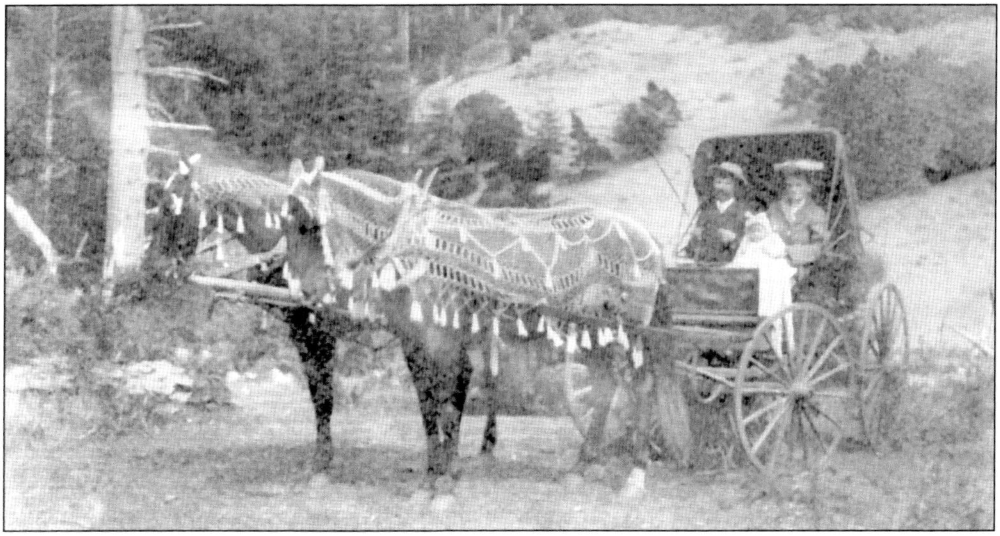

With caparison nets draping their horses, the Whitney family goes for an outing in 1905. Stephen Whitney holds the reins while his wife, Lillian (Martin) Whitney, positions her daughter Lena so that she can see the horses. The tassels on the nets fended off flies when the horses walked. (CP.)

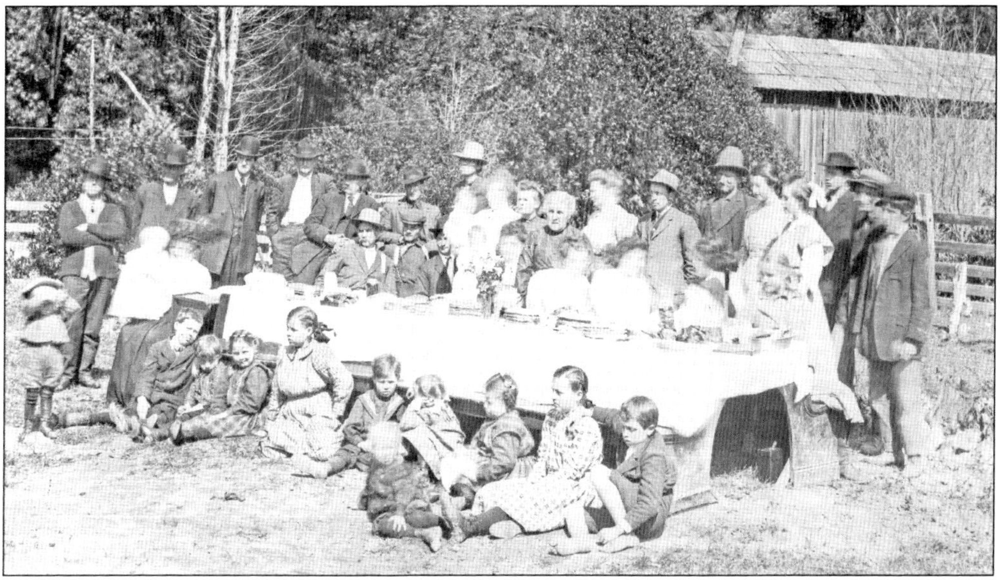

With the covered bridge over Brummit Creek in the background, a picnic is spread on tablecloth-covered school desks in the yard of the Sitkum School in the early 1900s. Chloe (Cook) (Harry) Laird, facing forward, has white hair and a dark dress. Born in 1841, she opened the Halfway House in Sitkum with her first husband, John Alva Harry. After his death, she married James Laird and continued operating the Halfway House. (DL.)

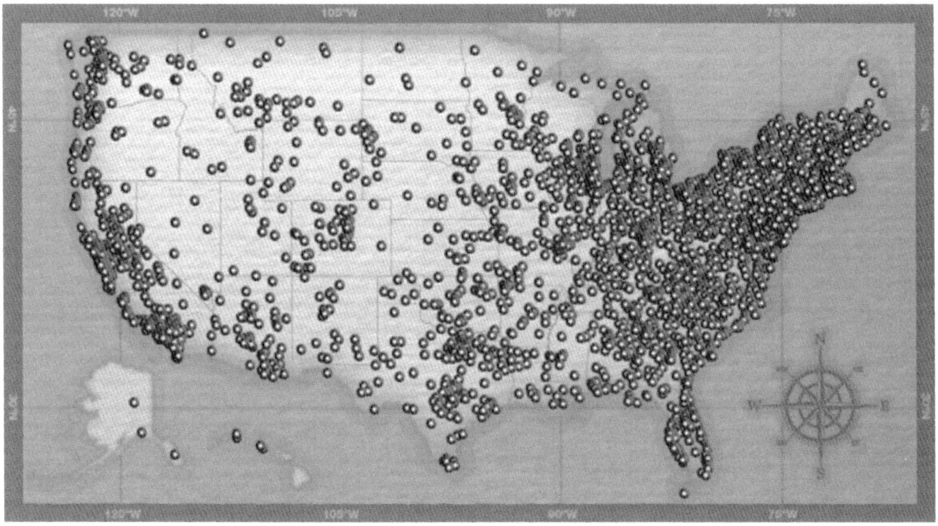